Cricket's Historians

Peter Wynne-Thomas

First published in Great Britain by
Association of Cricket Statisticians and Historians
Cardiff CF11 9XR
© ACS 2011
Reprinted April 2012.

British Library Cataloguing-in-Publication Data.
A catalogue record for this book is available from the British Library.

ISBN: 978 1908 165 12 1
Typeset and printed by The City Press Leeds Ltd.

Published in an unnumbered
paper back edition and in a
case bound limited edition of 40 copies.

Acknowledgements

Since I began researching for this book, I have contacted dozens of authors, initially to secure brief biographical notes of them, but in many cases asking for information on friends and colleagues, many now deceased. To list all those to whom I have spoken would start to create another Index. May I therefore thank them all for their co-operation?

There are nevertheless a handful of people who have been harassed almost continuously throughout the writing of this work and thus deserve especial mention and thanks. Martin Wilson fought his way through what I believed to be the final draft. Apart from adjusting my punctuation and other grammatical hiccups, he suggested pieces which required more explanation and indeed pieces which I somehow seemed to overlook. Rob Brooke and Keith Warsop both scanned the original mss from the venerable typewriter and suggested certain adjustments – not to the actual typewriter, but the man who pressed the keys. Derek Drake successfully researched biographical information on a number of mainly pre-1939 historians and cricket writers. Roger Page was kind enough to contact a number of Australian writers and obtain from them biographical notes. Peter Griffiths supplied the Appendix on the ACS personnel and publications, as well as working on the final publication prior to its printing. Finally I must thank the Committee of the ACS for agreeing to publish this ground-breaking volume. As I know from long experience in these matters, the problem with 'ground-breaking' books is the impossible one of estimating the potential sales!

Contents

Cricket's Historians
Introduction

The concept is a simple one – a book on how writers have portrayed the story of cricket, not only as cricket's history itself unfolded, but as researchers constantly uncovered hitherto lost facts relating to the game. The difficulty is to decide how broad a spread of writers should be incorporated. The number of books which have been published containing the story of the game from its inception to its present worldwide compass are relatively few and the task of reviewing their contents and some comments on the authors not too arduous, but none of those books, save the very early ones, would have been at all comprehensive without the input of dozens, not to say hundreds, of historical researchers working on a much smaller remit.

I do feel that those scholars should be recognised and therefore rather than concentrating on perhaps twenty or so writers and their work, I have deliberately included the work of several hundred specialists, who have made it their business to ferret out and publish the small facets of history, which welded together enable writers to give the overall pattern. Whilst reviewing this published work – in books, magazines and other documents – I have tried, not always with success, to provide a few biographical facts on the authors themselves. The pattern of an author's life always has some bearing on the written work he, or she, produces.

Writers on history in general, not specifically cricket, divide broadly into two groupings, those whose lives revolve round the dredging of old material in order to produce fresh data in their finished work and those who accept the data already to hand and try to re-interpret that data. The two groups are not exclusive, many, maybe the majority, are to a greater or lesser extent a combination of the two.

A third category which comes into play, not exclusively in cricket, but largely in this sport, at least in historical terms, is the statistician. Cricket statisticians are often considered by the cricketing public to be historians, but they are as a body neither historians or in the wider context of the definition, statisticians. One of the very few professional statisticians who did publish cricket statistical work was G.H.Wood, but he was exceptional. His career will be dealt with as this book unfolds.

As a generalisation, cricket statisticians like to see everything neatly divided into separate parcels. They can then happily play with the figures which are contained in each parcel, but history is not like that and the forcing of data into strict confines has been the cause of many a confrontation between the cricket historians and the statisticians. Figures are, whether one likes it or not, an integral part of cricket. The compilation of 'cricket records' has been a hobby of many ever since detailed cricket scores began to be published and these 'records' necessarily involve historical research. I have therefore written two books in one, in that I have followed the history of 'cricket records' in parallel with the general history of the game's development.

The two volumes of *Padwick* and Stephen Gibbs' *Post Padwick* provide the student with a splendid bibliography of cricket. One could argue that every title listed in those three volumes has some historical and/or statistical content, however tenuous, but it is not my intention to discuss by any means all or most of the works listed by Padwick – to do so would simply be re-writing Padwick with additional comments. I have therefore not, as a rule, included in this present work instructional books, autobiographies, most biographies (especially those dealing with contemporary players) and books on 'local' cricket clubs, except at county level, or the overseas equivalent.

On the other hand cricket periodicals have been studied and the history of the principal ones are discussed, because many contain articles of historic value and many of the contributors are historians or statisticians in one sense or another.

Two organisations have helped to foster an interest in cricket's history and statistics since the Second World War and have published 'in house' periodicals with historical contents. The Cricket Society was founded in 1945 and The Association of Cricket Statisticians and Historians in 1973, these societies' histories and development are explained and some other lesser such societies are mentioned in context.

In the final resort, what works are included or excluded are the choice of the author, but every endeavour has been made to at least inspect all the published material that is worthy of inclusion. Finally the work is laid out in chronological order, for no other reason than that the authors featured only had access to the data available at the time their work was written.

Peter Wynne-Thomas
Nottingham
December 2010

Chapter 1
The Pioneers of Cricket's History and Statistics

This story begins with a scorer, who went one step beyond recording matches in progress, in that he then published the scores of those games. Brief details of the results of cricket matches had started to appear in newspapers in the early years of the 18th century, in the last third of that century scores showing the totals for individual batsmen and how they were dismissed are published; actual match descriptions usually depend on whether royalty or major figures in the aristocracy either play or attend and riots or disputes are given larger coverage.

Poems describing specific games or cricket playing in general are published as small booklets or pamphlets as are the Laws of the Game, but in 1790, Samuel Britcher, the M.C.C. Scorer, compiles the first 'cricket annual'. This comprises the detailed scores of 14 matches played that season. His annual clearly proves financially worthwhile, since it continues until 1805 (the final issue for 1804/5 probably appearing after Britcher's death). The annual grows in size and some of the later editions contain over 30 match scores. The Laws of Cricket are also included in some editions as are poems. Several researchers including F.S.Ashley-Cooper, John Batten and John Goulstone have made attempts to identify biographical details of Samuel Britcher, but the most detailed published research on the scorer is by David Rayvern Allen. He published *Samuel Britcher. The Hidden Scorer* in 1982 and then in 2003 Allen updated his research and Christopher Saunders published not only Allen's revised effort, but also facsimiles of the 15 editions of the annual. Allen suggests that Britcher was born in Linton, near Maidstone in 1744, but is unsure of the year of his death. Perhaps further research will reveal more data on this key figure in the world of cricket statistics.

The importance of these scores is that statisticians were, from 1790, able to compile 'seasonal averages' for batsmen. No bowling details are shown, but scorers did not keep bowling figures until the 1820s – at least if they did none are extant. In one of the copies of the 1793 annual someone has written in some basic cricket averages. One assumes they were of use to the betting fraternity and perhaps the selection of players for representative matches. Averages are the start of 'cricket records'. How frequently 'averages' were compiled over the next few decades is unknown and, at the time of writing, it would appear that the next extant contemporary compilation is not until 1823. The Kingscote Cricket Club scorebook for that year has manuscript batting averages in it, with the following tabulation: 'name; had innings; got notches; average of notches for each innings'. The averages are calculated to the nearest half.

In 1799, William Epps of Rochester supplemented Britcher's annuals by publishing a book with the scores of notable matches from 1772 to 1790 – *Cricket: A Collection of All The Grand Matches of Cricket, Played in England, within Twenty Years*. In fact though the title page claims to include the season of 1771, the scores commence in 1772, similarly the title page gives 1791, but the scores end in 1790 – one assumes Epps did not have Britcher's first annual? The key point is that the issuing of Epps' book of scores demonstrates that cricket enthusiasts had an interest in 'historic' scores, as well as current ones. William Epps was a person of some standing in Rochester and at one time was a candidate for the office of Mayor. He was also a cricketer, for his name appears in Britcher's Match Scores.

Since Epps gathered together 19 seasons of historic cricket scores, he might justly be described as cricket's first historian, though he has to compete with Joseph Strutt for that honour. Strutt was born in Chelmsford in 1749; apprenticed to an engraver, he became a noted engraver in his own right. He then took up oil painting and achieved an acceptable standard in that art. At the same time he was engrossed in the study of antiquities, publishing his first book on the subject in 1773. In semi-retirement Strutt began to research the origins of sports. The result was the appearance in 1801 of *Glig-gamena angel deod, or The Sports and Pastimes of the People of England*.

Chapter 3 is 'Games of Ball' and one sub-section in that chapter relates to ball games in which an implement is used to strike the ball. The generic term Strutt uses for this sub-section is 'club-ball'.

This term is the one 'cricket' element for which Strutt is recalled today. Some misguided 'historians' misread Strutt, or half-read Strutt and claimed that 'club-ball' was a game in its own right. For the next 150 years, historians discuss 'club-ball' as if people prior to 1800 knocked on each other's doors and said, 'Come and have a game of club-ball'. Various lists of games, often prohibited, were published before 1800 and have been extensively quoted by sports historians. Not one contains 'club-ball'.

Strutt devotes a page or two to the origins of cricket, but pronounces it a 'modern' game. The first reference he could find appeared in a poem by Thomas D'Urfey, which Strutt dates as 1719; in fact the poem was reprinted in 1719 and first appeared in 1693.

A second edition of Strutt's book was issued in 1810, then an altered edition in 1831 and an updated and revised edition in 1903. It remained through the 19th century the standard work on English sport as a whole.

Statisticians were better served than historians. In 1823, Henry Bentley, a former cricketer at Lord's and now an umpire, published a 374-page book containing matches played between 1786 and 1822. He then issued a 20-page booklet on matches played in the season of 1823 and in 1826 published scores for 1824 and 1825, this time of over 40 pages. Why he chose 1786 as his starting point is not explained, though Lord's Cricket Ground was founded the following summer.

Recent studies of Bentley's principal book have confounded statisticians. Arthur Haygarth, writing in 1860, makes the point:

> 'This work (Bentley's Scores), however differs greatly
> from the scores kept by the Marylebone Club, and which

is correct cannot be said for certain. The matches in his book were copied from those of the M.C.C. These latter were, however, afterwards accidently burnt with the pavilion.'

The fire referred to was that which destroyed the Lord's pavilion on July 28, 1825, immediately after the Harrow v Winchester match.

Britcher was the M.C.C. Scorer; if Bentley supposedly copied the scores from the books kept in the M.C.C. pavilion, why are there so many differences between Britcher's printed scores and those of Bentley? An interesting point, but not one which can be entered into here.

Henry Bentley was born in Westminster in 1782 and died in Hereford in 1857. His playing career in major matches spanned 1801 to 1822.

Outside cricket's heartland of London and the South East, the first book of published scores was issued in Nottingham in 1830. The author, William North, a member of the Nottingham Eleven, does at least make clear his source:

'In order that the following collection may be found to be as complete and correct as possible, I have spared no pains, nor shrunk from any exertions that appeared to me to be necessary for the completion of a work that may be referred to with confidence. Should some trifling errors or imperfections be detected, I humbly entreat the candid reader to excuse them; of which I entertain no doubt, when it is considered that some have been almost unavoidable, from the mutilated state of many of the papers to which I have been compelled to refer.'

The book contains the match scores of games played by the Nottingham Club from 1771 to 1829, its actual title reads *A Correct Account of all the Cricket Matches played by the Nottingham Old Club* from 1771 to 1829 inclusive. The book runs to 52 pages. William North, by profession a school teacher and later Inspector of Corn Returns for Nottingham, died in 1855 aged 48.

It is of significance that the following year on November 18, 1831, the *Nottingham Review* publishes the career averages for the principal Nottingham batsmen, giving 'Average per Match' and 'Average per Innings'. The tabulation is attached to the obituary of a noted Nottingham cricketer, Joseph Dennis, and had been compiled in order to compare his record with those of his contemporaries. This set of averages was discovered by Keith Warsop in the 1960s. In view of the scribbled averages in copies of Britcher for 1793 and 1796, and the publication of both Epps' and Bentley's books of scores, it appears odd that these Nottingham averages seem to be the earliest ever printed. (*Sports History* No.10 contains a more detailed essay on early cricket averages).

From the data for statisticians, back to the historians; in 1833 was published *The Young Cricketer's Tutor, with The Cricketers of My Time* by John Nyren, but collected and edited by Charles Cowden Clarke. The book was dedicated to William Ward, the batsman who in 1820 scored a record 278 at Lord's. The section 'The Cricketers of My Time' had been previously serialised in the press.

John Nyren was the son of the captain of the Hampshire/Hambledon Club side, Richard Nyren, and was born in Hambledon in 1764. He was a fair cricketer, but in no way could compare with his father. John moved away from Hampshire at the same time as his father in or about 1791. He died in Bromley-by-Bow in 1837. Charles Cowden Clarke (1787-1877) was a well-known authority on Shakespeare, giving lectures and readings on the Bard throughout England. He retired with his wife to Nice in 1856 and they moved to Genoa in 1861 – Charles Clarke died there in March 1877 and his wife in the same place in 1898.

After a Dedication and an Introduction, there is a long chapter on how to play cricket and this also contains the Laws (as revised in 1830). In the second major section appears 'The Cricketers of My Time', which commences with some 400 words on cricket's origins, adding nothing of any substance to Strutt. The principal contents of this section are descriptions of players who appeared at Hambledon. However the final section 'A Few Memoranda Respecting the Progress of Cricket' claims to be an edited version of a manuscript, supposedly written 'some years ago by an old cricketer' and was given to the author by William Ward.

In this chapter is contained the detailed score of a match between Kent and All England played, so it states, in 1746. (How Ashley-Cooper corrected this erroneous date is noted later). This score predates Epps'earliest scorecard by a quarter of the century. Another paragraph in this manuscript tells how the wicket used to be two feet in width with a hole between the two stumps. In making a run the batsman had to ground his bat in the hole, but for the fielding side to run out a batsman, the ball had to be placed in the hole. The third piece of historical information was the introduction of the minimum width for a cricket bat, caused by White of Reigate coming to the crease with a bat as broad as the wicket, also the introduction of a middle stump, due to 'Lumpy' Stevens' accurate bowling.

Historians at first accepted these three pieces of information at face value, but gradually the details have been checked and cross-checked and more accurate data have emerged.

In 1838 *The Cricketer's Handbook* was published by Robert Tyas of London and J.Menzies of Edinburgh. The first chapter, 'Origin of the Game', is about 600 words in length: it quotes Strutt, then launches into a description of tip-cat. The remainder of the book just contains instructions on how to play and the Laws. Tyas issued a second edition in 1841 and a further edition appeared in the United States in 1844. Tyas then went out of business and a similar volume was issued by William Mark Clark, described as 'a dab hand at paste and scissors journalism, in 1844-45.

Clark entitled his book *Clark's Cricketer's Handbook in Three Parts*. The first part is 'History and Chronology of Cricket', which then splits into two sections, viz 'A Brief History of Cricket' and 'The Chronicles of Cricket'. The Brief History is some 2,000 words in length. It again quotes Strutt's reference of 1719, but also introduces 'creag' of AD 1300 and Barrington's Hand-yn and Hand-out of AD 1477. The book repeats the description of the wide low two stump wicket with the hole in between, into which the ball was placed. In the Chronicles section, the detailed score of the 1746 Kent v All England match is printed, but it states that the game is recorded in the *Gentleman's Magazine* of that year, a piece of information not given in Nyren's book, also the England second innings score is shown as 72, rather than the total of 70 given by Nyren. Clark also copies the 1777 Hambledon v England scorecard from Nyren; from then on Clark prints potted scores of sundry matches continuing to the date of publication. The book continues with sections on How to Play and on the Laws.

In 1851 William Bolland was the author of *Cricket Notes*. The first chapter entitled 'Early History' has 11 pages devoted to the pre-Hambledon period and describes Tip Cat as one of cricket's ancestors – more or less taking the detail from Tyas's 1838 book. In fact one of the few pieces of new 'information' introduced by Bolland is that the word 'cricket' comes from 'cross wicket' (i.e. the batsmen running between the wickets). The rest of the detail is derived from Strutt or Nyren. Bolland, who played cricket for M.C.C., was created the Perpetual President of I Zingari on the foundation of that club.

Since their inception in the closing years of the 17th century, newspapers have been a prime source of cricketing information. For those who do not have access to early 18th century papers, J.S.Penny's book *Cricketing References in Norwich Newspapers* 1701 to 1800 which simply prints word-for-word all the cricketing notices in the Norwich papers provides an excellent feel for the cricket news that Norfolk readers received prior to 1801 – in fact Penny failed to find any cricket notices before 1729. *Sussex Cricket in the Eighteenth Century* compiled by Timothy McCann and published in 2004 is a similar work.

James D. Coldham, in his essay on 'Some Early Cricket Reporters' (published in *The Journal of The Cricket Society* 1981-84 Vol 10 No 2 to Vol 11 No4), states that Pierce Egan (1772-1849) was the first 'sports reporter', working from 1816 for the *Weekly Dispatch*. However *The Sporting Magazine*, first published in 1792, contained cricketing notes occasionally. So too did *Annals of Sporting* from 1822 and *The New Sporting Magazine* from 1831. Were these simply sent in by readers, or were some contributed by journalists? John Wheble of Warwick Lane, near St Paul's was described as the 'projector' of *The Sporting Magazine*. He died in 1820 aged 75.

So far as cricket is concerned, *The Sporting Magazine* gave relatively superficial coverage to the game, as indeed did Pierce Egan, whose chief interest was in boxing. He did write a part-work *Book of Sports and Mirror of Life* which ran to 25 issues and in 1832 was reprinted as a book. One part was devoted to cricket, chiefly concerned with the Hambledon era. More important (from the cricketing viewpoint) was the foundation in 1822 of *Bell's Life in London* a weekly publication concentrating on sport and in particular cricket.

In the early part of the 19th century major cricket was very much centred on Lord's and the M.C.C., but in the 1820s Sussex and Kent revived the 18th century fashion for inter-county matches. Surrey lacked a patron to promote that county and Hampshire, though having several patrons, failed to find a 19th century equivalent of the Hambledon Club. The battle to be 'champion county' in the South East was thus confined to Kent and Sussex. In the Midlands Nottingham, having shown themselves superior to their neighbours, Sheffield and Leicester, renamed themselves Nottinghamshire and rose by the 1830s to challenge Sussex and Kent. In Norfolk, Suffolk and Yorkshire the idea of having a county side rather than just inter-town or village contests was starting to take root.

The press responded by giving more space to matches and the man who tried to supply the cricket data to the newspapers was William Denison.

His brief biography simply comments that he 'was a contributor to most of the morning journals'. Included among these journals were both *The Times* and *Bell's Life*. Born in Lambeth in 1801, Denison was a workaholic. Was Denison the writer of the sections on cricket's origins in both Tyas and Clark's handbooks? At the time of writing, no evidence has been found to substantiate this possibility. He himself announced in the 1840s, 'I never spent more than four hours in bed on any single night.' Cricket in that decade would not have occupied a journalist full time twelve months a year, so Denison also covered events in the House of Commons and, probably as a result, is rumoured to have made friends with a fellow cricket enthusiast and parliamentary journalist (and workaholic), Charles Dickens.

In 1840, national seasonal cricket averages were printed in *Bell's Life* for the first time – it is probable that these were the first seasonal averages ever to appear in the press. The cricket historian, G.B.Buckley, credited Denison with this compilation.

In 1844 Denison issued *The Cricketer's Companion*, which gave match scores and averages for the season of 1843. Ignoring Bentley's two supplements, Denison's book was the first annual since the final edition of Britcher though a supplement to the *New Sporting Magazine* of August, September and October 1833 had contained 14 full scores and around 250 summary scores. That supplement was not repeated in subsequent years. The new annual by Denison cost 1s 6d, but must have proved financially viable, since a second edition appeared. Likewise the 1845 edition required a second printing. That year Denison took on the additional role as a founding Hon Secretary of the newly formed Surrey County Cricket Club. An active player, Haygarth sums him up: 'He was a slow bowler, round-arm; but as a cricketer was nothing remarkable. His name will not often be found in these pages, but he participated in a vast number of suburban and other inferior contests, not recorded in this work (*Scores & Biographies*).

In acting as Surrey Secretary and publishing his cricket annual, as well as continuing with his self-imposed schedule of 'ordinary' reporting, Denison over-stretched himself. He resigned as Surrey Hon Secretary and the last edition of his cricket annual was issued in 1847. Interestingly in the same year, Denison is pictured with William Clarke's England Eleven in the well-known lithograph of the team. With Clarke's team attracting enormous crowds all over England and putting inter-county games on the back foot, perhaps Denison believed that reporting the England matches was what newspaper editors required? In 1846 he had issued a book *Sketches of the Players*, which gave comprehensive essays on the cricket stars of the day. Denison died in 1856, officially of bronchitis, but 'overwork' might have been a more accurate description!

Before following the saga of Denison's successors as ace cricket reporter and embryo cricket statistician, it is time to return to the way cricket's history was being considered and for that it is necessary to consider the work of the Rev James Pycroft.

Pycroft was born at Guyers House, Pickwick, Wiltshire in 1813, the second son of Thomas Pycroft, barrister-at-law. He was educated at a school in Bath before going up to Trinity College, Oxford in October 1832. Pycroft supposedly, as a youth, had had a hand in the formation of Lansdown Cricket Club in the 1820s, though his claim to be the founder in his autobiography is a slight hyperbole. Pycroft certainly played for the Club as a 14 year old in 1827 and according to Donald Bradfield, in his history of the club, for the "full side" in 1829. At Oxford Pycroft was a major force in the revival of the university match – this had not been played since 1829 and was revived, with Pycroft opening the batting, in 1836. The previous year, a book *The Principles of Scientific Batting, or Plain Rules, founded on the Practice of the first Professors and Amateurs for the Noble Game of Cricket* had been written by a 'Gentleman'. Appropriately the Gentleman was James Pycroft.

In 1836, Pycroft obtained his degree and went to Lincoln's Inn to follow his father into the legal profession, but four years later abandoned the Law and took Holy Orders, taking a position as a master in a school in Leicester. He was the author of a number of works related to teaching and education, but his fame rests on having, in 1851, published *The Cricket Field : or, The History and Science of Cricket*. The book was destined to vie with John Nyren's work as the most popular cricket book of the 19th century and if not the most popular in terms of copies ever sold, then certainly the one most read and studied.

In his Preface, Pycroft states that he has Nyren's book and Bentley's book of scores and has been to the villages in Hampshire and Surrey to talk to old cricketers. Also important in the contents of Pycroft's book was a manuscript written by the Rev John Mitford, recalling talks Mitford had with William Fennex (the noted cricketer of the 1780s and 1790s). Pycroft also checked Joseph Strutt's book. He unfortunately adopts Strutt's club-ball reference so that in Pycroft it reads 'For Club-Ball we believe to be the name which usually stood for Cricket in the thirteenth century'.

Pycroft then boasts that he has discovered a literary reference to cricket 25 years earlier than Strutt's first quote (D'Urfey in 1710 or 1719 depending on the edition), namely Edward Phillips in 1685, 'Would my eyes had been beaten out of my head with a cricket-ball the day before I saw thee!'

Just as Strutt had the incorrect date for his initial reference, so did Pycroft, the year should have been 1658, not 1685. These incorrect dates have caused successive 'historians' great confusion, almost ever since. Phillips' piece was published by N.Brooks under the title *The Mysteries of Love and Eloquence*. One assumes the muddled dating 1685 for 1658 was, initially, a printing error.

Pycroft goes on to seek out from Clark 'Handyn and Handoute' and 'Cat and Dog' as games related to or akin to cricket; as well as 'creag' in the reign of Edward the First in 1300 – 'Creag and cricket, therefore, being presumed identical.'

In broad terms those are the facts Pycroft noted in the first edition of his book. In later editions, more historical data were included – the book was issued in nine editions prior to Pycroft's death, which occurred in Brighton in 1895.

From the present-day viewpoint the most valuable section of Pycroft's book is his record of the game from the 1780s, which provides a first-hand account of cricket. As has been noted, Pycroft interviewed many old cricketers, including, most notably, William Beldham (1766-1862) of Surrey and Hambledon.

The best edition of Pycroft, for the student, is that of 1922, which is edited with very extensive notes, by F.S.Ashley-Cooper.

Several local cricket clubs published the scores of their matches in book form about this time, most notably Ripon (1837), Audley End (1844) and Lansdown (1852). In addition some Public Schools issued match score books – Winchester (1838) and Rugby (1842) being among the earliest. However both these categories simply issued the bare scores with very little narrative.

As previously noted, North's book of Nottingham scores was published as early as 1830, but in 1853 Nottingham went one step further and not only printed the scores but a 14 page history, plus 10 pages of players' biographies. The book *Nottingham Cricket Matches from 1771 to 1853* was compiled by John Frost Sutton. The Sutton family were publishers of the local newspaper *Nottingham Review*, which in the 1840s and 1850s gave excellent coverage to cricket. Sutton claims that, 'Nottingham has as great pretensions to giving birth to the noble pastime (cricket) as any other locality.' However Sutton later concedes that the Southern and South-Eastern Counties have been responsible for bringing cricket to its present state of perfection. Sutton's brief foray into the early years of the game owe all to Strutt and Pycroft and his first hard fact for Nottingham cricket is North's score for Nottingham v Sheffield in 1771. Sutton's history of Nottingham cricket from that date is excellent, as are his biographies of 25 Nottingham players, then very brief notes on a further dozen or so. This work was destined to be revised and updated several times.

Returning to the national scene, William Denison was succeeded as the main cricket correspondent of *Bell's Life* in the late 1840s by Frederick Lillywhite, to whose enterprise the world of both historians and statisticians owes a great debt. Born in Hove in 1829, Frederick's father was the famous Sussex cricketer of his day, Frederick William Lillywhite (1792-1854). The father was generally known as William Lillywhite. He had several sons older than Frederick, including James (born 1825) and John (born 1826). Unlike Frederick these two became notable county cricketers.

The family moved to London in 1844, when William took a post on the ground staff at Lord's. In the same year, *Lillywhite's Illustrated Handbook of Cricket* was published in London and Brighton. This is essentially an instructional book and does not advance either the statistics or the knowledge of the history of the game.

Of greater importance is *The Young Cricketer's Guide* published twice in 1849, which was then to re-appear the next year (1850) as *Lillywhite's*

Guide to Cricketers, edited by Frederick Lillywhite jun, who describes himself as cricket reporter to *Bell's Life in London*. The section in the book on how to play was by 'William Frederick Lillywhite' (the father with his christian names reversed.) The brief historical piece in the early Guides does not deviate from Strutt.

This was the start of the most popular cricket annual to date – it was to continue until Frederick Lillywhite's death and then was merged with John Lillywhite's *Cricketers' Companion* in 1867 – the latter will be discussed in the next chapter. For cricket statisticians, the Guide contains a three-page section giving 'The Average Runs etc of Players' with a note that the figures have been collected together by Lillywhite 'a task of great labour' for the express purpose of publishing in *Bell's Life*.

The batting columns comprise: 'Matches, Innings, Runs, Average each innings, Number over'.

The bowling columns are: 'Matches, Wickets Bowled, no. Caught, Caught From, Stumped From, Leg before wicket From, Hit Wicket From, Total, Average, Over'.

W.Ward and W.Dorrinton each have a page to themselves giving career batting match by match. Fifteen pages are devoted to a brief Who's Who of some 150 well-known current players, and there are sixteen pages on 'Celebrated Ground Grounds'.

The remainder of the book consists of the Laws and Instructions on how to play – it was not until the 1851 edition that potted scores of the principal season's matches were introduced into the work. The earlier Guides never gave detailed scores of matches. There was a reason for this, which is found in an advertisement in the 1851 edition, viz:

'J. & F. Lillywhite's Register of Cricket Matches states that for a £2 subscription, match cards of about 60 games will be sent to subscribers DAILY – by post i.e. up to 180 match cards in all.'

Frederick Lillywhite had a portable printing press, usually based at The Oval, but also travelling to other grounds on which major three-day matches were staged, and the sale of his cards at matches was one of his main occupations. Reprinting the full scores in the annual would harm the sale of cards.

Through the 1850s and into the 1860s, Fred's Guide (as the annual was commonly called) had no serious competitors. The format remained little altered, though a section devoted to Public Schools and local clubs expanded. Fred's father, William Lillywhite died in 1854, 'He expired very suddenly (having smoked a pipe the day before), of cholera at the sports shop off Caledonian Road in London, which he kept with his sons, John and Frederick.' William Lillywhite's career in first-class matches continued until the year prior to his death, when, at the age of 61, he briefly took part in the Sussex v England match Lord's arranged for his benefit – he bowled 11 overs before retiring from the match. His career with Sussex had begun in 1825 and in 1850 and 1851 he had taken part in a few games for Middlesex.

In 1859, Fred Lillywhite accompanied George Parr and his team on the first overseas tour by England cricketers – to North America. Lillywhite reportedly drove Parr to distraction with the problems of transporting the famous printing press from venue to venue, but the end product was the first 'tour' book, *The English Cricketers Trip to Canada and The United States*, with a lithograph of Fred Lillywhite peering out of his printing tent on the title page. It gave an account of the travel problems as well as the matches and the detailed scores.

At the same time as this was being issued, Fred Lillywhite had in preparation perhaps the most ambitious cricket publishing project ever attempted. It was to be multi-volume work containing the detailed scores of every 'major' cricket match, combined with biographies of every cricketer of note. The work of collecting all this information was undertaken by Arthur Haygarth. He, it would appear, had become involved with Fred Lillywhite in 1852-53 when the latter published a simple book, entitled *The Public School Matches*. This contained nothing, apart from a brief introduction, but the scores of matches played between Eton, Harrow and Winchester – no averages, no list of players. After the seasons 1852, 1853, 1854 and 1855 the book appeared with the most recent games added. It then reappeared following the matches of 1860, 1863, 1866,

1867, and 1868. After the death of Fred Lillywhite in 1866, the title was adjusted to *John Lillywhite's Public School Matches*.

Arthur Haygarth was born in Hastings in 1825. He was educated at Harrow and appeared in the school eleven in 1842 and 1843. Haygarth played in first-class matches for M.C.C. from 1844 to 1861, as well as many of the principal matches at Lord's and dozens of minor M.C.C. games. Haygarth had made a hobby out of collecting the detailed scores of past cricket matches and from the 1840s keeping his collection up to date as matches were played. The best description of the work possibly comes direct from the biography of Arthur Haygarth published under a Harrow Match of 1842 in the third volume of the great work entitled *Frederick Lillywhite's Cricket Scores and Biographies of Celebrated Cricketers*:

'Mr Haygarth is the entire compiler of this work (F.Lillywhite being the publisher), having been engaged, solely for his own amusement, several years in collecting and arranging scores of all good matches that could be procured. Has also added all the foot-notes and remarks, which are appended to the various contests throughout the book. The biographical notices of all famous cricketers (most of whom either had, or would soon have been forgotten, had not some account of them been transmitted to posterity through these pages) have also been written by him....To get materials for the work, he visited, in 1858, 1859 and 1860, many of the famous cricketing districts and grounds of former days, including Broadhalfpenny and Windmill Down at Hambledon, in Hampshire; the Vine at Sevenoaks; Penenden Heath, near Maidstone; Benenden; Bishops-Bourne, near Canterbury; Town Malling etc etc. All Clubs of note, also throughout the kingdom, have been applied to for their scorebooks; and, when obtained (most of them, however, not having been preserved), everything worth recording has been extracted... In addition, a very large sum of money has been laid out by the publisher, who now takes the opportunity to thank Mr Haygarth for his many years' laborious and gratuitous task of compiling so much valuable information…'

Lillywhite published the first two volumes, but, presumably because of financial problems, volumes three and four were paid for by F.P. Miller, the Surrey cricket captain. He found himself unable to break even and eventually MCC stepped in and over some years issued ten more volumes taking in the scores up to 1878.

Cricket was Arthur Haygarth's entire life. Due to his family's wealth he never, in his own words, 'entered or followed any profession or occupation'. The reason, he states, is simple: 'I was when young not allowed to pursue the vocation I wished, and the result was none at all, as I would not think of drudging at a profession which was not suitable to me in any way, and which, moreover I detested.' His independent means allowed Haygarth to play cricket, spending most of his early manhood at Lord's, except when he returned to Harrow to coach the boys. The remainder of his time was spent researching cricket match scores and biographies of players. From the historian's view the most valuable part of his work is biographical. In the fifteen volumes of *Scores & Biographies* there are over 4,000 biographies. Volume XIV had been published by MCC in 1895; Volume XV, entirely composed of biographies, together with an Index to biographies already contained in the previous volumes was published in 1925. In 2003, Roger Heavens published Volume XVI containing scores for 1879 and a few more biographies.

One important piece of data which Haygarth included in Volume I is a list of his sources for the scores he published. He includes in the list Epps, Bentley and Denison, but of Britcher he only had access to the annuals covering 1793 to 1802 (so missing the earliest and the last editions). Haygarth also lists the Marylebone Match Books 1791 to 1860, though those up to 1825 were destroyed in the Lord's Pavilion fire. The list gives newspaper sources, for example *Hampshire Chronicle* 1772 to 1807 and the *Brighton Gazette* 1819 to 1854.

In the Preface to the First Volume, Haygarth inserts the piece by the Rev Henry Teonge concerning cricket near Antioch in 1676, which extract had recently appeared in *Bell's Life*. Haygarth reprints two early versions of the Laws, though he does not place a definite date on either version – the first he states is the earliest published set of Laws and the second comes from the border of a handkerchief. Haygarth's survey of the history and origins of cricket add little to the sum total of Strutt, Nyren and Pycroft.

The scores open with Kent v All England, still dated 1746, then apart from the Nottingham v Sheffield 1771 match, jump to 1772 and run continuously thereafter, with copious notes, which like the biographies grow very important as the seasons pass. The notes on the meetings to form County Clubs remain essential material for the historian. The one facet that Haygarth ignores is the 'cricket record', both team and individual. There are no 'averages' in the biographical paragraphs. He frequently places notes at the foot of score cards pointing out that there are several variations to the version he has printed, but, especially in the case of the 18th century Hambledon matches, Haygarth fails to comment that the match titles often differ in *Britcher* or in the newspaper reports. In doing so he was largely responsible for the Hambledon/Hampshire controversies which erupted half a century or more after his death. After several years of ill-health, Arthur Haygarth died in London in May 1903. He had continued to gather together match score cards until 1898 and his manuscript collection remains at Lord's.

Haygarth's work is laid out in some detail because his 15 volumes remain a basic text book for researchers who delve into 19th century cricket. Very few major matches played during that century eluded him. In fact he complains at one point that he had made his task too involved because he included too many matches, but historians must be so grateful that he did. The efforts he went to in order to obtain biographies of the vast majority of notable cricketers provide a treasure trove for all those interested in cricket history. He attempted to obtain these biographies if possible direct from the player himself, an added bonus, even if professional players were prone to adjust their years of birth!

Before closing this Chapter the dramatic change in the newspaper industry during the 1850s requires a passing note. In 1855 the Stamp Act was repealed and in September that year the first one penny daily newspaper was launched – *Daily Telegraph* – in 1859 a rival to *Bell's Life* was established, namely *Sporting Life*, but initially the latter was, in cricketing terms, not up to the standard of the former. The only effect of the dailies was probably the demise of Fred Lillywhite's postal service of daily score cards from major match venues.

Chapter 2
Wisden challenges Lillywhite

The introduction of the daily newspaper did not seem to dent the popularity of Fred Lillywhite's Guide. The Winter Edition of 1862 has a headline on its cover: 'Sixteenth Edition, Making a previous sale of 88,000'. Fred Lillywhite made various claims in a number of editions about the sales figures. David Smith, in his study of the Guide, suggests dividing the figure by four to obtain a more accurate statistic. The 1863 edition contains 50 more pages than its immediate predecessor, but Lillywhite apologises for a price increase from 1s 3d to 1s 6d.

Two other publishers spied a lucrative market in the cricket annual business and in 1863-64 new rivals emerged. The first was the *Cricket Chronicle for the season 1863* compiled by Capt. W.Bayly. It ran to 518 pages, 5 ½" by 3 ¾" and was crammed with cricket match scores, many with bowling analyses, a few with reports. Nothing on quite this scale had been attempted before. The publishers were A.H.Baily & Co of London; the price 2s 6d. The publishers had launched *Baily's Magazine of Sports and Pastimes* in 1860, a monthly along the lines of the old *Sporting Magazine*. There was a chapter each month on cricket, but like *The Sporting Magazine* the newcomer mainly dealt with field sports. It was successful, and very good on the major Public Schools' cricket matches and results. It lasted until 1926, whereas the new annual failed. The 1863 edition was the sole issue. The identity of Captain Bayly has confounded historians; two possibilities are W.H. Knight and W.H.Leverall. The former certainly had connections with *Baily's Magazine*, whilst the latter worked for *Bell's*

Life, from which most, if not all, the scores were gleaned. The value for historians is that the annual includes a lot of matches not in Haygarth's volume covering 1863 and some quaint overseas matches at unexpected venues.

Almost simultaneously a second new cricket annual was issued, *The Cricketer's Almanack for the Year 1864,* costing one shilling. This 112 page softback, 6" by 3 ¾", was published by John Wisden & Co of 2, New Coventry St, London W. No editor was given either on the title page or in the brief introduction. It cannot be said to be competing with *The Cricket Chronicle,* since it did not include even the principal cricket match scores for 1863. Nor did the new publication compete directly with Fred's Guide (though Fred lowered his price back to one shilling) since no review whatsoever of the 1863 summer is included and no pen-pictures of current players. The main cricket content was a section on Gentlemen v Players which included the detailed scores of all matches between the two teams – this had never appeared in book form before. 'We have taken great pains, and been at considerable expense in collecting the information...' runs the preliminary note – Haygarth's first four volumes of *Scores & Biographies* were issued before this new annual appeared and included all the games up to 1854, so the compiler was being rather too boastful! A second section prints the 13 matches between the All England Eleven and the United England Eleven, which again had not appeared before outside the newspapers. A brief 'record' section lists individual hundreds made in 'great' matches since 1850 and the other cricket piece runs from 1787 to 1850 (why 1850?, presumably linked to the list of hundreds?) and lists prominent players with the date of their first match at Lord's and the score(s) they made. The Laws of Cricket are printed, but, taking up the same space, are the Rules of Bowls. The remainder of the book is a general 'almanack'.

This second new annual was printed by the same firm that printed Lillywhite's *Guide* – W.H.Crockford of Blackheath Road, Greenwich. Some historians have suggested that Crockford acted as the Editor, but would he have edited a possible rival to Fred's *Guide,* when the latter publication had been such a commercial success for him over a number of years?

To emphasise this point, it should be added that Fred Lillywhite had set up a sports business with Wisden at 2, Coventry St, in October 1855, but Fred Lillywhite and John Wisden had quarrelled in October 1858, the partnership had split, leaving Wisden in sole charge of their Coventry Street business. Lillywhite had moved to The Oval. John Wisden retired as a professional cricketer at the close of the 1863 season – born in Brighton in 1826, his cricket had been principally for Sussex, but in 1847 William Clarke recruited him for the All England Eleven. Wisden broke away from Clarke's side in 1852 and, with James Dean, formed a rival professional wandering side, the United England Eleven. Later he formed a partnership with George Parr (Clarke's right-hand man) to set up a cricket ground at Leamington, but this partnership was also later dissolved. Wisden does not seem to have been a man for business partnerships!

The second edition of his annual was a total change from the first. Almost all the book (aside from the Oxford v Cambridge match series) was devoted to the games played the previous season, as well as the scores of the 1863-64 matches by Parr's Team to Australia and New Zealand. Had Wisden seen that there was much interest in the principal scores given in *The Cricket Chronicle*, but not the mass of minor games also published there?

The third edition followed the format of the second, though adding the detailed scores of the All England and United matches against local 22s. What was lacking was any bowling statistics – Printed Match Cards of the day did not normally include bowling, but these details did appear in newspapers.

No doubt to the delight of cricket followers another annual was launched in 1865 *John Lillywhite's Cricketers' Companion for 1865*. This first edition was 160 pages in length and priced at one shilling. The page count was larger than Fred's Guide, which in 1865 only contained 124 pages. Unlike the cricket public, brother Fred was not amused by John's new venture. In format and content the two were very similar. Both had pen pictures of current players, but for his 1865 edition Fred Lillywhite decided to attack both his rivals: in 1864 he had printed the normal innocuous descriptions of John Lillywhite and John Wisden, but now he changed his stance:

> Lillywhite, John, born at Hove, near Brighton, Sussex, Nov. 10 1826. Has been a first-class bat, and of valuable assistance to his county and "England" generally, but is now "poaching" for ideas on another field, without license. May he be successful with his "gun" by "day" and his net by "night"… A most eminent publisher of cricketing works, following the steps of his brother Fred, having now been promoted and "gazetted" as "compiler".

> Wisden, John, born at Brighton, Sussex, Sept.5,1826. Was a "good 'un" but now "does nothing" for his county, England, or any other eleven, in fact, devotes his time to do a "deal of good" for promoting the manly game, for which he spends a vast amount of "coin" being a paid secretary to the Cricketers' Fund Society, chairman (in daily attendance) Mr Thomas Box, late of the Brighton ground. Wisden is also the "energetic" secretary to the "United Eleven" and expects an appointment to his County Club.

John Lillywhite himself acted as editor of his annual, probably for the first ten issues. G.D.West, whose books on both this annual and the later one issued by James Lillywhite, are a quite excellent historical survey of each, explains the tangled complex of the editorship. David T.Smith's similar study, published privately in 1991, of Fred's *Guides* has been mentioned before.

The three annuals again appeared in 1866, all three broadly staying with the layouts they had used in 1865, though (due to his comments in 1865) Fred Lillywhite lost the patronage of M.C.C. The circulation battle was not destined to continue for a third year, for on September 15, 1866, Fred Lillywhite died in Brighton, he was only 37. Whatever his shortcomings, he had provided cricket followers in the 1850s and 1860s with an invaluable guide to the cricket season and though his role in the publication of *Scores & Biographies* is frequently derided, the fact must be obvious that, without him, the volumes might never have seen publication. David Smith in his analysis of the editions of the *Guide* proves that Fred Lillywhite cut corners and reduced the production costs to a minimum, but does that really matter? Lillywhite was assisted by Arthur Haygarth, who not only wrote pieces in the Guide but provided facts, particularly on the biographies of current players. Perhaps Lillywhite ought to have acknowledged Haygarth's help, though the latter was a very wealthy man who treated the whole idea of collecting scores and biographical material as a hobby.

With the death of Fred Lillywhite, the Guide effectively died; John Lillywhite had purchased the copyright and *John Lillywhite's Companion for 1867* appears with the extended title:

'Lillywhite's Cricketers' Companion: With Which is Incorporated Lillywhite's Guide to Cricketers For 1867'.

The 1867 edition is 30 pages larger than the 1866 edition, there being a general increase in information given in each section, rather than any complete innovation. The 1867 edition contains an advertisement for the first four volumes of *Scores & Biographies* – 'which was commenced by his late father and continued by his late brother Frederick (and) has been placed in his hands for sale by Mr F.P.Miller (who has expended £2,000 upon it).'

Returning to *The Cricketers' Almanack* (Wisden) the issues for 1867, 1868 and 1869 are made largely up of detailed match scores, but no description of individual games, or any bowling analysis. The 1867 edition has a new section, 'The Births and Deaths of Celebrated Cricketers', culled without acknowledgement from Haygarth's researches printed in *Scores & Biographies* – about 400 players, are included. John Wisden does not publish pen pictures of current players. The 1869 edition contains an article for the first time, namely: 'Individual Innings of 200 or more Runs'. More significant however is that the article is credited to a compiler, W.H.Knight. The reason for the list was twofold, first E.F.S.Tylecote hit

404 not out (by a long way the highest ever) and five others exceeded 200 in 1868 – though Knight could only discover 23 double hundreds ever scored. (*Lillywhite's Companion* for 1867 and onward gives lists of 100s made the previous season and long lists of first-class averages neither of which appear in *Wisden*).

William Henry Knight is shown as the editor of Wisden in the 1870 edition. He was born in London in November 1812 and was a journalist on several newspapers, though he is only credited with cricket reporting for the *Sporting Gazette* (founded 1862). At one time he was the only officially recognised reporter at Lord's. Knight continued as *Wisden* editor until and including the 1879 edition – he died in Middlesex Hospital on August 16, 1879, 'long a martyr to a painful disease'.

Meanwhile, in 1872, yet another Lillywhite had founded a cricket annual. He was James Lillywhite, the eldest of the sons of F.W.Lillywhite, being a year older than John. James had played 18 major matches for Sussex between 1850 and 1860, in spite of the fact that, in 1855, he had moved to Cheltenham, taking up the post of coach at the town's College. He was to remain as a resident of that town for the rest of his life. The first issue of *James Lillywhite's Cricketers' Annual* was published by James Lillywhite & Co in the spring of 1872, but the second was published by James Lillywhite, Frowd & Co of 4, Newington Causeway, S.W.(sic) actually S.E., ten minutes walk from London Bridge, where the firm advertised a vast array of sporting equipment. The new annual is edited by Charles W.Alcock (Secretary of Surrey County Cricket Club).

The Annual had board covers with a distinctive red cloth covering – *John Lillywhite's Companion* had a rather flimsy green paper cover. The two annuals are therefore often referred to as Red Lilly and Green Lilly. Both sold at one shilling and the difference between the two was marginal. Doubts as to whether there was room in the market for two similar annuals must have vanished when the 1872 edition of Red Lilly was re-issued twice.

Charles William Alcock, the editor of the new annual, was born in Sunderland in December 1842, moving to Chingford, Essex with his family in 1855 and was educated at Harrow. On leaving school he joined his father's marine insurance business, at the same time contributing articles on cricket and football to the London papers. Alcock was also an active player, both of cricket and football. He captained Wanderers to victory in the first F.A. Cup Final and played for England v Scotland in 1875. Apart from his work on the cricket annual, he was editor of the *Football Annual*. His biography, entitled *The Father of Modern Sport*, was written by Keith Booth and published in 2002. Further references to Alcock will be made in due course.

Coupled with C.W.Alcock should be a second Harrovian, Robert Allan Fitzgerald. Unlike Alcock, Fitzgerald went up to Cambridge and both at school and university he had a highly successful cricketing career. He was in the Harrow side of 1852 and then won his blue in 1854 and 1856, being described as a 'quick run getter and an excellent field'. Having entered the legal profession and become a barrister in 1860, he was appointed Secretary of M.C.C. in 1863 and remained in that post until ill-health forced him to resign in 1877. He began his cricket writing by sending reports of Quidnuncs matches to *Bell's Life* and in 1866 wrote a comical tale *Jerks in from Short-Leg*, using the pen-name 'Quid'. He was in addition a regular contributor to *Lillywhite's Companion*, though unlike Alcock, he doesn't seem to have taken up the editorship. In 1872 he captained the M.C.C. Team which toured North America and wrote an account of that trip, *Wickets in the West*. Fitzgerald died in Chorleywood, Herts in October 1881 aged 47. His obituary in *Lillywhite's Companion* notes: 'His lively temperament, good heart, and keen sense of humour rendered him generally popular, and his loss is deeply regretted by a large circle of cricketers.'

James Lillywhite's Cricketers' Annual was only in its third year when the proprietor of the rival 'Green Lilly' died – John Lillywhite's obituary noted: 'Frank, cheerful and generous, he made many friends, but never an enemy; and his name will be passed down to future generations of cricketers, as that of one, whose thirty years' connection with the game, won for him the esteem of all.' John was only 47 and judging by that obituary a contrast to both his father and his brother, Fred! Green Lilly continued, but there seems to be an insoluble mystery as to the identity of the editor, following John's death. Several names have been put forward, Arthur Haygarth and James Pycroft being two of the best known. All that is definitely confirmed is that E.S.Pardon edited some of the 1880s issues. To complicate matters, in January 1879, James Lillywhite junior, the cousin of James senior (of the Red Lilly Annual) and of John (the founder of Green Lilly) joined the firm of John Lillywhite, thus changing the name to John & James Lillywhite & Co. then in 1883 James junior bought the whole business and Green Lilly for 1884 appeared under the title *James Lillywhite's Cricketers' Companion*. Through these changes in ownership, the Preface and Season's Review in each issue is simply closed by 'The Editor'.

Edgar Searles Pardon was born in September 1859, one of three journalist sons of George Frederick Pardon, who in 1870 had published under the pen-name Capt Crawley *The Book of Manly Games for Boys* which included fifty pages featuring cricket – G.F.Pardon died in Canterbury, whilst attending the cricket week, on August 4, 1884. He was then aged 63. He was a prolific reporter, reviewer, leader-writer and essayist. He borrowed the pseudonym Capt Crawley from *Vanity Fair* and was a friend of its author.

Edgar Pardon died in July 1898 aged 38. After Green Lilly closed, Edgar had assisted his brothers on the compilation of *Wisden*. His obituary commented: 'Not only English, but Australian cricketers found in him a faithful chronicler. To the Australian teams of later years, indeed, no one, perhaps, on this side was better known. Singularly fair, as well as temperate in his views, while never lacking the courage of his opinions, his writings naturally always commanded respect.'

Whilst the battle to be the best cricket annual was being fought between the two Lillywhite productions and Wisden, all of whom were broadly concerned with describing the current scene, the M.C.C., between 1876 and 1880, were supplying the historian's needs by publishing Haygarth's *Scores & Biographies* covering the seasons 1855 to 1876 (Vols V to XIII).

There were, in addition, several other individuals whose interest lay in cricket's history and one was Charles Box.

Box was originally the proprietor of a small school in South Malling, Kent, but the school failed. He had already published two books on cricket, first *The Cricketers' Manual*, which appeared in several editions between 1848 and 1851 – bibliophiles continue to debate exactly how many. The Manual was written using the pseudonym 'Bat' and the work does touch on the historical rise of cricket. In 1868 Box produced *The Theory and Practice of Cricket From its Origins to the Present Times.* By now he had taken up journalism as a full time occupation and been appointed the cricket correspondent of *The Times*.

Box's magnum opus appeared in 1877 *The English Game of Cricket* published by *The Field*. It was the first major work devoted to the history of the game, completely dwarfing the chapters in Pycroft and Nyren. After sections on cricket history generally, Box then treats each of the main cricketing counties separately, with a number of full match scores, as well as the batting averages for 1875. There follows chapters on England tours to America and Australia, also a Glossary of words and phrases, as well as a decent index. The complete work runs to 596 pages, 9½" by 7½". Box understood the problems of historical research as the following passage makes abundantly clear:

> 'Individuals who had to write for a living – no matter what the subject – seized upon the facts and theories propounded by Lambert and Nyren to garnish a substantial dish of veritable knowledge with fables and fancies, and thus make what in the esteem of the literary world would be 'dry reading' a subject of some interest. Strutt was rushed after as one of the hardest used books in the Museum, and among the thumb-worn and greasy pages few appear at the present day to have been more frequently scanned than those relating to cricket. But the paucity of information afforded, forced into play a lively imagination, and a great deal of nonsense was the result.

There was a market for the article; but as truth often lies in a well too deep for the indolent to search out, pretty stories were introduced to save such exercise.'

Charles Box retired from *The Times* in 1880 and then was appointed cricket editor of *The Field* until 1885; he died in Camberwell in July 1890 aged 84. In his chapter on the Origin and Progress of cricket, Box, though exceedingly verbose by today's criteria, does note the 1598 reference to cricket in Guildford and the earliest overseas reference in Aleppo. He also pours doubt on John Timb's note that Bishop Ken played cricket whilst at Winchester. In all, Box's work is worthwhile reading for those who wish to see how the writing of cricket history was progressing.

Another writer whose work deserves to be studied, but whose name, unlike Box's does not feature in *Padwick* is George Moir Crauford In the 1870s he wrote perhaps half a million words on cricket's history – certainly the Nottinghamshire section runs to 100,000 words – in his column in *The Sporting Life* using the pseudonym 'Gemse'. Whilst Charles Box's history is on the florid side, Crauford's is solid fact. He used Haygarth's *Scores & Biographies* as a general guide, but did not simply regurgitate Haygarth's biographies. Crauford toured the country interviewing old cricketers and by doing so picked up details of players that Haygarth missed – Haygarth, as a rule of thumb, normally confined his biographies to cricketers who played at Lord's, but Crauford in his researches dug out players from the 'country'. Since Crauford was writing a weekly column, he also had the advantage that readers wrote in with additions and corrections and these normally appeared at the top of his following week's piece. The umpire Robert Thoms acted as an adviser to Crauford. The latter died in London in July 1883 aged 43. A note, which appeared in *Cricket* regarding his death, stated that he was 'in the War Office', though one can hardly imagine that his journalistic work was part-time – these Victorian writers achieved so much more than their successors!

A much longer-lived 'amateur' journalist and author was Frederick Gale (known as 'The Old Buffer'). He would seem to be the nearest 19th century equivalent in cricket writing terms to the 20th century Neville Cardus.

Born in Pewseyvale, Wiltshire in 1823, Gale was educated at Winchester, being in the XI in 1841. A hard-hitting batsman, he played one match for Kent in 1845. He resided for many years in Mitcham, captaining the local village team; by profession he was a parliamentary solicitor. His cricket articles appeared in *Bell's Life, Baily's* and *Fore's Sporting Notes*. His first book, *The Public Schools Matches and Those We Meet There* was published in 1853 using 'Wykehamist' as his pen-name; Padwick lists in all 15 books or publications by Gale. He firmly believed in Hambledon as the Cradle of Cricket and his very extensive writings allied to his cricket lecture tours did much to perpetuate that myth.

Gale emigrated to Canada in 1891, selling his extensive cricket library at Sotheby's, but returned to England after a year and died in London in April 1904.

The existence of the three competing national cricket annuals – *Wisden* and the two *Lillywhites* – has been discussed; the various provincial ones will be noted later, but the very keen interest in sports and cricket in particular can best be demonstrated by listing the main national periodicals devoted to sports and pastimes in the mid-1870s:

- *The Sportsman* – published four times a week, subscription 19s 6d for six months, 'devoted a large portion of its space to Cricket Reports and Analyses'.
- *The Sporting Gazette* – published every Saturday, price 4d, 'Aquatics, Cricket, Football, Athletics were highlighted as its major sports'.
- *Land and Water* – price 6d weekly; 'Latest Reports from the Universities and a critique on passing Important events on the River, the Running Path, the Cricket Field and Billiard Table'.
- *The Sporting Life* – every Wednesday and Saturday, 'The only Penny Sporting Paper – Largest Circulation of any Sporting Paper in the World'.

In addition to these publications, all of which were advertised in *Lillywhite's Companion* of 1875, *Bell's Life* was still being printed, but its popularity was waning in face of the burgeoning opposition; *The Field* also covered cricket, but as the name implies was more to do with field sports. In 1875 the *Athletic News* was launched in Manchester as part of the Edward Hulton newspaper empire. Hulton began his career as a reporter for the *Manchester Guardian*; in 1871 he established *The Sporting Chronicle*. He chose T.R.Sutton as the editor of *The Athletic News*. Thomas Robert Sutton was only 21 on his appointment and he turned this paper into the best all-round sporting sheet in the country. Sutton died after a serious illness in Lytham St Anne's in July 1895, he was only 42 and still running the paper. In his youth he had been a more than competent footballer, playing both soccer and rugby. It should be mentioned that *Baily's Monthly* magazine and *Fore's*, a quarterly, both carried some cricket articles.

Aside from the three national cricket annuals, there were two rather unexpected ones. The first, John Lawrence's *Handbook of Cricket* in Ireland appeared in 16 issues between 1865 and 1881. It was published by John Fortune Lawrence, whose father (also John Lawrence) had moved from Southern England in 1833 to establish a sports outfitters in Grafton St, Dublin. Like John Wisden before him, Lawrence began the annual to publicise the goods sold in his shop. The compiler and editor of the annual was J.T. Hurford, Secretary of the Phoenix Cricket Club. Lawrence also helped in the publication in 1879 of a book describing the Irish Cricketers Tour to North America that year. The author was Henry William Brougham (1853-1908), who was a playing member of the touring side. He was, later, the father of Henry Brougham, an Oxford blue in 1911.

The second unexpected annual was *Scottish Cricketers' Guide* founded in 1870/71 by Percival King. King, born in Stockwell, Surrey in December 1835, had some trials for Surrey, but moved up to Edinburgh as a coach and opened a sports store in the city. The annual lasted until 1888/89. It gave good coverage to the main Scottish clubs with potted scores and averages.

Whilst Ireland and Scotland both had annuals which survived for a relatively long period, in Australia cricket annuals seldom became established. Ken Piesse, the well-known Australian cricket historian, researched the subject and his treatise was published in *The Journal of The Cricket Society* Vol 9, no.4 (Spring 1980) and following issues. Anyone seeking detailed information should consult Piesse's articles. In brief, the first annual *The Australian Cricketer's Guide* lasted three seasons, 1856-57 to 1858-59 and was financed largely by a Melbourne businessman, William Fairfax. The next attempt at a publication *The Victorian Cricketer's Guide*, was by the Cambridge University and Surrey cricketer, turned journalist, William Hammersley, which survived only two seasons, the last being 1863-64. Hammersley was the sports editor of the *Australasian* newspaper for 16 years, retiring in 1882. He died in November 1886 aged 60. The third annual *Australian Cricketer's Guide* was another to survive only two issues. The editor was Thomas Wentworth Wills, who played cricket for Kent and Victoria, but is better remembered for getting a blue at Cambridge, though never actually a student there.

Over in Canada *The Canadian Cricketer's Guide* appeared in 1858, then after a long interval twice more, in 1876 and 1877; across the border the magazine *The American Cricketer* was founded in 1877. It was to continue until 1929, its contents were almost exclusively contemporary.

Chapter 3
The Influence of W.G.Grace

By 1880, the cricket statistician was well catered for with regard to the detailed scores of the major matches played in England. In the previous chapter the principal national newspapers, magazines and annuals dealing with cricket, which were published during the 1870s were commented upon. With the aid of those plus Haygarth's *Scores & Biographies*, a statistician could possess the scores of almost all matches of 'first-class' county standard, since such matches began to be published on a regular basis in the 1770s. The provincial press gave local county sides even more detailed coverage, but the compilation of 'records' had scarcely begun.

Bell's Life, as has been pointed out, began the publication of 'averages' for leading players and these were taken up by some annuals, notably in the early days, Bat's *Manual* and Fred Lillywhite's *Guide*, but taking, as an example, the *Wisden Almanack* of 1880, whilst very good match descriptions and full scores of major games are given (Wisden in 1870 began to include bowling analyses with each match score) the Almanack does not even print a table of 'first-class' averages, only providing separate averages for each county, plus M.C.C. There is no 'Record Section' at all and merely a straight list of individual hundreds, of any class – similar to lists which appear in the Lillywhite publications. It may be that *Wisden* followed Arthur Haygarth's view that detailed 'records' were unnecessary and unwanted?

One man however was to force the hands of cricket writers and embryo cricket statisticians and that was W.G.Grace. Within a few years of his first public match, Grace became the outstanding sporting figure in England and his appearances, as well as his performances were news not only in cricketing circles, but also amongst the general public. It is a commonplace remark that Grace created all the batting records that his successors had to beat, but in fact for several summers in succession he beat his personal record for the previous season. Lillywhite's Companions over four consecutive years illustrate the point:

- Season 1868

  Mr W.G.Grace is at the top of the tree, with the wonderful average of 65-3 for nine innings, all played in leading matches of the season.

- Season 1869

  Mr W.G.Grace is of course, facile princips, his exploits with the bat having eclipsed all hitherto recorded.

- Season 1870

  Mr W.G.Grace is, of course, at the top of the tree; who would dream of disputing his claim to the championship? Such batting as he has displayed in 1870 has never been equalled. An aggregate of 1808 runs (the largest on record), compiled in 33 innings, and giving an average of more than 54 runs for each completed innings, is indeed a marvellous feat; and that the day be far distant when his peerless science and hitting cease to charm a crowded ring is our most earnest hope. (note: the writer's comment that Grace's 1808 was the largest on record – even if lists of high aggregates were not printed in the cricket annuals, clearly someone was looking back at previous performances)

- Season 1871

  Mr W.G.Grace is, of course, far in advance of everyone, and such an average as his has never yet been approached. His aggregate of 1808 runs and average of 54.26 in 33 innings in 1870, was then reckoned an unparalleled achievement, but the great batsman's doings during the past season have thrown all his previous efforts, great as they have been, into the shade. An aggregate of 2739 runs, amassed in 35 innings, yields an average of 78.9, so that with two more innings he has made nearly a thousand more runs than last year, and his average has increased to the wonderful extent of 24 runs for each time he has gone to the wickets!

Each of those quotes come from the paragraph which heads the first-class batting averages of the specific season.

In 1876 W.G. twice broke the individual innings record, which as the press reminded their readers had been held by William Ward (278) since 1820 – Grace hit 318 and 344, but the reporters were even more astonished by his innings of 400 against XXII of Grimsby, more than double the previous best against Odds.

It is little wonder that this torrent of records led inevitably to the composition of tables of records – initially batting by individuals, then by teams and also bowling tables. In 1880, the *Lillywhite Annual* included a chapter 'A Few Loose Strings' which expanded the traditional lists of the season's hundreds and top bowling analyses to feature 'Carrying Bat Through Innings', 'Long Scores for First Wicket', 'Small Scoring', 'Tall Scoring', though these lists only included feats in the season under review. This list of sundry records is perhaps a milestone in the development of the collation of such data. The rival *Lillywhite's Companion* featured 'Cricket Curiosities' which pointed out, among other items, that Cambridge University's score of 593 was the second highest ever in first-class cricket.

The encouragement of 'amateurs' to seek out and compile 'first-class records' on a bigger scale came with the creation of the weekly magazine *Cricket* in 1882. This was not the first weekly devoted entirely to cricket – that innovation had taken place in the United States in 1877. *Cricket* was also preceded in England by *Cricket and Football Times*, a weekly publication that first appeared on May 2, 1878 and was published from 115, Fleet Street, London. As its name implies the magazine covered football in the winter. This weekly was clearly designed to cash in on the visit that summer of the Australian Touring Team. The magazine never really took hold and closed in 1881. There is a minor mystery as to the person responsible for the cricket content. J.D.Coldham, in his essay on early cricket journalists, credits H.V.L.Stanton with the work, but Stanton was only 18 when publication began and, according to his obituary, trained as a solicitor before switching to journalism. Henry Valentine Labrow Stanton was born in November 1859 and established his reputation as a cricket reporter with *The Sportsman* newspaper, writing under the pseudonym 'Wanderer'. He joined that paper in 1884 and remained in post until the paper closed forty years later. From *The Sportsman* Stanton moved to *Wisden*, compiling the seasonal averages and other statistical data until his death in May 1933. Having a wry sense of humour, Stanton was in great demand as a guest speaker at social functions.

The publishers of *Cricket*, W.R.Wright of 17, Paternoster Sq, London, had the foresight to appoint C.W.Alcock as Editor. At least that would seem to be the case, but a note in the edition of March 28, 1895 states: 'The change of premises has in no way altered the proprietary of the paper, which remains in the hands of the Cricketer who has been editor and proprietor from the first.' Therefore Wright & Co were publishers, but not the owners and controllers of the magazine – in 1895, Messrs Merritt & Hatcher of 168, Upper Thames St, London E.C. took over as publishers from W.R.Wright & Co. It has already been noted that Alcock was Editor of the *Lillywhite Annual* and his knowledge of the politics of cricket (with ten years as Surrey Secretary behind him) could hardly be equalled.

W.R.Wright was not simply a publisher, he was also a cricket enthusiast. His firm printed the scorecards for The Oval, as well as a wide variety of sporting pamphlets and books. Wright later had a long spell as Editor of *Ayres Cricket Companion*, which annual will be treated separately.

The Alcock-Wright partnership, if it was such, pitched their new weekly at just the correct level. Unlike *Cricket and Football Times*, *Cricket* flourished from its inception and in the process attracted some very intelligent cricket statisticians and historians as correspondents. The influence of Alcock, in particular, is easily demonstrated by the single fact that, when he died in post, the magazine lost momentum and slid gently into deficit.

Looking at a typical 16 page weekly edition (the magazine was monthly in the winter), a portrait and biography of a cricketer (one of the Australian tourists) occupied the first page; the second page was a section of the serialisation of John Nyren's book; there were 12 pages of scores, both first-class, with reports, and local metropolitan club matches (local clubs paid for the insertion of scores); finally came the editorial and 'Pavilion Gossip' – Alcock being in a prime position to slant both these items, so that they were accurate and topical. In the issue which I picked at random, Alcock chides a paper called *Echo* both for the way it reports the Surrey v Australia game and for describing the two Surrey Reads as brothers. Alcock's editorial in this edition is headed 'Decadence in Cricket'.

In an edition in 1883, Alcock republishes a long piece on Yorkshire Records, which first appeared in the *Sheffield Telegraph*. The article is very thorough, even listing the heaviest and lightest Yorkshire cricketers! In 1884, on page 348, is the following note:

'It is not often too, that the statisticians of cricket have to record an innings....'

It would be foolhardy to suggest that this is the first reference to 'statisticians of cricket', but perhaps it is the first in a specific cricket paper?

In the same issue of *Cricket*, a short article appears containing the 'records' in the County Championship since 1873. The author is Thomas Keyworth, who was responsible for several other pieces in the weekly during the 1880s. He was acclaimed by historians many years later as a researcher of great importance, even though so little of his work was published. Keyworth was born in Sutton-cum-Lound, Notts in 1844 and was a Congregational minister. He worked in Toxteth, Liverpool in the 1880s, but had moved to Halifax by 1901.

A flavour of the growth in interest for cricket statistics is clearly shown in an 1887 item in the magazine *Cricket*; a reader writes:

"This is the age of statistics. I have amused myself and whiled away some hours of this winter's evenings by ascertaining the averages of those who have figured most prominently in the Gentlemen v Players matches during the last 40 years."

A list then follows of the top 26 batsmen and top 26 bowlers who appeared in the series. Through the first few years of *Cricket*, similar items, usually less extensive, creep into the 'Pavilion Gossip' section, or correspondence column of the magazine.

The first full-blown hardback book totally devoted to cricket statistical analysis, rather than simply publishing scorecards of games, was published in 1888 and featured the details of Surrey as a team and the county's cricketers individually. In the same year another author dealt with the statistics of Nottinghamshire, but this included the detailed scores of the county's matches and longish biographical sketches of the leading players. In 1888 the battle for the Championship crown was between those two county clubs. The Surrey book, entitled *Surrey at the Wicket* begins with a list of Surrey players from 1844 with, where known, place of birth, date of birth, height and seasons for Surrey. There follows on facing pages, each season's potted scores and the seasonal averages. The results are then given in a summary table, with the record against each opponent, followed by the runs and wickets for and against Surrey season-by-season. Career Records for all the players, both batting and bowling, and sundry other tables complete the book, which is 159 pages in length.

The Nottinghamshire book *Fifty Years of Nottinghamshire Cricket* is much more substantial, being 82 pages of biography plus 388 pages of scores and averages. The biographical section contains 62 cricketers and the more famous players have very detailed notes on their cricketing career – William Barnes' piece, for example, runs to 12 pages with portrait. The scores up to 1869 are without bowling or match description, but from 1869 bowling and match description, plus seasonal averages are included. There are however no record tables as such, save those incorporated in some of the longer biographies.

If the facts are presented in contrasting ways in these two works, then the authors are even more of a contrast. The Surrey book was privately printed for its author, in Madrid. Anthony Benitez De Lugo was the compiler's name; born in 1858, he was educated at St George's College from 1870 to

1875 (the college is now in Weybridge). He had followed the fortunes of Surrey as a schoolboy, but it was not until 1886 that he joined the County Club as a member. He died in Pau, France on March 16, 1907. De Lugo's other publications were a statistical analysis of W.W.Read's career and an updated but shortened version of his 1888 Surrey book, published in 1900. In addition he made a contribution to the 1904 sumptuous *Surrey Cricket : Its History and Associations*.

The information regarding De Lugo comes from an article by J.D.Coldham, published in *The Journal of The Cricket Society*, but recent research by experts in Surrey casts doubt on the actual authorship of the work.

De Lugo was, seemingly, the enthusiastic amateur statistician; the author of the Nottinghamshire book was C.H.Richards, a professional publisher and printer in Nottingham, whose father had printed scorecards at Trent Bridge since the 1860s. The Richards firm over many years was responsible for the printing and publication of numerous cricketing items and more about the family and its business will be detailed later. ·

At a national level, did the success of *Cricket* affect the three major annuals – the two Lillywhites and Wisden? When *Lillywhite's Companion* was published in 1885, its Preface noted that 'it has by far the largest circulation of any of the cricket annuals.' However on January 1, 1886, Messrs James Lillywhite of 10 Seymour St, Euston Sq, London, the Companion publishers, merged with James Lillywhite, Frowd & Co of 24 Haymarket, Charing Cross, London, publishers of *Lillywhite's Annual* and the *Companion* and *Annual* merged as one single entity for 1886. Charles Alcock was the editor of the combined work. Curiously the publishers were now given as jointly, Lillywhite, Frowd & Co and Wright & Co (Cricket Press) of 41, St Andrew's Hill, London E.C. – as has been noted the latter published *Cricket*.

Just to recap briefly on the Lillywhite dynasty, John Lillywhite who had launched the *Companion* died in 1874; James sen, the original partner in Lillywhite, Frowd, died in 1882 and James jun, who played for Sussex until 1883 and was responsible for the 1876-77 England tour to Australia and then joined with the Notts pair of Shaw and Shrewsbury in prompting several later tours, died in 1929. In 1888 James jun claimed he was more or less destitute, so he presumably had relinquished his interest in Lillywhite, Frowd? Lillywhite, Frowd continued as publishers of the *Annual* (Wright & Co ceased their interest in 1894) until it closed.

At the time the *Companion* and *Annual* merged, the other chief competitor, *Wisden* was going steadily downhill. W.H.Knight, the editor, had died on August 16, 1879. An obituary in the 1880 edition of *Wisden* ends,

> 'to none more so (is his loss felt) than the proprietors of
> this Almanack, who have lost in him a painstaking and
> conscientious compiler.'

George West was appointed as Knight's replacement. West who had been a sub-editor on *The Field*, was appointed to succeed Charles Box, as cricket correspondent of *The Times*, within a year of his appointment as *Wisden* editor. West also wrote on many other subjects apart from cricket. Unlike Alcock he did not seem able to ride several horses simultaneously and the *Wisden Almanack* was the one which suffered in consequence. John Wisden himself died in April 1884; Harry Luff bought both the Wisden sports outfitters business and the Almanack from the Wisden estate. Luff had already acted as manager of the shop in Cranbourn Street, Leicester Square and therefore knew the business. One of his first actions was to remove West as editor of the Almanack. West who hailed originally from Devon and claimed relationship with the famous sportsman, Squire Osbaldeston, continued his work on *The Times* until ill-health forced his retirement, not long before his death in 1896, aged 45. West had also been the editor of *Feltham's Cricketer*, an annual that came out twice – in 1877 and 1878. He was probably responsible for *Feltham's Cricket Directory for 1883*. This ran to 175 pages and apart from scores, did publish some records. These re-appeared with additions in W.G.Grace's book of 1891, which is noted in detail later.

With the Almanack at its lowest ebb, Luff decided to bring in Charles F.Pardon as the new editor. It proved an astute move. C.F.Pardon had founded The Cricket Reporting Agency in April 1880 and had a firm knowledge of sports reporting. He had been a member of George Kelly King's Sporting Press Agency as well as a sub-editor with the Press Association. Kelly King died in 1879 and Pardon took on staff from the now defunct Kelly King Agency for his new venture.

In the Preface to the 1887 edition of *Wisden*, Charles Pardon states:

'Messrs Wisden requested me to undertake to tell the story of the chief play of 1886, and that task I have been able to accomplish owing to the assistance promptly and generously rendered to me by Mr Sydney H.Pardon, Mr Edgar S.Pardon (both Charles' brothers), Mr C. Stewart Caine and other writers and reporters on cricket, who have now been associated with me for several years.'

In the 1888 edition of *Wisden*, Herbert E.Jewell is added to the list of assistants and contributors. Charles Pardon's reign as editor did not last long; he died in April 1890 aged 40. C.W.Alcock, editor of the *Lillywhite Annual* the main rival to Wisden, is unstinting in his praise of Charles Pardon. Alcock writes in *Cricket*:

He was an entity in the cricket world, better known, in fact, than the majority of the players, whose doings he had been accustomed so graphically to recount for several years….It was in a great measure to him that the public owes the vastly improved style of cricket reporting of late years….As a cricket writer he had no superior, combining freshness as well as vigour of style with a close observation, and, withal, practical knowledge of the game.'

Sydney Pardon, Charles' brother, took over as *Wisden* editor and the 1891 edition, under Sydney's name in the Preface has added to it 'Cricket Reporting Agency, 112, Fleet Street. Apart from the Pardons the only named contributor to *Wisden* in 1887 is Charles Stewart Caine. Born in Portsmouth in October 1861, he trained as a journalist with Kelly King's Agency and on its demised moved to the Cricket Reporting Agency, where he was destined to remain for the rest of his life – he edited *Wisden* for eight editions from 1926 and died in post in April 1933.

Herbert Edward Jewell, the correspondent who joined the named *Wisden* writers in 1888, was a member of Pardons Agency for 27 years. He worked also for the *Morning Post* and, aside from cricket, specialised in athletics. Jewell died in December 1922, aged 66. When the Pardons first took over the running of what was then an ailing annual, their initial move, no doubt to reduce costs, was to reduce the number of pages by 50, this, despite the need to cover the 1886 Australian Tour. The reduction was achieved by drastically pruning the match reports; for example all the Gloucester home game reports were cut from a full page to half that length and the report on the Gentlemen v Players game at The Oval shrank from three pages to 1 ¼ pages. The single innovation was the first-class batting and bowling tables, each split into two sections – amateurs and professionals. They are printed in order of merit, whereas *Lillywhite's Annual* gives a combined amateur and professional list, but in alphabetical order. The two sets of averages more or less match, probably stemming from the same original source.

Rather surprisingly *Cricket* does not publish a set of first-class averages at the close of the 1886 season, even though the top batting averages are printed in several issues as the 1886 season progresses. The magazine does print an irate letter from a reader complaining that no one seems to print averages to two places of decimals, but just gives the full figure plus the remainder (*Lillywhite's Annual* changes to two decimal places in their 1891 edition).

Having a high profile amongst cricket followers, Charles Pardon, with his *Wisden* editor's hat on, enters into the politics of the game with essays in both the 1889 and 1890 editions. He determined to establish a proper league table for the first-class counties, featuring the top eight sides, and, more in hope, a second division of the next ten counties and even a third division of the remaining counties that possessed viable County Clubs. In view of what has occurred in much more recent times, readers might find Pardon's two essays worth revisiting. Unfortunately, for him, the points system he devised resulted in a triple tie (out of just eight teams) for the

1889 contest. This rather farcical result seems to have pushed the counties into arranging a meeting to agree a points system among themselves and what was just as important, decide definitely which counties qualified to be in the top 'league'.

Apart from the eight principal counties during the 1880s – Gloucestershire, Kent, Lancashire, Middlesex, Notts, Surrey, Sussex and Yorkshire – three others had been included at times by some or all cricket publications – Derbyshire, Hampshire and Somerset. The eight were counted by the cricket press for the 1890 season, but Somerset managed to arrange enough fixtures against the top counties, to be 'promoted' in 1891. This classing of the top counties meant that keepers of cricket records, amateur and professional, could all compile their statistics using a standard base, at least for inter-county games. The classification of peripheral 'first-class' games was to remain unresolved until the 1947 season!

The 1889 edition of *Wisden* introduces for the first time a section of cricket records, it is rather vaguely headed 'Some Cricket Records' and is a series of 21 brief paragraphs, but it is worth noting that a number of these paragraphs have the tag, 'in a first-class match' appended to them. *Lillywhite's Annual* for 1889 expands its record section, entitled 'A Few Loose Strings' to 8 ¼ pages, but it deals only with events that occurred in 1888.

Another source of cricket data and in later years informative essays on various aspects of cricket history is the county annual or yearbook. For a long time, the Shropshire Cricket Club annual which covers the seasons 1865 to 1870 has been listed as the earliest known County Cricket Club annual. It is listed in Padwick, but the compiler apparently never actually saw a copy. The archivists' office in Shrewsbury does not possess a copy and a number of reputable cricket book dealers have been questioned but have not seen a copy for sale. The suspicion must be that, if it exists, either in six separate editions, or in a single version covering six years, the book is only in manuscript form.

Gloucestershire were most fortunate to possess a publisher who was also a great cricket enthusiast. James William Arrowsmith was born in Worcester in 1839, but moved to Bristol and in 1874 published a booklet containing the seasonal Gloucestershire match score cards. The publishing business was founded by his father, Isaac, but it was Arrowsmith who developed it into one of the major firms in Bristol. The annual continued until 1914; in addition Arrowsmith published several books which combined together a number of seasons of scores. He was elected to the Gloucestershire County Cricket Club Committee in 1888 and also became Chairman of the Gloucestershire County Ground Company. Arrowsmith died in Bristol in January 1913. A number of other cricket titles published by his firm will be noted in due course.

The first of the major County Clubs to publish its own Yearbook with the season's match scores was Kent in 1878. It is a very neat 4 ½" by 3 ½" hardback with a blue cover. The Rules and list of subscribers are followed by the detailed scores – batting on one page, bowling on the facing pages, then finally the seasonal averages. The Rt Hon Lord Harris is given as Hon Sec and recalling the later cricketing publications to which Lord Harris gave encouragement and assistance, one may perhaps speculate that Harris had a hand in this innovation.

Hard on the heels of the Kent Annual came a Nottinghamshire annual, though published privately as in the case of Gloucestershire by Arrowsmith, rather than by the County Club. In February 1878, Frank Spybey had published *Nottingham County Cricket Matches From 1865 to 1877*. These detailed scores unfortunately followed the early editions of Wisden and gave no bowling analyses. There are no averages and one simple table of 'records' – 'Individual Innings of Three Figures recorded at Trent Bridge'. However at the end of the same year, Spybey published: *Spybey's Annual Register of Nottingham County Cricket Matches*. For 1878 these scores do include bowling analyses and end with the season's averages. The annual ran for ten years and by its final edition included very detailed descriptions of matches and a table of Births & Deaths of Notts Cricketers. Frank G.Spybey was a tobacconist with premises in Long Row, Nottingham. He stood for the County Cricket Club Committee, but failed to gain election.

In 1893 he retired to the Isle of Man, dying there in June 1895.

F.R.Reynolds, on behalf of Lancashire cricket, not only copied Spybey's scheme, but improved upon it. In 1881 he published *Lancashire County Cricket*, which ran to 160 pages, plus adverts. The book covered all Lancashire matches from 1864 to 1880 on a season by season basis, with averages for each season (except 1864 and 1865) and a review of each season. The only additional information is the short section on the Laws. Reynolds did give the bowling analyses for all but a few lesser matches. Reynolds' book was updated in 1882 and 1883. The work has in recent years been reprinted by Red Rose Books. Three other publications dealing with Lancashire at this time were annuals, which did not last beyond a season or two.

Frederick Reginald Reynolds was born in Cambridgeshire in 1833 and played for his native county until 1867, even though he had been engaged as a ground bowler to the Manchester Club from 1860. In 1870 he was appointed Ground Manager and Assistant Secretary at Old Trafford. For ten seasons, 1865 to 1874 he played for Lancashire, being for the first five or so years one of the county's principal bowlers. Reynolds retired from his Old Trafford post in 1908 and died in April 1915. County Cricket Club Yearbooks with full scores and the now usual format were not published by the Lancashire Club until 1930 – in the case of Nottinghamshire, apart from three issues in the 1930s, the Club did not publish an annual, with detailed scores until 1948.

With C.W.Alcock at the helm it is hardly surprising that Surrey followed Kent as the second County Club to publish its own Yearbook containing detailed scores. The book had board covers of a distinctive chocolate colour. The book is twice the page size of the Kent one and is published by Wright & Co. The matches are printed but without any description. The members are listed, but no addresses. There is no record section, and only the basic seasonal averages.

Yorkshire County Cricket Club became the third first-class county to issue its own Yearbook. In 1878 W.Duthoit had compiled and published *The Yorkshire Cricketer's Guide For 1878*. This contained the county match scores, but the annual only lasted one issue. Duthoit was for several seasons on the County Umpires' List. In addition there was *Durham and Yorkshire Cricketers' Handbook*, established in 1882. It survived to 1900, but contained little statistical information. The official County Club yearbook was first published in 1893. It gave detailed scores for the previous season and a list of births & deaths of County players. This annual gradually expanded is in essence the annual which is still published by the County Club – no other county club has been so dedicated to their yearly publication. In the 1895 edition the fall of wickets data were added to the scores, also the names and addresses of Yorkshire C.C.C. members. Responsible for the annual was the long serving Secretary to the County Club, Joseph Beckett Wolstinholm. He had been appointed as Secretary in 1864, combining the job with the secretaryship of Sheffield United C.C., the club which played at Bramall Lane. He was also a senior partner in Wolstinholm and Stevenson, chartered accountants and stockbrokers. Wostinholm retired as Secretary to the County Club in 1902 and died in Malton in April 1909.

Of the two remaining 1890 first-class counties, Sussex County Cricket Club, considering its age and the example of neighbouring Kent, seemed uninterested in issuing a cricket annual. Alfred James Gaston, the noted cricketing bibliophile, published a seven page booklet, *A Pocket Synopsis of Sussex County Cricket* containing some Sussex statistics, these included hundreds for Sussex since 1868 and batting and bowling averages. A great collector of cricketana, he gave lectures with slides on cricket history and built up a substantial business buying and selling mainly cricket books and pictures. In addition Gaston wrote for the *Sussex Daily News*, under the pen name 'Leatherhunter'. He died in Brighton in October 1928, aged 74. Irving Rosenwater published a monograph on Gaston's life, *Alfred James Gaston : A Study in Enthusiasm* (1975). A second Sussex cricketing bibliophile, a contemporary of Gaston, was Alfred Daniel Taylor. He was responsible for a Sussex Cricket Annual which ran from 1901 to 1909 – he used the pen name, 'Willow Wielder'. Born in London in July 1872 he earned the title of 'cricketologist' and reportedly possessed the largest library of cricket books in the world by the time of his death in March 1923. Other books by both Gaston and Taylor will be noted later. Although Sussex was not the most productive of counties regarding the publication of statistics during the 19th century, the county does boast one very unusual item, *Sussex County Cricket Scores from 1855 to 1878.* It also includes Gentlemen of Sussex matches and some other Sussex related scores, but no bowling at all. No author, publisher or printer is given, though it is believed it was printed in India and compiled by George Ewbank and that only four copies were issued. The work runs to 288 pages and is hardback-bound. Ewbank, who was born in India, played a handful of matches for Sussex commencing 1855; he died in South Norwood in April 1885.

Middlesex, the last of the first-class counties of the time, was the only one not to have a 19th century publication containing the county's statistics, although technically it should be noted that the County's first book of scores was published in 1900!

Outside the leading 1890 counties, Derbyshire's first annual appeared in 1885 edited by E.Elliott and T.Thornhill; Norfolk had a very good annual, which appeared under various editors between 1889 and 1898, giving detailed scores of county matches and county trials, as well as a long list of cricket clubs based in Norfolk. Somerset's first annual commenced life in 1890. It also gave county scores, but was published by the County Club – the annual continued, with some breaks to 1967. Northamptonshire had a 30 page annual in 1887, but this did not reach a second edition. Three years later, a very comprehensive annual of 84 pages, edited by Arthur Daniell, was published but sadly it too survived for one issue only (1890). Staffordshire was more fortunate, the first issue being 1891, then apart from the two World Wars, production continued without a break. Hampshire's annual commenced in 1892, as *Hampshire County Cricket Club Guide*, edited, until his death in 1908, by the County cricketer, Edward Lee Ede.

Warwickshire's attempts at the publication of a yearbook, as opposed to an annual report have been very chequered, whilst Worcestershire have also struggled to publish anything worthwhile prior to the First World War – one appeared for a single year – 1907.

It has previously been mentioned that the progressive success of W.G.Grace seems to have pushed the national annuals into the beginnings of 'Record Sections'. The Champion himself inspired two ghosted autobiographies by William Methven Brownlee. A Scotsman, Brownlee moved to Bristol, where he established a flourishing business as a wine merchant. He was also a cricket enthusiast – he joined the Gloucestershire County Cricket Club Committee in 1896, but his books on W.G.Grace appeared earlier, in 1887 and 1891. It is the latter which is of importance to historians-statisticians. The final 70 or so pages, Chapter XII, titled 'Records and Curiosities' are the most valuable and detailed set of records for cricket as a whole (as opposed to De Lugo's Surrey records for example) yet printed. They commence with the results of all the 'first-class' inter-county matches from 1870 to 1890, followed by results of Gentlemen v Players matches and the career figures for the leading cricketers in those games. The players touring for England and Australia with summary results of 'Test Matches', though not labelled as such are printed. A brief section gives major batting and bowling feats, then the season-by-season batting and bowling figures in 'first-class' matches for the leading players, between ten and twenty in each list in each year. There are career records split into two decades, 1871 to 1880 and 1881 to 1890. No one is directly credited with this record section, though apart from Brownlee, C.P.Green of Malvern, Rev R.S.Holmes of Wakefield, Thomas Padwick of Redhill and Frederick Gale of Mitcham are thanked for their assistance. Of those Holmes is the most likely suspect – he will be treated in a later chapter.

The main sports reporting agency in Yorkshire in the 1880s was founded by George Townrow Groves and based in Sheffield. Groves was the editor of one of the most peculiar of cricket annuals, *Wm Whittam's Modern Cricket and Other Sports* Some idea of its eccentricities can be gauged by a note in the front of the book and by the Preface which follows. The note states:

> Copyists of any part of the book, without quoting the

> source, may safely anticipate Nemesis, all rights being strictly reserved.'

The Preface by William Whittam begins:

> 'The Editor tells me it is necessary to have a preface. Well, Gentle Reader, like the needy knife-grinder, who had no story to tell, I haven't the least idea what to say in the way of a preface.'

As for the actual contents, in the 1883 edition, the batting and bowling averages for Lancashire, Yorkshire, Notts, then Middlesex and Gloucestershire are printed, but not for Kent, Surrey or Sussex. Pen pictures of current Lancashire and Yorkshire players are shown, but not Nottinghamshire. Another section, which is perhaps unique to the annual and of interest to cricket historians, is a long list of the 'Principal Cricket Authors and Reporters'.

William Whittam was a printer of scorecards in Yorkshire; he died in Sheffield in January 1910 aged 76. G.T.Groves, who later moved to London, died in October 1916. His son, G.J.Groves, was also a sports reporter and a very good club cricketer, he played a few games for Nottinghamshire in 1899 and 1900.

Chapter 4
Test Match status is defined and Overseas Publications multiply

English cricket followers must have been delighted when a publisher made the decision to launch a rival to *Cricket*. For too long that magazine had held a monopoly, but in May 1892 *The Cricket Field* was issued. Edited by A.W.Browne, it was published by The Pastime Office, 11-12, Rose St, Paternoster Sq, London E.C. The first article in the initial edition was by W.Methven Brownlee, the subject, inevitably, W.G.Grace. The Pastime Office published weekly journals on Football and on Lawn Tennis, as well as covering the other popular sports. A.W.Browne was not a journalist specialising in cricket and therefore could not compare with his rival editor, C.W.Alcock.

The principal cricket man on the new magazine was Walter Ambrose Bettesworth. Born in 1856, Bettesworth was educated at Ardingly and then stayed at the school as a master. He had a brilliant school cricketing career and that success saw him graduate to the Sussex County side. In between scholastic duties he played 21 games for the county, spread over six seasons. In 1883 he moved to Blair Lodge School in Scotland and hit two double centuries in club cricket in Scotland. Bettesworth decided to retire from schoolmastering and plunge into journalism. He was a very talented artist notably with pen and ink sketches. His first book relating to cricket, *The Royal Road to Cricket* was published in 1891 and cashed in on the vogue for comical productions – C.W.Alcock comments: 'The sketches which accompany the letter-press are full of humour and of a quaint conceit'. Ashley-Cooper was later to say that Bettesworth was 'a man of rare charm and of much quiet humour.' A typical example of his generosity occurred during the First World War. He was too old to take an active part in the war, but he presented virtually all his large library of cricket books to the Royal Navy, the books to be distributed around the fleet. He must have recommenced collecting after the war, in a small way at least, as books from his collection were sold by Hodgson & Co on 25, April 1929, realising £43.6.0. Bettesworth reported matches for *The Cricket Field* and illustrated his words with very pleasant scenes of the games under consideration. Another feature which he contributed was 'Chats with Cricketers'. A number of these were later reissued in book form.

The Cricket Field which was more attractively laid out than its rival *Cricket*, gave more coverage to schools and colleges. Instead of having long descriptions attached to each county scorecard, the magazine gave separate weekly paragraphs for each shire. Its statistical content was largely confined to immediate matters and very few historical articles were printed.

Bettesworth remained on the magazine throughout its existence. It ceased in September 1895, after four years. Bettesworth then transferred his cricketing journalism to *Cricket*; in 1902 he combined that work with the post of cricket editor of *The Field*, remaining with the latter until his death on February 23, 1929. His most important cricket book was *The Walkers of Southgate*, published by Methuen in 1900. The book remains an essential work of reference to the family which effectively created and ran Middlesex County Cricket Club.

As an adjunct to the weekly magazine, the publishers of *The Cricket Field* launched an annual in 1893 – *The Cricket Handbook*, priced at 6d and 96 pages in length It was a complete contrast to the two old established annuals, *Wisden* and *Lillywhite's Annual* There were potted county scores, brief biographies of current county players, county averages and a full page photograph of one player per county. Perhaps the more recent annual which most closely resembles it was the original *Playfair*. No editor was given, but Padwick attributes the work to J.B.Payne.

John Bertram Payne was born in Hunstanton in 1864 and educated at Stonyhurst. He qualified as a solicitor in 1889, but never practised and spent a number of years as a tutor for public examination entrants. In the 1890s he was residing in Harrogate. He published an Index to the matches in *Scores & Biographies* (limited to 100 copies) in 1903 and in 1905 *Scores and Analyses 1864-1881*, a most valuable work which gave the detailed scores of 60 major matches that had not appeared in *Wisden*. In April 1927 Payne was appointed Secretary to Worcestershire C.C.C. but only remained there for nine months, the County Committee then deciding to employ an amateur county cricketer, C.F.Walters. Payne died in Redhill, Surrey aged 94 in July 1959.

The publishers of *The Cricket Field* magazine were not the only people who felt England needed a new annual. In 1892 two had been produced. William Dewar, born in Hull in 1844, published *The Cricket Annual 1892*. This hardback of 328 pages, 7½" by 5½" was in direct competition with *Wisden*, since it printed the full scores of all English first-class matches for 1892. The page layouts were much more attractive than those of *Wisden*, and the new annual included full-page team photographs of the major county sides, which ought to have attracted buyers, but sadly this was not the case and the annual never reappeared after its initial issue. Dewar, who lived in Leeds, was a sub-editor on a local paper – his son, also William, was a journalist.

Also in 1892 came the first edition of *Bussey's Cricketer's Diary and Companion*. As its name implies the book was published by the sports goods firm of George Bussey & Co of Peckham Rye. It was very small 8ov and designed for the waistcoat pocket. The annual continued, without a break, until 1931.

Yet another new departure in 1892 was Percy Cross Standing's book which contained the scores of Gentlemen v Players matches from 1806 to date (The first edition of *Wisden* had contained those matches up to 1863, but with no bowling details.) A versatile journalist and writer, Standing was born in Rickmansworth in 1871 and early in his career was employed by the *Daily Telegraph*, later moving to *The Times*. His work was by no means confined to the sporting field; he wrote a biography of the well-known Victorian painter, Alma Tadema, another book on *Guerilla Leaders of the World* and was an authority on Ibsen – many of his articles and essays have a theatrical theme. For some time he was also music critic of the *Morning Leader*. In 1890 and 1891 Standing was an assistant editor on the magazine *Cricket*. His best remembered cricket book is *Cricket of Today and Yesterday*, which originally appeared as a part work in 1902, but was reissued in two volumes, when additional articles were added by notable contemporary cricketers. His biography of Ranjitsinhji was issued in 1903. Then after a long absence from cricket writing, Standing compiled *Anglo-Australian Cricket 1862-1926* prior to the 1926 Ashes series. This book contains a separate chapter on each tour to and from Australia. Standing died in August 1931 – his death seems to have been ignored by the cricket press.

How did C.W.Alcock react to the emergence of a creditable weekly rival to his magazine? Was it mere coincidence that the first article by R.S.Holmes was published in *Cricket* on February 25, 1892? Robert Stratten Holmes was born in London's Oxford Street in 1850, his father having a retail bookshop in that thoroughfare. Holmes was ordained in 1874 and moved to Northampton; a useful all-round cricketer at club level, he made two appearances for Northamptonshire. He returned to London for a year in 1877, before moving to Liverpool, where he remained until 1890. It was not until he made his next move, to Yorkshire, that he began to write seriously about cricket. He was commissioned to produce a weekly cricket article for *The Wakefield Express*. With his father being in the book trade, Holmes had over the years built up a fairly comprehensive library of cricket books (he states in 1892 that he possessed 650 cricket titles, few collectors can have acquired more, at least until recent times) and these gave his articles a strong historical and statistical background. His first article for *Cricket* was an essay on George Parr. It must have impressed the editor, for two months later Holmes' weekly column 'Cricket Notches' appeared for the first time. Although these notches deal with current events as the season progresses, he alludes very aptly to related past happenings and players. Holmes first book on cricket, *Surrey Cricket and Cricketers 1773 to 1895* was published by the magazine *Cricket* in 1896. The work is in the main statistical and supplements De Lugo's book of 1888. In 1897 his second statistical work was issued – *The County Championship 1873 to 1896*, Arrowsmith of Bristol being the publishers. At 168 pages it is comprehensive. A section lists each county with total runs and wickets, for and against, season by season. Then follow the results of matches, county by county. Team Totals over 400 are listed as are those under 50. Individual hundreds, 'spectacles' and large partnerships are also featured. Finally for bibliophiles a list of books previously published for individual counties is added. However, just as Holmes had built his Surrey record book on De Lugo's pioneering work, he built his Championship volume on the work of Alfred Gibson, whose similar, if not quite so comprehensive, book on the Championship was issued the previous summer – an updated version of Gibson's work was published in 1896.

Holmes was however a pioneer in the compilation of a history of Yorkshire cricket. His book was published in 1904 and will be commented upon later. Holmes died as the result of a traffic accident, being knocked down by a lorry, near his home in Herne Hill on January 13, 1933. Irving Rosenwater believed Holmes to be one of the greatest of cricket historians.

Alfred Gibson was a complete contrast to the Rev Holmes. Gibson was a professional sports journalist. Though born in Scotland, in 1860, he came to London, where he was employed by *The Morning Leader* and lived in Camberwell. His best known sports book, which is highly sought after today is *Association Football and the Men Who Made It.*, published in four volumes in 1905. He used the pen name 'Rover' and as such was editor of the *Star and Morning Leader Cricket Manual* which first appeared in 1895. This and the *Athletic News Cricket Annual*, founded in 1888 and Manchester based, were to kill off the *Lillywhite Annual*, being very much cheaper publications.

C.W.Alcock was not averse to using the press in general to promote his own work and in 1895, the *News of the World* published in 18 parts, Alcock's *Famous Cricketers and Cricket Grounds.* When republished as a single volume it contained 288 folio size pages, the vast majority of which contained a single photograph of a current player with brief biography and usually a facsimile signature. The back page of each part had a photograph of a county cricket ground.

In 1897 *The Jubilee Book of Cricket* was published by William Blackwood & Sons, commemorating the Queen's Jubilee. The author was given as Prince Ranjitsinhji (C.B.Fry is generally considered to be the actual writer) and the work was destined to be as popular at the time as the books of John Nyren and of James Pycroft. According to Padwick there were 11 editions of the work. The first 276 pages are detailed instructions on the playing of cricket with many illustrations showing notable cricketers performing batting, bowling or fielding techniques. There follows 36 pages on the major Public Schools with a smattering of history and 50 pages on the two Universities, with good historical notes. The next section runs to 78 pages giving the history of M.C.C. and the 14 first-class counties. From the historian's point of view it is the section on the counties that is the major interest. Thomas Case is listed as the author of the Oxford University section, W.J.Ford of the Cambridge University section, but the county sections have no specific accreditations, except Essex (O.R.Borradaile), Lancashire (A.N.Hornby) and Leicestershire (T.Burdett). In 1905 A.J.Gaston stated he had been responsible for the Gloucestershire section and perhaps had a hand in other parts. He receives an acknowledgement in the Prefatory Note.

Reading through the essays for the anonymous counties, it would seem likely that Gaston wrote most if not all of them, gleaning from cuttings and information in a variety of books, which would have been in his possession (see Chapter 3)

Surprisingly the book does not contain a chapter on 'Early Cricket', but there are some interesting notes in the Kent section. The Hampshire section, which does deal with Hambledon, reproduces, with acknowledgement, a very long essay which had been published in the *Morning Post* in 1896, written by E.V.Lucas. Lucas was at the time building up his reputation as one the great essayists of the day. A Sussex man, he had begun as a journalist on the *Sussex Daily News*, but had moved to Fleet Street in 1893. Cricket was just one of his many interests. From 1904 he was a member of the *'Punch'* table and moved on to become Chairman of the publishers, Methuen. A Collection of some of his cricket writings are to be found in *Cricket All His Life* issued by Hart-Davis in 1950.

Returning to Lucas' essay on Hambledon, this simply recycles Nyren, though Lucas did visit Hambledon before writing his piece. Lucas died in 1938 aged 70 shortly after editing *A Hundred Years of Trent Bridge*. It is little strange that no obituary of him appeared in either *The Cricketer* or *Wisden*. However much more recently Lucas has been described as 'a cynical man, very bitter about men and politics, also the possessor of the finest pornographic library in London.'

So the Hambledon myths received a tremendous boost by the vast sales of Ranjitsinhji's book. In the same year as the book appeared another unusual volume was issued by the Brighton publishers, D.B.Friend & Co, the title *Curiosities of Cricket*. The author had combed *Scores & Biographies*, *Cricket* and many other publications, including newspapers, to list some 750 'Curiosities'. What was almost as important as the actual content, the author quotes the exact source for each item. The book is the basis for many of the authors who have since indulged in such compilations. J.W.McKenzie republished the work in 1978 with an Introduction by Irving Rosenwater. There was some dispute as to the authorship of the original work. Rosenwater goes through the contortions which mark many of his published researches and arrives at A.L.Ford, rather than A.J.Gaston, who had been suggested as the author by C.W.Alcock soon after the volume first appeared.

Ford was the ultimate anorak cricket book collector. According to Ashley-Cooper, a typical book in Ford's large cricket library would be indexed by Ford as follows. The title 'A Book about Cricket' was indexed under 'A', 'B' and 'C'. One wonders how large the Index was!

Alfred Lawson Ford was born in 1844 and was a useful as well as very enthusiastic practising cricketer. Playing the game until the age of 60, he claimed he bowled in every game in which he was involved as an adult. A cousin of the famous Walker family of Southgate, much of Ford's cricket was for the Southgate Club. He began to collect cricket books as early as 1853, but apart from the anonymous 'Curiosities' the only other title which he compiled was an *Index to Scores & Biographies* Volumes s I-XIII. This was published in 1885. Ford died in October 1924 in Lynmouth, Devon, having retired there.

A third book of 1897 that commands attention is *Scores and Annals of the West Kent Cricket Club*, published by Eyre & Spottiswoode and compiled by Philip Norman. It was 395 pages in length and very well produced. Philip Norman was a member of a well-known Kent family: two of his brothers played for both Cambridge University and Kent; his father also represented Kent. Philip Norman himself, born in Bromley, Kent in July 1842, was in the Eton XI in 1859 and 1860. He played for Gentlemen of Kent in one first-class match in 1865 and though invited to play for the full Kent team, he declined. The West Kent history was held up by Ashley-Cooper as a model for anyone wishing to undertake a similar project. Philip Norman was not only a noted antiquarian but also a talented artist, who had exhibited at the Royal Academy. The book contains the detailed match scores of the West Kent Club, as well as short biographies of players, as they made their first appearance.

Many years later, Philip Norman was persuaded by Lord Harris to compile a similar work entitled *Eton Ramblers Cricket Club 1862-1880*. Norman compiled the work with the same thoroughness with which his early book had been written. What is of great value in the book, aside from preserving the scores, are the biographies of the players, because Philip Norman clearly knew many of them personally. The book was published in 1928. Philip Norman died in London in May 1931.

Club histories were becoming relatively common in the final years of the 19th century. It is beyond the scope of this work to comment on the vast majority of them, but in addition to Philip Norman's books, one which certainly deserves mention is *Annals of the Free Foresters*. Its authors are noted as W.K.R.Bedford, W.E.W.Collins and Other Contributors. The book, published by William Blackwood & Sons, was issued in 1895.

The Rev William Kirkpatrick Riland Bedford was born in 1827 and educated at Westminster; he founded the Free Foresters in 1856 as a wandering but Midland-based club, Bedford being the Rector of Sutton Coldfield. In the 1860s he compiled two books of Free Forester match scores and in 1894 wrote a three part reminiscence of his early cricket, which was published in *Cricket*. He died in January 1905.

His principal co-author was William Edward Wood Collins, educated at Radley and Jesus College, Oxford. A very talented all-rounder, he failed to obtain a blue and indeed played very little first-class cricket, though proving, when he did turn out, how useful a player he was. In a minor match for Northwood (Cowes, Isle of Wight) he once hit 338 not out (out of 535) in three hours and five minutes. He also represented England once at rugby football. Collins was a well-known writer on a variety of topics, many articles by him were published in *Blackwood's Magazine*. A series of his cricketing essays *Leaves from an Old Country Cricketer's Diary* were published by William Blackwood & Sons in 1908.

The book on the Free Foresters gives detailed scores of the principal matches and potted scores of the remainder with seasonal averages. There is a good selection of photographs, both team and individual and some biographical sketches, rather similar in style to those in the West Kent book.

On statistical matters in the 1890s there was some controversy regarding which England v Australia matches should be considered as 'Test Matches'. The main debate centred on a number of matches played by England touring teams in Australia in the 1880s. The definitive list, as still employed by statisticians today, was set out in 1894 by C.P.Moody. A well-known Australian journalist, Clarence Percival Moody, born in August 1867, began his career as a sports reporter with the *South Australian Register*, writing on both cricket and Australian Rules Football. His ground-breaking book on Test status *Australian Cricket and Cricketers 1856-1894* was soon accepted as the 'official' line by statisticians. The book contained the scores of both inter-colonial matches and Australian international games. This acceptance is clearly illustrated by the comments of J.N.Pentelow in his book *England v Australia. The Story of the Test Matches*, published by Arrowsmith a year or so later. Pentelow comments:

> 'Since I first conceived the idea of this book, Mr Clarence Moody's *Australian Cricket and Cricketers...* has come into my hands. On reading the short chapter therein in which he deals with the test games with England, I was so struck with the cogency of his reasonings as to what were and what were not test games, that I immediately set to work to reconsider the whole matter; and finally I came to a determination to follow Mr Moody's list.'

Pentelow then proceeds to quote Moody. Pentelow's book gives the detailed scores (without maiden overs) and brief reports of the Tests from 1877. His record section includes leading averages up to the end of the 1894-95 series.

Moody's two other cricket titles both published in 1898 were George Giffen's autobiography *With Bat and Ball* and *South Australian Cricket*. After the First World War he moved to New South Wales and reported mainly on horse racing. Moody died in Manly, New South Wales in November 1937.

The individual colonial cricketing entities published annual reports, the Tasmanian one beginning as early as 1866-67. In 1895-96 another attempt in Australia was made to launch a national cricket yearbook, *Australian Cricket Annual*. This was 190 pages in length and fairly comprehensive. The compiler was the journalist, John Corbett Davis. He had been born in London in 1868, but emigrated to Australia as a boy and trained as a journalist in Sydney. In addition to his journalistic work Davis was very much involved in the administration of cricket both in New South Wales and by the Australian Board of Control. He managed the New South Wales Team, including on a tour to New Zealand in 1889-90. He was at times editor of a number of Australian newspapers. Unfortunately his Australian cricket annual survived for just three editions. Elected a life member of the NSWCA in 1927 for his administrative work. he died in Bellevue Hill, Sydney in February 1941.

Across the water in New Zealand cricket publications were also rare, except for the annual reports of the major Associations. The first inter-colonial game in Australia had been in 1850-51, whereas in New Zealand similar matches did not begin until March 1860 when Wellington played Auckland, however the first game ranked 'first-class' was in January 1864 Otago v Canterbury. The first publication which printed 'historical' scores of matches appeared in 1879. The book entitled *Cricket Notes : Interprovincial Matches* gives the games played in the Otago v Canterbury series. The author is unknown. F.E.Brittain, a local cricket club secretary, compiled a cricket annual in 1889-90, mainly covering Wellington cricket. It survived for three issues. William H.Newton edited *New Zealand Cricketers' Annual* which had a run of four issues 1895 to 1898.

The West Indies had one annual which did survive its first few years. This was *Barbados Cricketers' Annual*, edited and compiled by J.Wynfred Gibbons. Established in 1894-95 it continued without a break until the First World War – after the first two issues, the publication was undertaken by the *Globe* newspaper. The annual gave a good coverage of cricket and the cricket clubs on the island.

In the United States, Jerome Flannery, who was born in Dublin in 1865, but emigrated with his family to the United States as a child, was the founding editor of *The American Cricket Annual*, first published in New York in 1890. The annual ceased in 1902, but resumed as *Spalding's Official Cricket Guide* in 1904, Flannery continuing as editor. Flannery, a very useful club cricketer, played for, at various times, Manhattan, Morris Park and Brooklyn cricket clubs. He died on May 7, 1908 in Brooklyn. The annual was an excellent production; the 1893 edition, for example, gives the detailed scores of the Gentlemen of Ireland tour, details of the Halifax Cup matches, chapters on American clubs district by district, a piece on Canadian cricket and on English cricket, the latter including County Championship tables for both first-class and second-class counties. When the Spalding sports company took over production the standard was maintained and the annual was well illustrated with team photographs.

This American Spalding's annual should not be confused with *Spalding's Cricket Annual* edited by J.A.McWeeney. The latter was published by the British Sports Publishing Company of 2, Hind Court, Fleet Street, London E.C.; it came out in five editions 1907 to 1911. Although we are presently concentrating on 19th century publications, it is convenient to detail this early 20th century annual now.

The annual varied in page numbers, but on average there are about 200. Rather unusually, the frontispiece of each edition contains a large photograph of the editor. The detailed scores of matches played by the current year's County Champions are printed, but only potted scores for the remainder. No brief biographies of players are given and there is no 'record' section. The book is one of the 'Spalding's Athletic Library' series.

In Canada, the Introductory Preface to the second edition of the *Canadian Cricketers' Guide* commences with:

> 'Eighteen years ago the first edition of the 'Canadian Cricketers' Guide' was sent out, and so favorably was it received, that the intention to issue the work annually would have been carried out, had not more pressing engagements rendered it impossible for the chief compiler to devote to the work the requisite time and care. Now that the game is so universally played (the clubs of Ontario alone being counted by hundreds), it seems imperatively necessary that a yearly record of its progress towards earning the epithet 'national' should be sent abroad.'

This second edition appeared in 1876, edited by T.D.Phillips and H.J.Campbell. The Rev Thomas Dowell Phillips was born in Bristol in 1833 but emigrated to Canada in his youth and played for Canada v United States in 1858, opening the batting. His final game in the series was in 1879. In 1880 he joined the Canadian side which toured England

– the tour ended in disaster with the arrest of the captain. Phillips died in California in 1915.

His co-editor, H.J.Campbell was a pupil at Trinity College School and in 1876 had moved to Trinity University. He was a useful fast bowler, but unlike Phillips, Campbell was never selected to play for Canada. The annual they produced gave details of the main clubs in Canada and a handful in the States, plus the detailed scores of three 1875 international matches. The third and final appearance of the annual was in 1877.

Canada did however see the production of the most extensive cricket history published outside England. *Sixty Years of Canadian Cricket* by John E.Hall and R.O.McCulloch, printed in Toronto in 1895, was 588 pages in length and very comprehensive. It contained a large number of portraits both of players and officials.

As in other countries, 19th century cricket literature in South Africa was largely confined to annual reports from clubs and occasional, short-lived annuals. The exception was the *Natal Cricketers' Annual*, which was founded in 1884-85 and from 1888-89 continued as *South African Cricketers' Annual* until it ceased in 1907. Most of the issues were edited by John Thomas Henderson, a Natal journalist, who used the pen-name 'Cover Point'. He was born in Gateshead in 1856 and died in Durban in 1935. A useful cricketer, he appeared once for Natal in a first-class match in 1889-90. The annual began, as its original name implies, by just covering Natal club cricket, but in its later format was a substantial volume of some 200 pages, incorporating match scores, various statistics and photographs and covering all South African cricket by white players. There were no issues between 1892-93 and 1904-05.

The first significant book published on cricket in India was *A Chronicle of Cricket amongst Parsees and the Struggle: Polo versus Cricket*. The book is undated, but was published about 1882. The first section quotes mainly from Pycroft and Box on the origins of the game, then relates how cricket began to be played by the Parsees. There then follows the story of the fight to stop polo players using and ruining the main cricket ground in Bombay. It is so eloquently described that those who wish to study the relationship between the Europeans living in Bombay and the Parsees ought to read the long essay in detail.

In 1901, M.E.Pavri, the best known Parsee cricketer of the period, was the author of *Parsee Cricket*. This gives a Who's Who of notable Parsee cricketers, past and present, with statistics and a history of the Parsee game in Bombay, as well as instructions on the playing of cricket. Dr Mehallasha Edudlji Pavri was born in Surat in October 1866 and toured England with the 1888 Parsee side, being the outstanding bowler on that trip. He spent some time in England and appeared in one first-class game for Middlesex. Pavri died in Bombay in April 1946.

In 1905 J.M.Framjee Patel was the author of *Stray Thoughts on Indian Cricket*, which is more comprehensive than Pavri's book, in that it also covers the European cricket in Bombay. Lord Harris, the former Governor of Bombay, provides the Introduction. One point which is apparent is the difference between cricket played in the Bombay area and that played in the then capital of India, Calcutta. In the latter cricket was a purely European pastime. Framjee Patel captained the Parsee side which beat the English touring team in 1889-90 – a game considered the greatest triumph for Parsee cricket. He went on to organise the first All India tour to England in 1911, but was disappointed when Ranjitsinhji decided not to accept the captaincy.

Chapter 5
Ashley-Cooper, Pentelow and their Contemporaries

Whilst Frederick Gale and his many imitators were busy, as Charles Box had said 'confusing a very few historical facts with a growing volume of fable', there was hidden in the bowels of the British Museum, a man who was beginning the process of blasting away the clichéd mists of time.

Henry Thomas Waghorn, who was born in Tunbridge Wells in April 1842, joined the Army at the age of 15, but in 1868 retired from service life to become an attendant in the British Museum Library. Twenty or so years later he had been promoted to the task of supervising the 50 staff, whose job it was to search the shelves for books requested by readers. Why did Waghorn decide to comb the 18th century British Museum newspaper collection for cricket references? One assumes that his search began about 1888 when he had been given a supervisory role. His searches seem to have been made in the same kind of haphazard manner that characterized many of the early Egyptologists, digging up artifacts along the Nile and almost by accident stumbling over some very significant discoveries. His first batch of cricket newspaper references was published in 1899, under the title *Cricket Scores, Notes &c. From 1730 to 1773*. The book was 140 pages in length. Quite frankly it shows up as the work of an uneducated, though madly enthusiastic, amateur. The newspaper references are in chronological order with a month and a year, but no precise day and no indication of the original source. There are many misprints regarding place names and surnames, due, perhaps, to poor original hand-writing or poor proof-reading. It is however easy to criticise with hindsight what was a pioneering cricketing work.

Lord Harris, to whom the book is dedicated, is thanked for helping with the publication of the volume. In his biography of Waghorn, Irving Rosenwater suggests that Waghorn had made the acquaintance of Lord Harris because Harris's half-uncle had been Waghorn's Company Officer in 1868 and had therefore provided the standard testimonial on Waghorn's leaving the service. This possible link seems rather far-fetched.

There can be no doubt however about the interest Lord Harris took in cricket's history – he effectively sponsored several important historical cricketing books, apart from Waghorn's. These books will be commented upon in due course.

In the 1890s, as Waghorn continued his checking of old newspapers for references to cricket, a much younger enthusiast began a more thorough exploration of the archives. Frederick Samuel (Ashley-) Cooper was born in Bermondsey in March 1877. Little is known of his early schooling and life, despite some very detailed digging into the obvious possible sources by, among other researchers, Irving Rosenwater, until his name appears in the magazine *Cricket* in 1896, when he reveals a specific interest in the statistical career of W.G.Grace. Several biographical essays on Ashley-Cooper have been published, so a short resumé of his life is all that should be required here. In 1897 he joined the Surrey C.C.C. as a member and through both this membership and his writing for *Cricket* became a friend and colleague of C.W.Alcock. Inevitably his visits to the British Museum Library resulted in his making the acquaintance of Waghorn. In his book *Cricket Highways and Byways* published in 1927, Waghorn's photograph is printed and Ashley-Cooper describes him as 'this friend of long standing', though Waghorn's two books of early cricket references are not mentioned in the reference. Ashley-Cooper's researches into old newspapers were much more systematic than those of Waghorn. A prime example of this occurred in November 1898, when the magazine *Cricket* published Ashley-Cooper's discovery that the famous England v Kent match was played in 1744, not as given in Haygarth's *Scores & Biographies* (and elsewhere) in 1746. In his explanation, Ashley-Cooper states that he just happened to be looking through the *Gentleman's Magazine* for 1744 and tripped over an advertisement in the July issue, offering Love's epic poem, which in effect describes the match. A little more digging by Ashley-Cooper located the basic match details, but not the detailed score. Was Ashley-Cooper haphazardly scanning the 18th century press, or perhaps he had previously read *At The Sign of The Wicket*, a book published in 1894 and written by E.B.V.Christian (who would become a long-term correspondent of Ashley-Cooper's), in which Christian notes that Love's poem was published in 1744?

It is strange that when Waghorn's book *Cricket Scores &c* appeared in 1899, Waghorn stated that he was unable to find the England v Kent match! If Ashley-Cooper and Waghorn were acquaintances, as would seem most likely by 1898, clearly Ashley-Cooper hadn't specifically shared the information with the older man, and Waghorn had not seen the article in *Cricket*. A book of essays, *The Lighter Side of Cricket*, edited by Christian was published in 1898, with an essay by Ashley-Cooper, in which Ashley-Cooper still adheres to the year of 1746 for the match. One can therefore date his discovery of the true facts with some accuracy. In January 1900 the magazine *Cricket* began to print Ashley-Cooper's newspaper researches covering the seasons 1741 to 1751 (subsequently reprinted as a pamphlet of 15 copies.) The data came from the British Museum newspaper collection, but the large majority of the references were not in Waghorn's published work.

Like Ashley-Cooper, E.B.V.Christian was a Surrey member (joining in 1889). Born in Deal in 1864 Edmund Brown Viney Christian was a qualified solicitor. His first piece in *Cricket* was published in 1891 and entitled 'Cricket in the Law Courts', which drew attention to several cricketing court cases not previously reported in the cricket press. The basic history section for the volume *Surrey Cricket : Its History and Associations* was written by Christian, but he frequently had cricket poems and essays of a less serious nature published, a typical title 'WG as a Solar Myth' gives of flavour of his work. In 1930 he published privately *The Epic of The Oval*. His Surrey membership lapsed in 1936 and he died at his home in Tulse Hill, South London, in October 1938.

Ashley-Cooper, as has been shown, knew Alcock, Waghorn and Christian, he also made friends with Arthur Haygarth. An idea of the esteem in which he held Haygarth can be gathered from a paragraph of dedication in a new edition of Nyren's *Cricketer's Tutor*, which Ashley-Cooper edited in 1902. He writes:

> 'To Arthur Haygarth, Esq., in deep appreciation of his zeal and enthusiasm in compiling the whole of the Fourteen Volumes of 'Cricket Scores and Biographies', a labour of love to which he has devoted all his time and energy since commencing his self-imposed task whilst at Harrow School in 1842'.

Up to this point in time, the writers who have been described were either amateurs, such as Haygarth, Christian, Holmes and Keyworth, or full time journalists such as Denison, Alcock, and the Pardons, the latter normally covered a variety of subjects even if they specialised in cricket. However the arrival of Ashley-Cooper saw the first cricket historian whose sole source of income came from his cricket writing, without being his own publisher – Fred Lillywhite being a prime example of the latter. The income which Ashley-Cooper was to derive from his attention to cricket's statistics and history was never going to make him a rich man, but his total devotion to his subject made him indispensable to the rest of the cricket publishing fraternity. He appears to have corresponded with almost everyone in the field, from 'big names' such as Pelham Warner to, for example, Isaiah Thomas, whose fame rests on a single early guide published in Belize. Within a few years virtually every cricket publication that was worthwhile and was reliant on statistics or historical data of national or international scope needed Ashley-Cooper's input.

Having a friend and patron in C.W.Alcock, Ashley-Cooper was commissioned to provide the statistics for the *Lillywhite's Annual*. It is not certain in which edition he first provided the data, but it is possibly as early as 1895. In 1898 he was firmly established in *Cricket*, with his weekly column, 'At the Sign of The Wicket'. This provides the reader with a blend of historical information and current statistics. Two years later Ashley-Cooper first provided the statistical section for *John Wisden's Cricketer's Notebook*. This was a diary with cricket information attached and Ashley-Cooper's notes continued until the final issue in 1913. At the same time as providing these notes he was placed in charge of both the Births & Deaths section and the record section of the *Wisden Almanack*. The Births & Deaths section comprised 24 pages in 1900. Ashley-Cooper expanded it to 88 pages by 1914. As regards the Records section, this had first appeared in the 1889 edition and consisted of two pages, entitled 'Some Cricket Records'. It was almost entirely devoted to batting – highest individual innings, highest team totals and highest partnerships, all specifically labelled where appropriate as first-class or not. The brief paragraph on bowlers simply lists some of the bowlers who have taken ten wickets in an innings. The *Lillywhite Annual* of 1889 in as previous editions confined its records to those achieved during the season under review.

Searching for a precedent for the new *Wisden* record section, one is found in Spybey's Nottinghamshire annuals commencing in the 1885 edition. This gives Notts' records against each of the county's opponents plus a list of hundreds for and against the county, commencing with Tom Marsden's 227 in 1826. Spybey adopted *Wisden's* Births & Deaths section in his 1879 edition. Ashley-Cooper began correcting and expanding the Wisden Record Section in 1901, when it grew to 14 pages and included for the first time, a list of County Champions, albeit from 1875. In 1906 Ashley-Cooper divided the Record Section into easily identified headed paragraphs, rather than the solid mass of type which it had been since 1889. The 1906 version ran to 23 pages. This was to set the standard which in essence remains in the almanack to this day.

Ashley-Cooper's first major publication was *Gentlemen v Players*, issued by Arrowsmith in 1900, though in the same year he made a very large contribution to Bettesworth's *The Walkers of Southgate*. Ashley-Cooper's principal chapter entitled 'The Walkers on the Cricket Field' gives in chronological sequence each match in which one or more of the Walkers appeared, with their statistics for that match. The list specifically states 'First-Class and Other Important Matches'. If something out of the ordinary occurred in a match, then Ashley-Cooper appended a note. In a separate section I.D.Walker's statistics are summarised. This is prefaced with a note which gives an idea of the statistical record keeping problems with which compilers were faced in 1900:

> 'So incomplete are the records of the matches in which
> the elder members of the Walker family played – among
> other things the bowling analysis is often not to be found
> – and so difficult is it to say what were first-class matches,
> that it would be quite useless to give averages even if they
> were obtainable. But in the case of Mr I.D.Walker it is
> possible to give a complete record. The following tables
> were compiled by himself'.

This is not the place to try and break down the season by season first-class batting data that Walker gives, but what is rather peculiar is that Walker lists 465 first-class innings (presumably completed innings) and this is exactly the number credited to him in the statistics compiled by the ACS, BUT he claims 11,655 runs, whereas the ACS make the total 11,400. The differences are an exercise for a rainy day!

The next major work to which Ashley-Cooper made a substantial contribution was *Surrey Cricket: Its History and Associations*. As previously mentioned De Lugo compiled the Record Section for this work, but Ashley-Cooper was responsible for two chapters, 'Early Surrey Cricket 1598-1845' and 'Cricket Curiosities' which make up 89 pages. The whole volume is 552 pages in length, easily the most comprehensive County history to date. The editors are given as The Rt Hon Lord Alverstone (Surrey President) and C.W.Alcock.

In view of the popular notions of cricket history peddled by Gale, Lucas etc, it is very worthwhile reproducing Ashley-Cooper's opening paragraph to his early Surrey piece:

> 'Surrey, in short, is the Cradle of Cricket, an honour which
> many commentators have declared to belong to the little

Hampshire village of Hambledon and to Hambledon alone. As records are in existence, however, which prove that organised elevens of Surrey, Sussex, Middlesex and Kent played matches many years prior to the formation of the Hambledon Club, it is difficult to see what claims the latter has to be the birthplace of cricket, or even the locality in which the game was first brought to some degree of perfection. Thus the statement that Hambledon was the Cradle of Cricket goes for nothing.'

Ashley-Cooper follows this with some detail on John Derrick and the Guildford 1598 cricket reference. He then moves to cricket being played on Clapham Common in April 1700 (a newspaper reference not in Waghorn's *Cricket Scores*). A detailed list of the 49 matches played by Surrey against England in the period 1793 to 1831 is given. The chapter as a whole adds much to the general reader's knowledge of early cricket, a subject not really tackled since Box's history of 1877, except by Waghorn's notices and Ashley-Cooper's own 1742-1751 work.

Whilst no contemporary could compare with Ashley-Cooper for his depth of historical research, a rival was bent on compiling and publishing statistical work, which might have equalled Ashley-Cooper's in volume, had not he been so occupied with churning out 'ripping yarns'. J.N.Pentelow's first cricket book had predated Ashley-Cooper's work by several years. The title was *The Blues and Their Battles*, published in 1893 and covering the university matches. When R.S.Holmes gave up his column in *Cricket* due to pressure of his 'day job', Pentelow took over the column, though its title switched from 'Cricket Notches' to 'Between The Innings'. The first appearance of this feature came in January 1896. He had already had a series entitled 'The Australians in England' published by Alcock in *Cricket* in 1892, so Pentelow's appearance as a regular correspondent was not a surprise to readers of the magazine.

John Nix Pentelow was born in Somersham, St Ives, Huntingdonshire in 1872. He began his career as a school teacher, but had a flair for writing and whilst teaching submitted stories to such magazines as *Boy's*

Own Paper and *The Captain*. Pentelow apparently employed numerous pen-names when delivering his adventure stories to editors – Irving Rosenwater published a monograph on Pentelow, but he had to confess that he found it impossible to discover a complete list of pen-names used by the writer. The success of his writing allowed Pentelow to abandon teaching and become a freelance writer and journalist. In his column in *Cricket* Pentelow rarely strayed from current events and those of the immediate past. In the winter of 1898-99, Alcock used both Pentelow and Ashley-Cooper as columnists, but as soon as the 1899 season approached, he retained Ashley-Cooper's 'At The Sign Of The Wicket' and Pentelow's 'Between The Innings' disappeared. Whether or not this caused a serious rift between the two statisticians is not known. If it did then it was short lived, since a few years later they were working in harness and their friendship lasted until Pentelow's death.

Ashley-Cooper and Pentelow might be considered the principal professional cricket statistician-historians at the turn of the century, but there was still ample room for amateurs to compile and publish work. Albert C.Coxhead, born in St Pancras, London in 1847, was a tea merchant. He contributed bits and pieces fairly often in the 1890s to *Cricket*, then in 1899 had published *Cricket Records with a Commentary*, a 100-page hardback. The work consisted of a long series of progressive records, such as the highest individual innings and the highest team total, each taken from the earliest available score sheet through to 1899, in all there are no less than 78 tables of figures. He was perplexed by the problem of whether matches were or were not of first-class status and makes the following comment:

> 'For a long period such an invidious distinction (between first-class and non-first-class) was not known; for another it was unauthorised and ill-defined, and of recent years, although useful and indeed necessary in appreciating the records of any one season, yet in comparing season with season, it is obviously illogical and probably often unfair.'

Despite this remark Coxhead still splits matches into first-class or non-first-class, starting with the famous 1744 Kent v England game. Coxhead quotes the correct year of the game by naming his source – Ashley-Cooper's article in *Cricket*. It is rather ironic that Coxhead's book was printed in the same year as Waghorn's (as noted, the latter still couldn't correctly date the game). It should be pointed out that Coxhead's tables of statistics are fortified by some very lucid footnotes of a type which have sadly long fallen out of fashion. Unlike *Wisden* and other contemporaries, Coxhead has no truck with the prefix 'Mr' in front of amateurs' names, he comments:

> 'Doctor Grace or Mister Read somehow rings as false
> as Mister Spenser or Mister Milton, (Shakespeare was a
> professional).'

A.C.Coxhead became wealthy enough to retire from the tea trade and move to a Sussex village. In 1901 he describes his occupation on the census form as 'author', but according to the British Museum catalogue he was the author just one cricket volume as described and a handful of very modest works relating to music and painting.

Another amateur statistician, whose cricket reputation rests largely with a single volume was John Henry Lester. His work entitled *Bat v Ball* was published by Boots, but financed by A.W.Shelton, a member of the Notts C.C.C. Committee and a very keen cricket historian. The majority of the book, 236 pages, was occupied with a list, batsman by batsman of every fifty scored in first-class cricket. Then followed the seasonal batting averages for all those batsmen, but only for the seasons in which they hit an individual fifty. There were also season by season bowling averages for bowlers who took 25 or more wickets in a season. The author includes Ashley-Cooper's career records for the leading players in the Gentlemen v Players series. Births & Deaths were listed, but taken from *Wisden* (with acknowledgements). The Introduction was by Herbert Jewell, who has been previously noted as a member of the Cricket Reporting Agency. It was stated that the book required a sale of 10,000 copies to break even. Evidently it did not do so – no up-dated version ever appeared. Lester died in November 1914 aged 62.

A rather similar project was being undertaken by another amateur cricket statistician whose first work was issued around the same time. He was destined to bombard the public with statistics and historical notes for half a century, but unfortunately his work did not achieve the accuracy of Coxhead and Pentelow, let alone Ashley-Cooper.

Home Seton Charles Montagu Gordon, born in Brighton in September 1871, was educated at Eton, but did not obtain a place in the XI – in fact he played no cricket of any consequence. He became Sir Home Gordon, when he succeeded his father as the 12th Baronet in 1906. He contributed occasional articles to *Cricket* from the end of the 1880s and from 1900 wrote frequently for the *Badminton Magazine*. However he confessed that he was fascinated by cricket statistics. After some 12 years of endeavour, Home Gordon published in 1902 *Cricket Form at a Glance 1878-1902*. The two main statistical tables are set out landscape, with, after the player's name, year of birth and team, a column for every season from 1878 to 1901 and the runs scored with average each season, plus a career total in the final column, or wickets taken, average for bowlers. Inclusion qualifications are that a player batted, or bowled, in a minimum of two seasons. By this system 1,158 batsmen are detailed. The book also includes catches and stumpings for all wicket-keepers who played in three or more seasons. Other tables analyse the performances of players for and against the Australian touring teams. In all the statistical sections occupy 314 pages, in addition to a Preface by Lord Hawke and the author's Introduction. The author states that the original data has been gleaned principally from the scores published in *Wisden*, but 'fully ninety-five per cent of all the averages have been entirely reworked and sought out by myself'. It is unfortunate that Gordon goes on to state that he has excluded four or five matches previously considered as 'first-class' from his statistics, but fails to name the matches. The hours spent in the compilation of this dense mass of figures must have been enormous, but the end result is very patchy. By not including every player, Gordon could not balance his figures, which makes checking very difficult.

His notion that first-class cricket commenced in 1878, based purely on the Australian tour of that year, has caused much comment over the years, and few statisticians would agree with him. Whatever the criticisms that can be levelled at Home Gordon's statistics in his 1902 book, it must be pointed out that he was a pioneer in his creation of mass first-class career records. Lester, in his book, had given the career records of 100 leading batsmen in first-class cricket and fifty leading bowlers, but he had taken his figures back to 1864 for the batting and 1866 for bowling, it is very difficult therefore to compare Lester's figures with Gordon's. Lester does state that his tables are only a portion of the total number of career records which he had prepared. Lester includes eleven-a-side matches by English teams in Australia, which Gordon does not. At this early stage in the creation of first-class records therefore the year from which these should be calculated is controversial – it remains so to the present time! In 2000 *Sir Home Gordon, Bart. – An Affectionate Retrospect* was published by Christopher Saunders, Irving Rosenwater was the author. Readers who wish to discover more of Home Gordon's cricketing life should consult that work. Home Gordon published two further updates on his *Form At A Glance* book, in 1924 and in 1938, but he acknowledges that these works were not financially viable – unfortunately they do not seem to increase much in accuracy either.

Chapter 6
Some Sumptuous Volumes and County Histories

The major contribution to the history of the game published in the decade or so prior to the First World War was *Imperial Cricket*. Edited by Pelham Warner, it was issued by The London & Counties Press Association Ltd of Covent Garden, W.C. in 1912.

Lord Hawke's Introduction has a jingoistic tone to it, that might well deter present day readers, but it would be a mistake to judge the book by its opening, which commences:

> 'Imperial Cricket has a good genuine ring. The greatest
> game in the world is played wherever the Union Jack is
> unfurled, and it has had no small share in cementing the
> ties that bind together every part of the Empire.'

Ashley-Cooper begins the book proper with 48 pages on 'Cricket and The Royal Family'. It is a typically thorough piece of Ashley-Cooper research. However after the death of Frederick Louis, apart from notes on the Prince Regent at Brighton, the Royal Family is decidedly peripheral to the main thrust of cricket history.

The chapter which concentrates on the history of the game in general comes from the pen of Andrew Lang. Born in Selkirk in March 1844, Lang was educated at Edinburgh Academy, St Andrew's and Balliol College, Oxford. Although not a notable cricketer himself, he had a deep interest in the game and strong family connections. His brother, T.W.Lang, gained a blue at Oxford and played occasionally for Gloucestershire in the 1870s.

Andrew Lang, a poet, novelist, prolific essayist and literary critic, had written the Introduction to Richard Daft's *Kings of Cricket*. In his essay for *Imperial Cricket,* Lang flirts with the notions of some early types of cricket being played in both Scotland and Ireland, but he firmly dismisses the theory that cricket was brought over to England from France at the time of Joan of Arc. Lang plumps squarely for the Guildford reference of 1598 as the first definite mention of the game. Lang had twice before written on cricket's history, in the *English Illustrated Magazine* (Vol 1, 1884), and in the introductory chapter to the 1888 volume on Cricket in the Badminton Library.

Unlike Box's history, the book does not have chapters on each major county, although Warner provides a chapter on Lord's and the M.C.C. and John Shuter and H.D.G.Leveson Gower write on The Oval & The Surrey County C.C. Neither chapter adds anything to what has been written before – the details of Surrey cricket and of the Oval had been dealt with in the volume mentioned in the previous chapter. Where the book covers a totally new field is in cricket outside the British Isles. Australia, South Africa and New Zealand are reviewed, as one might expect, but also Egypt and Sudan, West Africa, East Africa, Ceylon, Hong Kong, British Malaya, Samoa, Fiji and the Solomon Islands, each chapter written by someone familiar with the specific area or colony. The chapters are illustrated with photographs of grounds in the places mentioned. There is an excellent index, the work of Ashley-Cooper. Pelham Warner thanks Ashley-Cooper for effectively editing the final proofs, whilst the former was in Australia with the 1911-12 M.C.C. touring side. The book would be overshadowed as a reference work in the 1920s by Altham's history, but *Imperial Cricket* provides a much larger canvas than that work was to cover.

The magazine *Country Life* had published in its series 'Library of Sport', a 454 page work simply entitled *Cricket.* The Editor is Horace Gordon Hutchinson (1859-1932), whose fame rests with golf. He captained Oxford v Cambridge, then won various golfing trophies as well as writing extensively on the subject. He is regarded as the Father of Golf Instruction.

He had eleven authors writing chapters in this *Country Life* tome, but chose to write the chapter 'Some Points in Cricket History' himself. It is merely information borrowed from Nyren and Pycroft. There is a chapter entitled 'Foreign Cricket' which looks interesting, but is just Pelham Warner describing his overseas trips. The merit in the book lies solely in the vast number of historical illustrations. Many have not before been published in the covers of a hardback book. The titles are unfortunately often rather vague. No one of Ashley-Cooper's calibre has been employed in this ambitious work.

As has been pointed out, the editor of *Imperial Cricket* was Pelham Warner. Warner had, seemingly, become a cricket writer by accident. He had been educated at Rugby and Oriel College, Oxford and read law. His father was the Attorney-General of Trinidad and young Warner was born in that colony in October 1873. He had made his County debut for Middlesex in his first year at Oxford and played in 15 Tests for England between 1898-99 and 1912, being captain for ten of those games. Lord Hawke invited Warner to tour West Indies the winter he came down from Oxford and volunteered Warner to cable reports of the tour to *The Sportsman*. From then on Warner reported for various newspapers and later converted his reports into books. When he retired from County cricket after the 1920 season, H.A.Gwynne appointed Warner as cricket correspondent of the *Morning Post*, which, at that time, was considered the major national cricketing paper. From the viewpoint of the history and statistics of cricket, Warner's role as the founding editor of *The Cricketer* should be considered his lasting memorial and he will therefore feature in a subsequent chapter, related to that notable magazine.

Linked to *Imperial Cricket* must be *British Sports and Sportsmen* a 16 volume work, volume 5 being on cricket and football. The books were published by *The Sportsman* and came out in various years beginning in 1906. The cricket-football volume did not appear until 1917, Pelham Warner being the editor. The first chapter of Volume 5, is entitled 'Old-Time Cricket', which purports to be a history of the game to 1869, but it is very thin – the year of 1746 for the 1744 Kent v England match has not been revised, this however is just one example of work written by a general sports journalist, G.E.Hopcroft, whose knowledge of cricket history was seemingly minimal. The one major feature of the 579 page book, that is still of value, is headed 'Prominent Players', giving biographies of some 300 amateur cricketers and footballers who flourished in the early 20th century.

Both *Imperial Cricket* and *British Sports and Sportsmen* were published in sumptuous volumes for subscribers. Another volume on a similar scale was *Fifty Years of Sport at Oxford and Cambridge and the Great Public Schools*, edited by A.C.M.Croome. Volume One features Athletics, Cricket and Rowing from 1861 (the book appeared in 1913). The cricket section contains the detailed scores of University matches from 1861, but is perhaps more valuable for photographs of nearly all the University Elevens. Volume Three appeared in 1922 and gave details of Eton v Harrow, Eton v Winchester and Harrow Wanderers.

Arthur Croome was educated at Wellington and Oxford, gaining his cricket blue in 1888 and 1889. He played for Gloucestershire from 1885 to 1892 and his county career is famous for an incident in the match at Old Trafford in 1887, when he ran to save a boundary and impaled his neck on the spike of some metal railings. Prompt medical help from W.G.Grace saved his life. Croome became a master at Radley, but then moved to journalism, writing on cricket for *The Times* and golf for the *Morning Post*. He succeeded Sydney Pardon as the chief cricket correspondent of *The Times* in 1925, but died in 1930. Sir Home Gordon commented:

> 'With his writings on cricket he took tremendous pains, whereas he would dash off his golf articles as fast as he could scribble them. To my mind he attained the very highest standards of cricket journalism in his daily accounts of the Test Matches…'

In retrospect it seems a pity that Croome's cricket writing did not appear more often in hard covers.

Having reviewed three large tomes that were beyond the pocket of the ordinary cricket follower, we return to the mundane area of the station bookstall. After the demise of the weekly *The Cricket Field*, the magazine *Cricket* remained the only national weekly magazine devoted to cricket. The *Sportsman* newspaper launched *Bat, Ball and Wheel* on May 5, 1898 but it survived just less than a year. As its name implies the magazine covered many sports, though the cricket element was very strong. It dealt however with current affairs and not with historical or statistical matters. The magazine *Cricket* therefore continued unrivalled on the weekly stage, but suffered a tragic loss and indeed a slow, painful demise with the death in February 1907 of its editor C.W.Alcock. The following notice was published under 'Pavilion Gossip' in the March edition:

> 'The death of Mr C.W.Alcock at Brighton on Tuesday last will have occasioned much grief to all readers of 'Cricket', for it was he who founded this paper twenty-five years ago and had been its Editor since its inauguration. How profoundly he will be missed only those who have been intimately associated with him can adequately realise.'

There are no figures to indicate the relative sales of *Cricket* in 1906 compared with its first two decades, so it is impossible to discover whether the publication was already sliding downwards at the time of Alcock's death. One small indication of a possible decline was the absence of club scores in 1906. In the 1880s and 1890s it was not uncommon for the magazine to run additional pages to accommodate these scores – clubs paid for the insertion of their matches. One also assumes that players whose names featured in these games also tended to be subscribers, or bought the magazine at bookstalls.

Ashley-Cooper was appointed to succeed Alcock as editor of *Cricket*, presumably the ownership of the magazine was in the hands of Alcock's widow – Alcock did not leave a will. Not the worldliest of men, Ashley-Cooper was completely the wrong person to try to run the magazine. Sales began to slip, even if they were not already doing so and the contents became less and less topical. Pentelow bought the magazine, but by 1910 the circulation had dropped to 2,400 – breakeven was roughly double that number. One of the major problems was that the daily papers gave increasing space to current cricket matters and there was also a mass of weekly local papers. Ashley-Cooper wrote his column 'At The Sign of The Wicket' through most issues of 1910; Pentelow's 'Some Chapters of Australian Cricket History' was serialised in the winter issues; R.S.Holmes and W.A.Bettesworth were frequent contributors. P.F.Thomas (of whom more will be noted in the next chapter) wrote many articles and some pretty frightening poems. For the historian of today the contents of the magazine as a whole are quite brilliant, but the number of budding historians in 1910 interested in minutiae can almost be numbered on the fingers of one hand.

Pentelow relieved Ashley-Cooper of the editorship in 1912. A letter written by Pentelow quoted in Rosenwater's essay on Pentelow paints a grim picture:

> 'I have put over £1,000 into the paper – or shall have done when I have paid off Merritt & Hatcher's account. Every number has been a dead loss to me. I have had promises of help in hundreds. I don't mean help in money, but in getting readers. Out of them all perhaps 50 have come to something. Those fifty are really staunch friends: but they are not numerous enough, and the continual disappointments sour me. 'Cricket' has a fine past – has it a future? I begin to fear not. So few seem to care. Most of the keen readers are overseas; but at best we can never hope to keep the paper going by overseas subscribers.'

The point made about keen overseas readers is certainly reflected in the contents of the paper in 1912 and 1913, many more overseas items are published, but it must have been obvious to Pentelow that they could hardly attract new readers in the British Isles. Merritt & Hatcher, the firm Pentelow owed money to, was the magazine's printers, who had taken over in 1895 when Alcock had fallen out with W.R.Wright.

At the end of 1913 a saviour presented himself, theoretically, in the guise of Archibald Campbell MacLaren, erstwhile captain of England and Lancashire. As one of the greatest of English cricketers at the turn of the century and still active as a player – he was aged 42 – MacLaren's name alone ought to have boosted sales. The magazine, now in the joint ownership of MacLaren and Pentelow, was relaunched in 1914 as *The World of Cricket*. Pentelow however initially seemed unaware of MacLaren's unreliability in financial matters and Pentelow's debts doubled in the nine months during which he and MacLaren ran the magazine. Michael Down in his biography of MacLaren noted that 'Pentelow was apparently left to take care of all the financial debts and the worry appeared to age him overnight. Although only forty years old his hair turned white, his shoulders bowed and his face lined.' Pentelow paid off his debts by writing schoolboy fiction, almost night and day.

Under the new title *The World of Cricket* the price of the magazine had been increased from 2d to 3d on May 2, 1914. The weekly editions were suspended on August 15; an issue appeared in September, others in October and November. One was scheduled for December 12, but never materialised. It was a sad end to Alcock's creation.

Moving from the weekly to the annual, the end of the sequence of Lillywhite annuals had come with the 1900 edition of 'Red Lilly'. C.W.Alcock wrote in the introduction to this 1900 issue:

> 'The fact that the Annual has reached its twenty-ninth anniversary is proof of itself – were any needed – that the Red Lillywhite is going strongly. Fortunately no proof is wanting. That time has not withered its infinite variety for the cricketer we have the most gratifying evidence from all sections of the cricket public. In this number some slight alterations have been made, as we believe, in the general interest. For a great part of the statistical matter we are indebted to Mr F.S.Ashley-Cooper, who has lent throughout ready help. To the Secretaries of Cricket Clubs whose doings are recorded herein we have also to express our hearty thanks.'

In fact two long standing items had disappeared from the 1900 edition, the who's who of current county cricketers and the register of the principal local cricket clubs. The price of the *Lillywhite Annual* was one shilling. The 1900 edition of *Wisden* was also one shilling, but almost twice the number of pages. Rather oddly, Alcock gives a glowing review of the 1900 *Wisden* in *Cricket*, but a very cursory paragraph on the 1900 *Lillywhite*. As well as competing on size with Wisden, the Lillywhite Annual had competition from the very cheap annuals that were flooding the market.

The best known of these annuals were the *Athletic News Cricket Annual* and the *Morning Leader Cricket Annual* (both are mentioned in Chapter 4). Another competitor, *Ayres Cricket Companion* was founded in 1902 and began life as a rather odd collection of cricket data mainly related to the past cricket season. It was sponsored by the sports goods firm of F.H.Ayres and was edited by W.R.Weir (a pseudonym for W.R.Wright). The price was 6d (half that of *Red Lillywhite* or *Wisden*). By 1914 the annual had more than doubled in page length, its price remained unchanged and the increase was largely due to Public School reports, which did not appear in the earliest issues. It also featured the history of a school in most editions. Once the First World War broke out and first-class cricket ceased, the annual was reliant on Public School data and it was to stay with that class of cricket for the remainder of its issues. It finally closed in 1932.

Several other annuals appeared in the Edwardian era, but mainly they are of only passing interest, however one which deserves a mention was *Cricket, Who's Who. The Blue Book of Cricket*, issued by Cricket Publishing Co. of Cannon Street, London E.C. The editor was Henry Vaughan Dorey, born in London in 1870 and on the 1901 census, living in Harpenden, Herts and being described as a 'General Manager'. Dorey was editor of several other cricketing publications including England v Australia in the 'Tests' in 1910 and an expanded version in 1912 that had South African Tests added. The books are a little more than the detailed Test scores and averages after each series – sometimes the Test averages, at others the first-class averages for the touring party. Dorey was also connected with the cricket poet, Albert Craig and shortly after Craig's death published a set of his poems plus *A Short History of the Poet's Career*. Dorey was presumably a director or the proprietor of the publishing company which moved from Cannon St to 353, The Strand and also went under the trade name of Cricket and Sports Publishers Ltd.

In 1904, a year after the publication of *Surrey Cricket : Its History and Associations* came Yorkshire's response, *The History of Yorkshire County Cricket 1833-1903* by the Rev R.S.Holmes, with an Introduction by Lord Hawke. Hawke's piece is relatively substantial, running to eight pages. The volume is 298 pages in length. The Rev R.S.Holmes had retired from his weekly column in *Cricket* in 1895, but he did continue to do some cricket work, in particular keeping the Record Section of the Yorkshire Yearbook up to date. However in this History, it was Ashley-Cooper who provided the season-by-season career records for Yorkshire players. Holmes seems to be more intrigued by the peripheries of Yorkshire cricket, rather than the successes and failures of the County Club itself – less than 50 pages are devoted to the 'proper' County Club seasons, from 1861 to date. Holmes had discovered some illuminating newspaper pieces on Tom Marsden, for example. There is a chapter on Yorkshire players appearing for England and on the AEE and their imitators in Yorkshire – he blunders when he states that no bowling analyses are available for the match in which George Wootton took all ten wickets – the analyses are in the Yorkshire scorebook, which Holmes claims to have checked. Holmes lists the winners, for example of the Heavy Woollen Challenge Cup, the season by season results of Yorkshire Seconds and even a list of Yorkshire bat manufacturers. Holmes therefore gives much information of value for present historians, but rather strays from the apparent principal aim of the History.

It is appropriate here to introduce the author of the second volume on Yorkshire County Cricket, even though it did not appear until 1924. 'Old Ebor', otherwise known as Alfred William Pullin was born in July 1860. Leaving school he worked on various Yorkshire newspapers for about ten years and was then appointed chief cricket and rugby correspondent of the sister papers, *The Yorkshire Post* and *The Yorkshire Evening Post*. Pullin was not a Yorkshireman by birth, but came with his family to Wakefield from Wales, when his father took up a clerical post in the City. During the cricket season, whilst with the *Post*, A.W.Pullin travelled with the Yorkshire side to all away matches and was regarded as a non-playing 12th man. He wrote a series of essays for his newspaper on interviews he had over the years with former Yorkshire cricketers and these essays were re-issued in book form under the title *Talks with Old Yorkshire Cricketers* in 1898 – clearly this volume was of great assistance to Holmes when he came to write his history five years later. Almost as a follow-up to his Yorkshire book, Pullin had published in 1900, *Talks with Old English Cricketers*. This work is constantly mined by historians and quotes from it appear with great frequency, not always acknowledged.

A brief note on Pullin's opposite number in Lancashire. James Alfred Henry Catton, born in Greenwich in April 1860, was raised in Lancashire. A full time journalist, he worked briefly with the *Nottingham Guardian*, before joining the Manchester-based *Athletic News*. He was appointed Editor in 1895 and from 1903 to 1924 was also Editor of the *Athletic News Cricket Annual* under the pseudonym 'Tityrus'. Like Pullin he travelled to away matches with the County team. Later he moved to London where he worked on Fleet Street newspapers, as well as being in charge of the Record Section for *Wisden* for four years from 1933. He died in London in August 1936.

Lord Harris, the mentor of Kent cricket, was not to be outdone by the volumes which were published on Surrey and now Yorkshire cricket. In 1907 came *The History of Kent Cricket* published by Eyre & Spottiswoode with Lord Harris as the nominal editor. Harris notes: 'But in chief I have to thank Mr Ashley-Cooper for a measure of assistance without which the work could not have been as interesting as I hope it may be found.'

Ashley-Cooper's principal contribution was the compilation of 'The Register of Kent County Cricketers 1729-1906'. This is 118 pages in length and quite outstanding – its basis is the biographical work published by Haygarth in *Scores & Biographies*, but Ashley-Cooper adds much data and each essay is self-contained. Several 'family trees' are also incorporated. Directly following this long chapter, Ashley-Cooper gives the season-by-season statistics for each player. One might have expected the chapter entitled 'Kent Cricket 1705 to 1750' to come from Ashley-Cooper's pen, but it is entrusted to W. South Norton. Norton acknowledges the use of H.T.Waghorn's second volume of newspaper references, which had been issued in 1906. William South Norton himself is thanked by Arthur Haygarth for his assistance in the compilation of *Scores & Biographies*. Norton played for Kent from 1849 to 1870 and was for some time Hon Secretary of the Kent County Club. He was born in Town Malling in June 1831 and died at Charterhouse in 1916. The volume is well illustrated and previously unpublished photographs of many players are a particular asset for historians.

Another county to publish an ambitious volume was Middlesex, but this employed a totally different format to Surrey, Yorkshire and Kent. The basis of the work was the scorecard of every Middlesex match. The actually history section was confined to 16 pages. There is a brief career record section, but not giving season by season statistics for each player. The title is *Middlesex County Cricket Club 1864-1899* and the book was issued in 1900, thereby preceding the titles previously described. The author was William John Ford. Born in Paddington in 1853, educated at Repton and Cambridge, he was in the XIs in both. He made occasional appearances for Middlesex, but emigrated to New Zealand where he was Principal of Nelson College. On his return to England he continued as a schoolmaster, but later also contributed to many sporting journals.

In 1902 he followed his Middlesex book with a much more profound work on Cambridge University Cricket Club. There are 150 pages of historical detail, even before the first match score. The early scores are published for the first time, having eluded Arthur Haygarth's grasp. It is a little unfortunate that Ford chose to print only the detailed score information for the Cambridge players and omitted that for the opposition. The book also contains some informative photographs. Ford died in April 1904.

The book which should be used in conjunction with Ford's Cambridge history is *Oxford and Cambridge Scores and Biographies* compiled by J.D.Betham and published in 1905. The work commences with the scores of the University Matches, but then follows this with excellent brief biographies of the players involved, including their occupations and dates of death or current addresses. It is important to note that Betham did not simply cull his data from Haygarth's work, but obviously undertook much original research. John Dover Betham, born in 1874, was a wool manufacturer and died in Sedbergh in 1918. This is his only cricket book, but he did assist the editor of *Wisden* in the information given annually for the cricketers whose deaths are recorded in the annual.

Nottinghamshire's production of a history was a hybrid – Edwin Browne, the County's Assistant Secretary, had published in 1887 a 33-page history plus the match scores of the season 1887. The efforts of Sutton and the annuals issued by Frank Spybey have been discussed in Chapter 3, but the publishers who went much farther than either of those pioneers, or indeed Browne's effort, were the Richards family, also noted in Chapter 3 They had the rights to print scorecards on the Trent Bridge Ground and in 1890 published *Fifty Years of Nottinghamshire Cricket 1838-1887*. The first date given is the year William Clarke founded the Trent Bridge Ground. The initial part of the book comprises biographies of 62 Nottinghamshire cricketers, the lengths of which are variable. Arthur Shrewsbury is allowed 11 pages, T.F.King is given five lines. As mentioned in Chapter 3 bowling analyses and match description details commence with the 1869 season along with the seasonal averages and in the later years Championship tables are also printed. The book does not include a narrative history. On the title page, Richards sub-titles his work 'Volumes One and Two of Notts Cricket Scores & Biographies.' In 1903, Richards issued a continuation to this work, which was titled *Nottinghamshire Cricket Scores and Biographies 1888 to 1900 Volume 2*. Again this starts with biographies and then the detailed scores, 33 of which are pre-1888 and had been omitted from the first mentioned volume. What I have stated here is a simplification – a number of the biographies were issued as separate booklets. Those readers who wish to look deeper into the Richards' publishing schedules should consult Duncan Anderson's *Bibliography of Nottinghamshire Cricket Literature*. The Richards firm was taken over about 1886 by the founder's son Charles Henry Richards (1850-1909). The latter's daughters continued to publish scorecards at Trent Bridge into the 1930s. To further confuse the picture the firm also issued some Nottinghamshire Yearbooks with full detailed scores, as well as a pocket-size *Notts Cricket Guide* which continued except for the First World War period until 1932 – again Duncan Anderson's book needs consulting.

Across the Erewash, Walter J Piper, the cricket correspondent of the *Derby Daily Telegraph*, had published in 1897 *The History of Derbyshire County Cricket Club*. This gave the match scores of County matches from 1871 with reports plus a short introduction explaining how the County Club was formed. The year prior to the appearance of this history, Piper, in conjunction with the County cricketer and sometime captain, L.G.Wright, acted as editors and compilers of *The Derbyshire Cricket Guide* This gave a review of the past season and a feature on one or two county players, but its principal contents were details of local clubs and leagues. Levi George Wright (1862-1953) played 317 matches for Derbyshire between 1883 and 1907. Piper died in July 1940.

Despite the enthusiasm of A.D.Taylor and A.J.Gaston, both of whom were noted in Chapter 3, plus a great patron in Lord Sheffield, Sussex never issued a history to rival those of Kent, Surrey or Yorkshire. The best that was managed was *The History of Cricket in Sussex* compiled by Gaston and dedicated to Lord Sheffield. It was a very modest 73 page book. Of those 73 pages, 17 are full page portraits of notable players. The great 18th century development of Sussex cricket disappears in three pages and James Ireland, who resuscitated Sussex as a County team in the 1820s, and his Prince's Ground are not even mentioned! However Ashley-Cooper did have two books on the county published. First came *Sussex Cricket and Cricketers*, which was a reprint of a series of articles he wrote for *Cricket*. It was limited to 30 copies. Second was *Sussex Cricket Champions 1815-1901*, which gave statistical and other information on the Sussex players.

In 1911, on the back of their maiden Championship success, Sydney Santall wrote a book *History of Warwickshire Cricket*. He had previously compiled a slimmer volume *Warwickshire as a First-Class County in 1904*. Born in Peterborough, where he was educated at the King's School, he played for Northants as an amateur before joining Warwickshire as a professional; later he was the County coach at Edgbaston. Santall built up a very comprehensive cricket library and wrote frequent letters and articles about cricket to the press, notably these appeared in the columns of *The Cricketer*. He died in Bournemouth in March 1957.

Of the lesser counties, the best history published prior to the First World War, rather surprisingly since the county did not aspire to 'Minor County Championship' status, was on Herefordshire. The author was Edwyn Anthony, a local journalist, born in Hereford in 1871. The book begins in 1836 and describes each season, including scorecards of significant matches and latterly seasonal averages. A hardback of 200 pages it is a work to be commended.

It should be noted too that the Victoria County Histories contain pieces on cricket related to each specific county – their scholarship is variable.

Two histories of M.C.C. were published in the early years of the 20th century. The first, by the Sussex historian, A.D.Taylor, appeared in 1903, but in 1914 that modest volume was completely superseded by *Lord's and the M.C.C.* by Lord Harris and Ashley-Cooper. E.B.V.Christian is thanked for his help obtaining the data relating to the purchasing of the three sites which the Lord's Ground has occupied. The fact that all subsequent histories of Lord's and the M.C.C., and there have been several, owe virtually everything to Ashley-Cooper's meticulous research, which the 1914 volume contains, speaks for itself. A few additional facts have emerged over the last century, but that is scarcely surprising. The long standing debate regarding the founding of M.C.C. is not discussed, save for the comment that the White Conduit Club was 'the acorn from which sprang the gigantic oak known as the M.C.C.' Apart from the text there is a splendid array of photographs and other illustrations, portraits of almost everyone of consequence involved in the Ground and/or the M.C.C. appear.

In Australia, after the closure of J.C.Davis' annual in 1898, the individual states published their annual reports, but there is little of importance published on a national level and certainly no attempt at a history of cricket in the country as a whole.

South Africa was more fortunate, having in Maurice William Luckin, a keen record keeper and historian. His great work *The History of South African Cricket* – 848 pages in length – was published in Johannesburg in 1915. It is comprehensive, including the scorecards of all the principal cricket matches played in South Africa and giving detailed histories Province by Province. There is a good selection of individual and team photographs, but only scattered biographical notes on a few personalities. Luckin was born in Romford, Essex in 1876 and emigrated to South Africa at the age of 19. He played two first-class matches for Transvaal in 1910-11 and from 1914 to 1918 was Secretary of the South African Cricket Association. He was to issue a second volume of South African Cricket in the 1920s.

In India M.E.Pavri published, in 1901, *Parsi Cricket*. This book with earlier Indian publications was dealt with in the previous chapter. Guha in his history of Indian cricket, published in 2002 under the title *A Corner of a Foreign Field* rather plays down the importance of Pavri as a player, I suspect because Pavri rather overstates the role that Lord Harris played in Indian cricket!

Throughout the rest of cricket world, various annuals and books of instruction were published in the early years of the 20th century; whilst valuable in their way, they do not come within the scope of this present book.

Chapter 7
The Cricketer Magazine

A major innovation, after the First World War, for cricket statisticians (and in the long run, historians) was the founding in 1921 of *The Cricketer* magazine. There is a stark contrast between its founding and that of its predecessor, *Cricket*. As has been noted, *Cricket* was created by C.W.Alcock in 1882. He had a decade of cricket journalism and cricket administration behind him. His ethic of hard work clearly inspired his contributors and his colleagues and this combination meant that *Cricket* was a success from the very beginning.

The Cricketer was conceived by G.N.Foster, who was appointed the Managing Director. A member of the famous cricketing brotherhood of Malvern and Worcestershire, though latterly he played for Kent, he had Pelham Warner as the titular editor and F.J.Sellicks, an experienced sporting journalist, as the day-to-day editor. Francis Joseph Sellicks was born in Saffron Walden in 1868 and was a notable rugby footballer for Richmond (he just missed a blue at Oxford). He had begun his working life as a schoolmaster prior to taking to journalism and worked for the *Morning Post* (Warner's paper) as the rugby correspondent. He was to remain at *The Cricketer* for seven years, his only signed articles being on rugby.

Judging by the first winter annual issued by the magazine, it seemed to be a case of too many chiefs and too few indians. The cast list of writers reads: Lord Dartmouth, Sir Home Gordon, E.V.Lucas, G.L.Jessop, H.S.Altham, A.C.M.Croome, C.Aubrey Smith, F.S.Ashley-Cooper, Sydney Horler,

H.Grierson, Sir A.Conan Doyle, Sir Edwin Stockton, A.A.Milne, Rev F.H.Gillingham, A.C.MacLaren, D.L.A.Jephson, etc etc. The contents during that first summer appeared to lack what might now be termed the 'wow factor'. The serials which ran through many of the issues included 'Batsmanship', in 15 parts by D.J.Knight; 'How to run Public Schools Cricket' also about 15 parts long, by H.S.Altham; 'Some Facts and Phases of Cricket in the Country' by W.E.W.Collins – Part One 'Psychology', Part Two 'The Extreme Psychological Moment', etc etc.; 'Fielding' in six parts by G.N.Foster. Exactly what audience the magazine was designed for is difficult to tell, but it seemed to be Public School sports masters – a fairly limited market. The county scores and Test Matches details were printed, but there was very detailed coverage of these games in the press.

The statistical content of the magazine was entrusted to R.O.Edwards, rather than Ashley-Cooper, whose contributions only amounted to a handful of historical articles in the first years of *The Cricketer's* existence - perhaps Ashley-Cooper required payment, whereas the 'amateur' contributors wrote for amusement?

Major Reginald Owen Edwards was the regular contributor on Minor County topics. Born in October 1881 and educated at Christ's Hospital, he played briefly for Norfolk and Cambridgeshire. The famous story about his being always accompanied on his travels by a set of *Wisden* and the set being the only item saved when his baggage was stolen on a trip to Russia has become somewhat embellished over the years. What in fact occurred was that the Editor of *Wisden* asked him to provide statistics concerning Tom Hayward. He took the *Wisdens* which covered Hayward's career with him to Russia in 1920, when he was assisting the White Russians against the Bolsheviks. He was detained and searched by what he described as 'Trotsky's Intelligence Branch', they saw no value in the *Wisdens*! (Seven pages of Hayward's statistical career did appear in the 1921 edition of *Wisden*). Following his Minor Counties column, he contributed regular features on current affairs in the same magazine under the heading 'Vin Ordinaire'. Edwards died on November 16, 1925, aged 44. He had been badly gassed in France during the 1914-18 War and had suffered ill-health as a result.

By the close of its second year *The Cricketer*, unsurprisingly in view of its contents, was really struggling to break even. Appeals to readers to buy shares, plus a move into the offices of the *Morning Post* saved the magazine.

Sales however did not improve and a second crisis in 1928 was only averted by dismissing both Frank Sellicks and the advertising manager. A.W.T.Langford was given the dual roles. Arthur William Tanfield Langford was born in Ilford in 1896; he followed his father, William, into journalism and after some weekly papers, wrote for the *Morning Post* and later the *Evening Standard*. A useful club cricketer he played for Jesters, Hampton Wick, Nomads, Grasshoppers and M.C.C. His major contribution, initially, to *The Cricketer* was a weekly column on the club cricket scene in the Home Counties. As will be mentioned later he was effectively to run *The Cricketer* almost single-handed from 1939 to his retirement.

Amid these battles to keep the new magazine afloat, the management had one idea which was to become a lasting legacy from the magazine's first decade, and that was to invite H.S.Altham to write, in weekly parts, the history of cricket. The series began in the edition of May 6, 1922 and concluded in the edition of August 22, 1925. The 91 episodes ended with the 1912 Triangular Tournament.

Harry Surtees Altham was born in Camberley, Surrey in 1888 and educated at Repton and Oxford. He was awarded his blue in 1911 and 1912. He played 10 matches for Surrey prior to the war and 24 for Hampshire in the immediate post-war period. He had joined the staff of Winchester College in 1913 and, except for his service in the 60th Rifles during the war, remained as a Winchester master until 1948. Whilst at Winchester he was an ardent cricket coach and, following his retirement, he more or less founded and then chaired the M.C.C. Youth Cricket Association, still being in post at his death. He held other cricketing posts, most notably Chairman of England Selectors in 1954.

Altham's part-work was reissued, having been revised, as a book *A History of Cricket* by Allen & Unwin in 1926. It became a standard text-book of the subject, perhaps not quite on the scale of Nyren and Pycroft, but demand was sufficient for it to be reprinted and updated several times, the last being in 1962. It is therefore worthwhile looking at its contents in some detail.

Following the tradition of many historical text-books of the time, Altham concentrated on the 'kings and queens', rather than the general spread and development of cricket from its birth to many parts of the world. An accomplished writer, he provided well constructed essays on the England v Australia Test series, on Gentlemen v Players, Oxford v Cambridge, the first-class counties and the Public Schools. In the original part-work, overseas countries are almost entirely ignored, save when a major England touring team visited. He acknowledges his debt to Rockley Wilson, the England and Yorkshire cricketer, who was also a master at Winchester. Wilson possessed an extensive cricket library and Altham used it as a source for most of his material. In the Preface to the History, Altham notes:

> "Some time ago a kindly critic remarked to me, 'After all,
> I suppose your history will only be a potted Wisden'. That
> impeachment I readily admit, for the book is indeed one
> vast plagiarism."

Altham's bibliographic list of references however does extend well beyond *Wisden*, with over 150 titles given. Included in the list is Warner's *Imperial Cricket*. As has been commented upon, this book gives excellent coverage of cricket throughout the Empire, and it seems a little odd that it didn't inspire Altham to branch out beyond his narrow confines. Altham did have Ashley-Cooper on hand to eliminate any factual errors and he is generous in his praise for the latter. He was also most fortunate that P.F.Thomas's learned booklets were being issued during the serialisation and some of Thomas's data could be incorporated into the hardback version of the work.

Although Ranjitsinjhi and Grace had nominally written long historical chapters in their published works, the last proper history of the game had been Charles Box's volume as far back as 1877. One is left wondering what sort of history Ashley-Cooper might have written. He was the fount of knowledge behind a number of pre-war books dealing with specific aspects of cricket's history – his work on the Kent history is an excellent example. In 1920 Ashley-Cooper had been appointed Secretary of Nottinghamshire C.C.C., a disastrous appointment, but out of it did come his only full length county history – that on Nottinghamshire, published in 1923. The book was about the same length as Altham's work, but much drier, not to say rather stodgy. As one would expect, Ashley-Cooper's Nottinghamshire contains a mass of previously unpublished detail (in complete contrast to Altham's book).

The 1920s was the golden age of Ashley-Cooper. No other contemporary historian/statistician held such an elevated reputation and indeed merited it. In my opinion his outstanding book of the decade was his annotated reprint of Pycroft's *The Cricket Field*. This was published by St James's Press Co.Ltd in 1922. I haven't performed an exact word count, but Ashley-Cooper's erudite notes are possibly as long as the original book. The work begins with a ten-page essay that places Pycroft in the context of his time. There are, in addition, over 30 full page illustrations.

Another worthwhile volume from Ashley-Cooper's pen was *Cricket Highways and Byways* published by George Allen & Unwin in 1927. It is a collection of essays and included among them is 'A Girdle Round the Earth' which gave the origins of cricket in virtually every country where the game was known to have been played. It was only superseded as late as 2009, with the publication of Martin Wilson's *First Cricket In*, which listed the earliest references to the game in each county and country.

A year after Ashley-Cooper's annotated *The Cricket Field*, he tackled the history of Hambledon by using two original manuscripts, one being the Hambledon Club Minute Book and the second the Club's Accounts. These he reprinted, adding biographies of both the Hambledon players and members, as well as an historical essay and a list of the 105 'Hambledon' matches, with notes and reference to Haygarth's *Scores & Biographies* for readers wanting the full scorecards. Ashley-Cooper employed the match titles as given in Haygarth in order to arrive at his total of 105.

Fierce arguments have since raged among historians as to the correct nomenclature of the Hambledon matches, many or most of which are considered as Hampshire matches promoted by the Hambledon Club. In retrospect it is rather surprising that Ashley-Cooper did not air this subject to any great depth.

Under the guidance of Lord Harris, Ashley-Cooper compiled *Kent Cricket Matches* 1719-1880 which effectively linked up to the Kent County Cricket Annual and thus gave that county's supporters the chance of possessing the detailed scorecard (or at least a summary, in the case of the early games) of every County game. Ashley-Cooper included seasonal averages from the time they became practical. With regard to the 18th century data, in particular, it is a fine piece of research and despite the passing of some 80 years, only a small handful of additional matches have been discovered. The biographies of the Kent players for these pre-1880 matches had appeared in the Kent History.

Ashley-Cooper was commissioned to compile *Middlesex County Cricket Club Volume II 1900-1920*, this being a follow-on from W.J.Ford's work. It is pity that the opportunity wasn't taken to include biographies of Middlesex players – this comment has been made already when noting Ford's book, but Ashley-Cooper must have been in a much better position to provide biographical notes than was Ford.

During the Great War, Ashley-Cooper had had two books published. *W.G.Grace Cricketer* sets out the immortal player's record innings-by-innings. He included the M.C.C. matches versus Hertfordshire and Staffordshire as 'first-class' together with others of doubtful first-class status, following the lead of the Lillywhite annuals of the 1870s. Ashley-Cooper's decision cemented a stance which has, like the Hambledon question, caused headaches for modern historians.

In the same year, 1916, Ashley-Cooper wrote the biography of E.M.Grace. This, like all the author's work, contains valuable historical nuggets, but the statistical section might have been fuller.

Ashley-Cooper's output was prodigious. Between 1916 and 1931 his bibliography lists some 60 titles. After his brief spell as Nottinghamshire

Secretary, he retired to a cottage in Milford, near Godalming and in his own words: 'I go into my study after breakfast and except for an interval for lunch of about an hour I work all day. It is a great delight to me.'

Apart from his books, he wrote two or three historical or statistical signed articles each year for *The Cricketer*, as well as supplying news items and obituaries. His pride and joy was probably his work for the *Wisden Almanack* updating annually both the Record Section and Births & Deaths. Also on a yearly basis he provided 'Feats, Facts and Figures', a feature running to about 20 pages for the *Athletic News Cricket Annual*.

In 1931 owing to deteriorating eyesight and general poor health, Ashley-Cooper was forced to abandon work and sell his incredible cricket library. Ashley-Cooper died at his home in January 1932. He remains a unique figure in the world of cricket research, history and statistics, fortunate in his early friendship with C.W.Alcock and then his worldwide circle of cricketing correspondents.

Only a few months prior to Ashley-Cooper's death, one of the most unusual cricket historians had passed away. Percy Francis Thomas died in Cricklewood, Middlesex on October 13, 1931. He was born in Woolwich in 1866 and the 1901 census shows him as running a confectioners shop in Hackney. Whilst Ashley-Cooper gives the impression of a very serious minded individual, though one who would willingly help other statisticians, Thomas, who usually wrote under the alias 'Hippo-Pott-Thomas', or its acronym, 'H.P.T., was described as a man of humour, that however, hid a very enquiring mind and a broader knowledge of life than Ashley-Cooper possessed.

An early flavour of Thomas's thinking and disposition is shown in a letter to *The Cricket Field* in December 1893. I quote a short opening section:

> 'Sir – The latest development of the classification question prompts me to trouble you with some comments which I hope, as one of the barbarian instigators of the upset, you will permit me to make, in however small type (Thomas had proposed a scheme for the classification of the

counties in the columns of *The Sportsman* newspaper).
What Mr Ellison intends by his extraordinary motion
I cannot conceive. If he wishes to cancel the miscalled
'Championship' and 'invidious distinction' of class
altogether, the only certain way of doing so seems to
be to abandon the competition and county cricket
altogether…'

The actual letter is some 1,000 words in length.

Some five years later, Thomas contributes a cartoon to the magazine
Cricket depicting a tree with men climbing up it, each man representing a
county. In view of the present (2010) complex method of awarding points
in the Championship, his attached note bears reproduction:

'This – a figurative design without a numeral figure upon
it – is the latest thing in glance guides. Cricketers who
have been satiated with points and decimals, systems
and proportions, ought to welcome a result table that
makes no call upon their mathematical faculties for its
comprehension. What could be plainer? From Lancashire
at the top of the tree, honourably snatching at the laurels
of victory; to Derbyshire at the bottom, making equally
sure of the wooden spoon, every county is portrayed in
the true position to which the M.C.C. warrants it to have
climbed.'

Thomas's contributions to *Cricket* became more frequent and his poems
more verbose during the magazine's final years. Those are however a
sideshow. His greatest piece of published research and logical thought
came in a series of booklets in the 1920s. The six booklets go under the
general title of *Old English Cricket* and were issued by C.H.Richards of
Nottingham between 1922 and 1929 – there is an excellent index, which
is combined to cover all six booklets. Despite the paucity of known
contemporary references, Thomas sets out to prove that the Weald between
the North and South Downs in south-east England was the birthplace
of cricket. The mass of additional data discovered since Thomas's time

merely reinforces his hypothesis. Another avenue explored in the booklets is the origin of the Laws of Cricket. He takes apart the earliest known published set of Laws and produces a convincing possible earlier version. There is no space here to explore the other themes aired – a study of his booklets is obligatory for serious students.

On another plane, Thomas issued from 1924 to 1931 a very bizarre cricket annual, latterly titled *The Cricket Spectator, An Annual Miscellany for the Lover of the Game*.

Whilst Ashley-Cooper was producing one publication after another and Thomas pursuing his strange if interesting ends, the other pre-war cricket stalwart, J.N.Pentelow was chiefly engaged in schoolboy fiction working for the Amalgamated Press and their weekly publications, *The Magnet* and *The Gem*. He was for a time editor of these famous comics and as such in charge of Charles Hamilton (alias 'Frank Richards') author of the Greyfriars/Billy Bunter sagas. In fact he is believed to have written some episodes when Hamilton's copy failed to appear. Pentelow did not totally neglect his cricketing past. In 1921 he wrote two cricket supplements for *The Magnet*. The first was a brief 'History of Australian Tours to England' – Australia toured in 1921. The second was much more substantial – 'Who's Who in the Cricket World'. This ran to 88 pages and was the most comprehensive work of its kind to date, far exceeding the small potted players' biographies which were published in the cricket annuals of the time. Pentelow also wrote occasional articles for *The Cricketer*, but the principal conduit for his cricket writing was *Ayres' Cricket Companion*. As has been noted, W.R.Wright was the Editor of this publication, but Pentelow took over when Wright died 1927.

Pentelow died on 5, July 1931 aged only 59, so it is a sad coincidence that perhaps the four most worthwhile cricket historians/statisticians of the first quarter of the 20th century (Waghorn, Ashley-Cooper, Thomas and Pentelow) died within eighteen months of each other. There was a void to be filled, but before looking for successors, an update on the career of that other pre-war statistician, Sir Home Gordon, would seem appropriate. The revised editions of his *Cricket Form At A Glance* were mentioned in Chapter 5. He enthusiastically embraced the creation of *The Cricketer*. In the 1922 and 1923 editions he supplied the detailed annual first-class cricket statistics, then after a few seasons, gap produced similar figures after the 1931 summer. By now Arthur Langford had the problem of coping with Home Gordon's efforts and later commented:

> 'He was a real problem. His copy was extremely difficult to read, and he left no room for corrections, which made things exceedingly awkward as he was alarmingly inaccurate. I hope it is not unkind to say that although he mixed with all the great players, English and overseas, covering a period of more than 50 years, he knew very little about the game...He was, too, injudicious, and I do not think it is any secret that the members of the Sussex Committee were fearful of expressing any views within his hearing in case they appeared inaccurately recorded in his articles.'

Returning to the major national cricket annuals, *Wisden* remained as the dominant publication for cricket statisticians. It had continued to appear through the war years, mainly featuring Public Schools matches. Ashley-Cooper remained in harness, looking after the Births & Deaths section, but with virtually no first-class cricket, the Record Section was put in abeyance. There was, due to war casualties, a very much enlarged Obituary Section. E.B.Noel covered Public Schools, having assumed this role in 1913. Evan Baille Noel was born in 1879; educated at Winchester and Cambridge, he was in the school eleven for three years, but only played for the Freshmen at Cambridge. On coming down he moved into journalism and from 1903 to 1909 was Sporting Editor of *The Times*. His principal cricket book, entitled *Winchester College Cricket*, was published in 1926. A 250 page hardback, in the main, it concentrates on Winchester matches against Eton and Harrow. He gave his wife a copy for her birthday! Noel died in London in 1928, he had been Secretary of the Queen's Club since 1914.

The long standing editor of *Wisden* was still Sydney H.Pardon and he had been in control for 35 years when he died on November 30, 1925. His final edition (1925) was over 900 pages in length, twice the size of his first edition in 1891. Stewart Caine, whose details are given in Chapter 3, took over the editorial chair. While Pardon had seen *Wisden* transformed, Caine, whose reign lasted until 1933, was content to continue the format developed by Pardon. His successor was to see the issuing of just two editions. Sydney James Southerton, the younger son of the famous England cricketer, James Southerton, was born in Mitcham in 1874. He acted as official scorer for the 1893 Australian touring team to England, before joining the Cricket Reporting Agency the following year. Tragically he died during a dinner at The Oval in 1935, having just proposed the toast to 'Cricket'. Like Caine he was happy to retain the trusted format.

The *Athletic News Cricket Annual* had a change of editorship in 1925 when J.A.H.Catton left and Ivan Sharpe was appointed. Sharpe, a well-known soccer player, had represented Great Britain in the 1912 Olympics and finished his soccer League career with Leeds United in 1923. As a journalist with the *Athletic News* newspaper he covered a number of sports including soccer and cricket.

Historians do not seem to appreciate the mass of information which the *Athletic News Annual* contained. Its spread was far wider, in terms of English cricket, than *Wisden*. Looking at the 1928 edition, for example, the following cricket leagues are featured: Bassetlaw, Birmingham, Bolton, Bradford, Central Lancs, Durham Senior, Glossop, Huddersfield, Lancashire, Liverpool, Lancs & Cheshire, Manchester, North Staffs, North Yorks & South Durham, Ribblesdale, Tyneside, South Lancs, Ulster, West Lancs, and Yorkshire Council. Not only is each of the League tables printed, but in many cases the league averages and/or individual club averages, also the fixtures for the coming season. None of this appears in *Wisden* and exceedingly little in *The Cricketer*.

Ashley-Cooper's 'Feats, Facts and Figures' section for 1927 is included and supplemented by 14 pages of first-class records and a Who's Who of the 1928 West Indian tourists.

The main rival to the *Athletic News* publication was the *Daily News*

Cricket Annual, whose editor was Frank Thorogood – his reign lasted until 1939, though the annual's title changed due to the merger of the *News* and the *Chronicle* newspapers. A charming man, whose writings echoed his general demeanour, he was the *Daily News*, then its successor, the *News Chronicle*, cricket correspondent until the Second World War. Thorogood died in Carshalton, Surrey in 1950, aged 78. Looking at the 1934 annual, the Record Section was a mere six pages dealing with first-class data and, since it previewed an Australian tour, an additional four pages of England v Australia Test Records – no author or compiler was given. The main content of the book was the pen portraits of county players. These were sometimes quite detailed; Walter Hammond's for instance was 500 words in length; in contrast to the very brief, purely statistical based pen pictures in today's *Playfair* annual, which is a direct descendent of the *News Chronicle* one. Several other newspapers launched cricket annuals, but they were short-lived.

The inter-war overseas market in cricket publications saw two major reference works issued. Luckin published his second volume on South Africa covering the years 1919 to 1927. In New Zealand Reese published *New Zealand Cricket 1841 to 1914* in 1927. It had been intended that the book would be printed in 1915, but the outbreak of war caused the long delay. The work is as comprehensive as Luckin's Volume One. As well as essays on the early development of cricket in the various provinces and the first-class match scores, there are detailed scores of many lesser games. Thomas Wilson Reese was born in Christchurch in 1867 and from 1887-88 to 1917-18 played representative cricket for Canterbury. He was considered one of the outstanding fielders of his day. Two of his brothers also represented Canterbury, one of whom, Daniel, wrote an interested autobiography which was published in 1948. T.W.Reese died in Christchurch in 1949. He issued a second volume of New Zealand cricket history in 1936. This covers the seasons 1914 to 1933.

In Australia, there was still no national volume of history, but in 1930 at his own expense, Charles Bernard O'Reilly, a local Adelaide journalist, published *South Australian Cricket 1880-1930*. This gave the detailed match scores of South Australian matches and averages, but only five pages of historical notes. Sales of the book were very poor and several hundred copies were burnt by O'Reilly's daughter, when the South Australian Cricket Association declined to buy them for a nominal sum.

In Ceylon, cricket followers were fortunate to possess Samuel Peter Foenander, who began adult life as a school teacher, but switched to journalism, becoming Sports Editor of the *Ceylon Observer*, he was also Ceylon's correspondent for *Wisden*. Educated at Wesley School, he had been a very talented wicketkeeper at the turn of the century. Foenander had a splendid cricket library and compiled a number of booklets on Ceylon cricket as well as the *Ceylon Cricketers' Companion* which for the three years it lasted (1925-1927) gave a very full account of cricket on the island during those seasons. He died in Colombo in 1967 aged 84.

India's answer to Foenander was the splendidly named Ponchaji Nussarwanji Polishwalla. Based in Bombay he published *A Brief History of the Past 50 Years of Indian Cricket* in 1914 in Gujarati. He also edited *Indian Cricket Annual*, which is as diverse as the years in which it was published (between 1917 and 1928, but by no means every year). Polishwalla's *All India Cricket Annual 1934* commemorated his thirty years in cricket journalism, again with odd statistics and unusual snippets of fact.

The American equivalent of Polishwalla was Karl Andre Auty. He had an unusual scholastic career, being at the Grammar School in Dewsbury, then at HMS Conway, the Sorbonne in Paris and Nottingham University. He arrived in Chicago where he played cricket and published a cricket annual covering cricket in the state of Illinois, the annual also covered Rugby Football in the state, in some years. Apart the match scores of local games, a wide variety of unexpected articles and some even more unexpected illustrations are included. Auty possessed a large cricket library; he died in Chicago in November 1959 aged 81.

Despite being raised to Test status, West Indian islands are barren ground for inter-war cricket literature of an historical nature.

Chapter 8
Differences in Style

In the 1920s, Ashley-Cooper and P.F.Thomas were the principal
historians who published the results of their cricket researches, but in
both cases much that they issued was as a result of their discoveries made
in the previous two decades. They leant heavily on the cricketing notes
that Waghorn had published, also in pre-war days. Historians such as
C.I.S.Wallace and A.H.J.Cochrane had a great interest in how cricket
evolved and wrote occasional articles on the subject, however the one man
who continued the pre-war work of Waghorn and Ashley-Cooper in depth
and had his researches published in book form was G.B.Buckley. His first
volume was published by Cotterell & Co of Birmingham in 1935, entitled
Fresh Light on 18th Century Cricket. Buckley (or his brother, Francis, whom
he thanks in the Preface for 'having discovered and collected many of these
Cricket notices') spent much time combing the newspaper collections of
the British Museum, the Bodleian and 35 other provincial libraries listed
in his two volumes.

The most important difference between the work of the Buckleys and
that of Waghorn is that the former records the name of the newspaper
from which the extract comes and the date. In some examples the
Buckleys quote the reference in *Waghorn* and then add to it, but the notes
are not necessarily the full newspaper detail. A second volume, *Fresh Light
on Pre-Victorian Cricket* was issued by the same publishers in 1937 and
this time although the main research took place at the British Museum,
quite a number of provincial libraries were also used. This second volume

contains three Appendices which bring together other information found during the researches. The titles of matches are discussed and the possible qualifications for players to appear in certain teams. Also explored are the Articles of Agreement which ran in conjunction with the basic Laws.

G.B.Buckley contributed articles to *The Cricketer* from 1937 to 1962 and some of his additional notices were later printed in *The Cricket Quarterly*. These were part of two volumes of manuscripts that were left to M.C.C. George Bent Buckley was born in Yorkshire in 1885. He trained as a surgeon in Manchester and after serving in the R.A.M.C. during the First World War, he moved to Weston-super-Mare, where he set up a private practice. He retired in 1938 and died, after a long illness, in April 1962.

Buckley's work was for a very small select band of readers. Most of the cricketing reading public of the 1930s were more enamoured by two more romantic writers. Some readers of this present work may protest that neither of these authors really belongs in a volume of this sort, but excluding them would present a false picture of the time when nostalgia was the order of the day and both writers at least flirted with cricket's history, even if they could not be described as either historians or statisticians.

In 1922, a volume *A Cricketer's Book* was published by Grant Richards. The book contained a collection of essays, combined with the reports of the 1921 Test series between England and Australia. One of the essays concerns the change in bowling styles from Hambledon to the 1920s, but the remainder are, for the most part, describing current or recently retired cricketers. The essays were first published in the *Manchester Guardian* and the author was Neville Cardus, the *Guardian* cricket correspondent. He was building a reputation as a journalist who described the playing of cricket in a new style, giving the reader his impressions of play and even imagined conversations between players. Cardus became the English equivalent of the French Impressionists, but in words rather than paint.

After this initial book, Cardus often wrote essays on cricketers and matches that he had never himself witnessed – historical sketches. In 1930 he was commissioned by Longmans Green & Co to write *Cricket* for their English Heritage series. It contains a chapter entitled 'Laws and

Evolutions', which begins with the 1744 Laws, but soon after states:

> 'I do not propose in this book to go all the way into the origins of cricket. Mr Altham and 'H.P.-T.' have attended once and for all (in our time) to the archaeology. If you tell me that the game was evolved (or was not evolved) from Club-ball, Creag, Cat and Dog, or Stob-ball, I am not more intrigued than I am when somebody tells me (while I am listening to Schubert) that the art of song was probably born when primitive man first bayed the moon with a howl and thus intensified speech by emotion.'

So Cardus made clear that he left the researches into early cricket to others, but he, himself, was responsible for one historical notion, that the Edwardian era was the 'Golden Age of Cricket'. In this small respect, Cardus influenced the perception of the game's history for future generations. Most adults consider that the cricket they watched as a schoolboy or schoolgirl was the 'Golden Age'. Cardus was no exception; it was simply that he had the ability to write fluently of his own childhood memories of county cricket at Old Trafford and the players that performed on that famous ground in the early years of the 20th century.

John Frederick Neville (he later added his mother's maiden name 'Cardus') was born in Manchester in 1889. He was engaged at Shrewsbury School as assistant cricket coach in 1912 and on the outbreak of war added to his duties that of secretary to the headmaster, Dr Cyril Alingham. He left this post when Alingham moved to Eton, in 1916. The following year he joined the staff of the *Manchester Guardian*; his cricket reports for that paper commenced in 1919. Between 1940 and 1947 he lived in Australia, but in 1945 *English Cricket* was published by Collins. This is a 48 page gentle introduction to the bones of cricket in England by Cardus; it does not delve further than the Kent v England match of 1744, but does contain reproductions of some early cricket illustrations. Following his return to England Cardus wrote two volumes of autobiography, which are largely as romantic as his other writings. He died in London in February 1975.

A final passing note regarding Cardus. The Introduction to his 1930

Cricket volume was written by Sir John Collings Squire, author and poet. His principal contribution to cricket writing was the reviewing of books on the game, but he was also a cricketer, though of the J.M.Barrie variety, keen rather than talented, and ran his own side 'The Invalids'. He died in Heathfield, Sussex in December 1958 aged 74.

Second only to Neville Cardus as a descriptive writer was R.C.Robertson-Glasgow, whose articles began to appear in *The Cricketer* in 1924. Born in Edinburgh in 1901, Raymond Charles Robertson-Glasgow was educated at Charterhouse and Oxford, where he was awarded his blue in 1920. He played for Somerset – he amusingly noted that he qualified for the county by changing trains at Taunton – on and off from 1920 to 1935, being a fast-medium bowler. In 1933 he was appointed cricket correspondent to the *Morning Post* and later wrote for the *Daily Telegraph*, *The Observer* and *The Sunday Times*. A charming person with a great sense of humour, which was reflected in his prose, sadly he developed into a manic-depressive and died by his own hand in 1965. Whilst a study of his writings reveals a fairly profound knowledge of cricket's history, his essay 'The Origins of Cricket' gives some idea of his lack of reverence for historians, who take their subject too seriously. The essay appropriately appeared shortly after the first publication of Altham's *History*. The former begins:

> 'It has long been a problem of acute interest to the thinking man, whether cricket (Pila Complex) was the grandmother, sister, or granddaughter of Fives (Pila Palmaris);'

His two collections of essays, *Cricket Prints* and *More Cricket Prints*, are outstanding, but encompass only players that Robertson-Glasgow met and knew. I must add that the illustration on the cover of the second volume is of the Notts batsman, Joe Hardstaff, – he is not the subject of one of the essays!

I left the *Wisden Almanack* in the last chapter in the early 1930s apparently flourishing and unchanged in its format over the past half century. However time was catching up the Cricketer's Bible as it was now termed. Sales started to drop and after the 1937 edition, the Wisden firm reached an agreement with J.Whitaker & Sons Ltd (publishers of the famous Almanack of that name) that they should take the *Wisden Almanack* into their stable.

After the death of S.J.Southerton in 1935, the editorship had passed to Wilfrid H.Brookes, another partner in the Cricket Reporting Agency and a general sports reporter. He had worked as a sub-editor on *Wisden* since 1921. He survived the switch to Whitakers, but only for two editions. Brookes died in Putney in 1955 aged 60.

At first glance there appear to be radical changes for the 1938 edition, but in reality, although the various sections have been shunted around – Births & Deaths and Obituaries go from the front of the book to the back for example – the actual content is largely unaltered. Births & Deaths have shrunk from 91 pages to 80; obituaries from 27 pages to 15, but on inspection this is due to a tightening up of the linage and a reduction in the type size, rather than a reduction in the number of words. The Record Section fell from 61 pages to 50, but again very little content is lost. Historians and statisticians were thus largely unaffected by these adjustments, however the actual seasonal reports on individual counties and the match reports were reduced, though each match still had its own page and bowling analyses were still printed in tabular form. One new section was ten pages listing cricket books in print. The cover design changed and the few photographic illustrations were printed on art paper. Whether these largely cosmetic exercises were responsible for an increase in sales, or whether it was due to better marketing by Whitakers is open to question.

From the historian/statistician viewpoint, the main sections of the Almanack are the Records section and Births & Deaths. Ashley-Cooper who had created the 'modern' concept for both had on his death been succeeded by J.A.H.Catton, as has been mentioned, but Catton was more a journalist than statistician and merely tacked the last twelve months' figures on to Ashley-Cooper's tables. J.D.Betham, whose details were given in Chapter 6, continued to assist with the Births & Deaths Section. A new name appeared in the credits in the 1934 edition of *Wisden*, F.J.C.Gustard.

THE ENGLISH CRICKETERS TRIP TO CANADA AND THE UNITED STATES BY FRED LILLYWHITE.

Fred Lillywhite in his printing tent.

The Rev. James Pycroft

Arthur Haygarth

H. T. Waghorn

H. S. Altham

The Rev. R.S.Holmes

A.D.Taylor

C.W.Alcock

F.S.Ashley-Cooper

A.A. Thomson and R. Yeomans

Prof. J. Mulvaney

L.E.S. Gutteridge

R.S. Rait Kerr

Tony Webb and Tony Percival

E.E.Snow

Neville Cardus

Sir Home Gordon   *A. Weigall*

Gordon Ross and Roy Webber

H.G.Deane and Lord Harris

R.L.Arrowsmith

David Frith

A.H.Carman

J.D.B.Coldham

He had been studying cricket history and its related statistics for some years prior to that, his first letter in *The Cricketer* in September 1922, was sent from the Y.M.C.A. in Tottenham Court Road, London. It was nothing more than his selection of the teams to represent the North and the South that season. His first published book appeared in 1925 and dealt with the statistics of Somerset cricketers; in 1929 he compiled a history of Somerset with biographies of all their players, but this never appeared in print. Gustard developed a great friendship with Pentelow and due to his guidance, the first of many articles by Gustard was featured in *The Cricketer* in 1931; the following year he had a regular column in the magazine and in 1933 began his informative series, 'The History of Cricket Overseas'. The first article was concerned with Australia and he began by tackling head-on the, then, vexed question of the start date for first-class cricket in that country. Gustard elected to choose the Tasmania v Victoria match of 1851. This milestone is nowadays automatically assumed as the logical answer, rather than the first New South Wales v Victoria game of 1856, for which some historians opted.

Gustard deals with the Test Playing countries of the 1930s in turn, before he moves on to South America. Here he suggests the first Argentina North v South match in 1891 as the commencement of first-class cricket. Continuing through the non-Test playing countries, Gustard gives 'first-class' averages for leading players in the United States, Canada and Bermuda. He takes a much more liberal approach to the subject, than later statisticians would. Clearly he is swayed by the possible expansion and development of top class cricket in these countries. The Second World War was to alter these perceptions.

In May 1934, Gustard suggested a list of overseas current teams that should be regarded as first-class – one such example is the representative Egyptian eleven. Gustard's views drew swift responses from readers of *The Cricketer* in particular from Sir Home Gordon, E.L.Roberts and Antony Weigall – the last two will be featured later.

Unfortunately Gustard was taken seriously ill in 1936. Following an operation he seemed to have recovered, but he had a relapse in 1937 and died in April 1938 aged 35. If he had lived he might have filled the void left by the death of Ashley-Cooper, for Gustard combined his interest in statistics with his study of the history of cricket – an essential combination for any sensible resulting outcome.

The only substantial book compiled by Gustard was *England v Australia*, which was issued just prior to the 1934 Test series. The work begins with ten pages analysing the Australian touring party and then gives well-rounded short biographies of each player with their season-by-season first-class figures. Twenty-two possible England Test candidates are similarly treated. D.R.Jardine is omitted as he had announced his retirement during the winter tour of India. G.O.B.Allen was also omitted, but because he would be unavailable due to injury. The record section includes Test career figures for all players in England v Australia Tests and averages for Australian tourists to England from 1878 including the AIF tour of 1919. The full scores of the 1930 and 1932-33 Test Matches are also given.

With the death of Gustard, the guardianship of the *Wisden* Cricket Records passed to the immensely enthusiastic statistician, E.L.Roberts. His original work was to expand the books on Test Cricket which had been published in the 1920s by William P.H.Sparks and William H.Coleman. These works were scorecards of Test Matches and series averages. In his initial book in 1932, Roberts gave summaries of Test scores, the run aggregates in each series by each team, individual centuries scored and some statistical notes. Two years later he expanded this work to include a Who's Who of all Test cricketers, but this was a very perfunctory list. No christian names were given. Births (and deaths) were only given for a selection of players, even though those details, in many cases could have been found in *Wisden*, occasional players were described as left-handed or left-arm bowlers, but Woolley was not so described. The work was simply not consistent. A rival work to Roberts' 1934 book was *The Story of the Tests in England 1880 to 1934*, with the tag 'containing information never before given in any publication'. The book acknowledges the use of Sparks' work, in giving the detailed scores of England v Australia in England matches, with notes, some of which deal with unusual coincidences or happenings.

There are no complete sets of averages, just the leading ones in 'average' order. The author, Cecil Kent, states that he checked the Test reports in *The Times*. The match scores in these books gave no more than the detail printed in *Wisden*, so no fall of wickets, second innings batting order and not necessarily the names of captains and wicketkeepers or even who won the toss.

Returning to E.L.Roberts, Edward Lamplough Roberts was born in Ecclesall, near Sheffield in 1880. Leaving school he went to work in a surveyor's office, though by 1921 he had moved to Sutton Coldfield and then further south to Purley, where he remained for the rest of his life. His first article in *The Cricketer* appeared in 1931 and then nearly every year to 1953 he contributed at least one article and often three or four. Padwick lists 21 titles compiled by Roberts, several of which appeared in more than one edition.

In two seasons, 1938 and 1939, he compiled a *Test Cricket Annual*. A number of his smaller booklets were sponsored by commercial firms, notably the bat manufacturers, Gunn & Moore. His flow of published works was on a par with Ashley-Cooper, but did not contain the erudite snippets of the latter, for he had little depth to his knowledge. Today his best known work is probably *Cricket in England 1894 to 1939*, published in 1946. The principal contents are details of each English first-class season between those dates. On one page are the top twenty batsmen of the year and the top twenty bowlers; on the facing page are notes on the season.

During the early years of the Second World War, Roberts worked for a 'pittance' (in the words of the Assistant Editor, Langford) to help keep *The Cricketer* going. It was typical of the man, kind and helpful to his cricketing friends and fellow statisticians. The last of his numerous contributions to *The Cricketer* came in the Spring Annual of 1953 – the detailed statistics of Alec Bedser. Roberts died in February 1954.

Another 1930s statistician of note was Samuel Canynge Caple. Born in Clifton, Bristol in 1910, he was educated at Clifton College and the Royal Academy of Dramatic Art. From 1928 to 1935 Caple appeared on the stage, but then switched from the acting profession to journalism. His name appears in the correspondence columns of *The Cricketer* with increasing frequency from 1933 and the following year he published *The Cricketers' Who's Who*. This volume was easily the most comprehensive work of its kind. Issued as a hardback of 214 pages, it contains the biographies of 291 contemporary players, some of which are very detailed. G.T.S.Stevens' biography is some 1,200 words in length. As well as English county cricketers, Caple gives details of 39 prominent overseas cricketers. His involvement in The Cricket Society as well as his post-war publications will be dealt with later.

A book which contained information on cricketers and still remains a very valuable reference work for historians is *The Elevens of Three Great Schools 1805-1929* Compiled by W.R.Lyon, it gives the match scores of the games involving Eton, Harrow and Winchester with biographical data on virtually all the players and longer notices on the more important. The work was published by Spottiswoode, Ballantyne & Co.Ltd in 1930.

A second work of reference that has remained the staple diet for historians is *The Language of Cricket* published by the Oxford University Press in 1934. The author was Wilfrid James Lewis and it is the best cricket dictionary yet produced. A number of so-called cricket dictionaries have emerged in post-war years, but it is an enormous pity that the OUP did not employ someone to update Lewis's book as new words and indeed fresh research have become available. Unlike some of his imitators, he gives the earliest known references to the words included in the work. Lewis was born in Headington in 1868, the son of a college servant. He was employed by the Oxford University Press to work on the *Oxford English Dictionary* from 1889 to 1933, when he retired. After retirement he continued to assist on a part-time basis and died in Oxford in December 1947.

The start of the long road towards clubs or societies for groups of people interested in cricket, but not connected to a club which ran a cricket team as such, seems to have begun with a letter to *The Cricketer* in August 1929. C.J.Britton of Harborne, Birmingham wrote proposing the formation of a club or society for collectors of Cricketana. The aim would be 'to preserve by publication or otherwise, records or manuscripts which might otherwise be lost'. Britton had an encouraging response and The Cricketana Society was launched on October 21, 1929 in Bride Lane, Fleet St, London. Pelham Warner chaired the meeting; C.J.Britton acted as convenor and G.Neville Weston was appointed Secretary.

Britton published two books on cricket, *Cricket Books : The 100 Best* in 1929 and *G.L.Jessop* in 1935. Both were modest productions. The Society seems to have made very little impact, though its fortunes were fleetingly boosted by Dr T.R.Hunter in 1933, when he issued a small annual *Willow Leaves*. This survived for three years.

George Neville Weston was born in Kidderminster in March 1901. Educated at King's School, Worcester and Wolverley Grammar School, he qualified as a solicitor in 1923 and established his own practice in his native town. In the year he became Secretary (and Treasurer) of The Cricketana Society he privately published *My Cricket Collection* and *Cricket Literature*. Neville Weston published a number of other booklets limited to a handful of copies, but he turned interestingly to cricketana related to W.G.Grace and a quest to catalogue all the matches in which the great cricketer appeared. In 1973 Weston published a book of 188 pages dealing with Grace's statistics in minor matches. Weston, who retired to Norfolk in 1970, died in August 1984.

In 1938 Allen & Unwin published an updated version of *A History of Cricket*, the new version being revised by E.W.Swanton. Swanton was born in Forest Hill, South London in 1907 and educated at Cranleigh. From school he went straight into journalism. His first cricket reporting was for the London *Evening Standard* in 1928, when the chief cricket correspondent was J.A.H.Catton. It was not until 1932 that a piece by Swanton was published in *The Cricketer*. In February 1938, Swanton was asked by Altham if he would collaborate in a second edition of the *History* and, according to Swanton, the revised version was for sale 18 weeks later. The book remained faithful to the structure set out by Altham, but to accommodate some of the additions, the bibliographic section of the first edition was scrapped. Swanton had made friends with Altham on the club cricket circuit. Swanton appeared for the Cryptics among other wandering sides and was a talented club batsman, good enough to play three games for Middlesex. Swanton later became a major figure in cricket journalism and literature after serving in the Second World War.

A more talented writer than Swanton was Bernard Darwin, grandson of Charles. Born in Downe, Kent in 1876, he was on the staff of *The Times* from 1907 to 1953, writing principally on golf. His best known cricket book is *W.G. Grace*, a 141 page work published in the 'Great Lives Series' issued by Duckworth in 1934. The book was reissued in 1948 and again in 1978.

At the behest of Sir Home Gordon, Darwin also wrote 18,000 words for the book *Eton v Harrow at Lord's*. The work was compiled by Sir Home Gordon and published by his own company in 1926. Since Ashley-Cooper's book covering the same ground had only appeared in 1922, this fresh volume added very little. Irving Rosenwater described Darwin's essay as 'a mixture of scholarship and fancy which, if not entirely successful or memorable, was naturally couched in the most felicitous prose.' Darwin died in 1961.

Another author who occasionally ventured into cricket was the poet, Thomas Moult. He had been born in Derbyshire in 1885 and had ghost-written Jack Hobbs' book, *Playing for England*, a very popular biography which appeared in 1931. In 1935 Moult edited *Bat and Ball*, which was an anthology with essays by many well-known writers. Moult contributed his own piece running to some 20 pages, this was entitled 'The Story of The Game', but is no more than a pleasant summary of cricket's history. Moult died in Essex in November 1974.

Cricket annuals, both national and county, ceased with the outbreak of war in 1939, but one major English title continued throughout the period of hostilities namely the *Wisden Almanack*.

The 1940 edition was very much in line with its immediate predecessors, since it reported the season of 1939, but the editions between 1941 and 1946 were reduced in size, in line with those that were published during the First World War. In the 1941 edition one innovation was the introduction of 'Some Dates in the History of Cricket', compiled by H.S. Altham. The dates of the foundations of the major cricket grounds and the major counties were an important feature of this new section. Readers might amuse themselves by comparing this first 'Dates' with the one published in the 2007 edition. The comparison shows how the emphasis has altered over the years.

In the 1942 edition, Hubert Preston writes a brief history of the County Championship. In view of the present regulation allowing players to be loaned between counties, it is notable that Preston announces that the County Championship began in 1873 when 'the farce of men playing for more than one county in a season having been stopped...'

Preston makes no attempt to research the oddities in the 'official' list of Champions, but does point out some defects without going to first-hand sources to try and remedy the faults. Preston however does rather criticize the expansion of the Championship after 1890, since the increase in numbers meant that each county could no longer play all the opponents twice. Another new section in 1942 was a complete list of all Test cricketers and every series in which each played. Norman Preston compiled this, whilst E.L.Roberts added an appendix which listed all Test captains. A list of the 244 centuries scored by Jack Hobbs is another interesting compilation, but no author is credited.

It was in 1944 that Hubert Preston took over as Editor from Haddon Whitaker; at the same time the publishers changed from Whitakers to Sporting Handbooks. Haddon Whitaker had taken over for the 1940 edition when Brookes resigned, but he was happy to stand aside for Hubert Preston, who was the senior partner of the Cricket Reporting Agency. Preston, born in 1868, had spent 50 years helping in the compilation of *Wisden* and was now a venerable 74. Profoundly deaf, he was naturally a man of few words and could be considered a safe pair of hands. He was assisted by his son Norman Preston, another partner in the Reporting Agency.

In 1944 the first official *Index to Wisden* was published, by Sporting Handbooks. The compiler was Rex Pogson, who was an expert on Lancashire cricket. Pogson had issued in 1938 *Australia v The Counties*

(1878-1938) which was a basic statistical record of the matches named in the title. In 1944 he published at his own expense *Gloucestershire Cricket and Cricketers*, a 36 page paperback, which rather curiously is simply a narrative covering Gloucestershire's performances in the inter-war years. His modest Foreword comments:

> 'If it be read at all, Gloucestershire men will read it and
> for them it will contain little that is new.'

His *Wisden Index* was useful in that it listed in alphabetical order all the obituaries which the almanacks had contained over the years. Pogson died in Lytham St Annes in April 1976, aged 61. Sporting Handbooks also issued Pelham Warner's *Cricket Between two Wars* in 1942, but due to paper rationing the type of reference work (such as Ashley-Cooper's books on the Graces) that appeared during the 1914-18 war were nowhere to be seen during the 1939-45 conflict. It is interesting however to look at the list of 'books in print' that was included in the early wartime *Wisden's* – there was a great deal on offer.

Chapter 9
Roy Webber and the Society of Cricket Statisticians

The Edwardian era has been designated the 'Golden Age' of cricket; however in terms of spectators attending Test and County matches in England the ten years directly following the Second World War were the most popular. The crowds who flocked to the matches arranged by the overseas tourists were quite extraordinary, especially the Australians of 1948 under Bradman, but even the rather lower key New Zealanders of 1949 attracted the public in huge numbers to both their Tests and County games. In 1947 three million people watched first-class cricket; in 1948 the Australians made a profit of £75,000 – more than double that of any previous tour and, most tellingly, the New Zealanders made a profit of £15,000, despite only having four Tests, each restricted to three days. Every previous New Zealand tour had recorded a loss.

The publishing of cricket books boomed. A simple measurement gives an idea in comparison to the 1930s. The Australian tours of 1930, 1934 and 1938 resulted, according to Padwick, in 14, 14 and 11 titles respectively. The tours of 1948 and 1953 created 31 and 29 items. The South African trip of 1935 had just three items listed in Padwick; the 1947 tour realised 12.

Many of the books and booklets in these numbers were simply popular works of only passing consequence to the serious statistician or historian – though every publication contains something of value, even if the value is a negative. Its very existence is worthy of note. The previous chapters have featured the handful of cricket historians and statisticians whose works ended in publication, but beyond those published writers was a large body of people who tinkered with cricket statistics purely for their own amusement or who to a lesser extent browsed through old newspaper files, like Waghorn but not in such a determined and methodical way. The Cricketana Society of the 1930s had been an attempt to reach these amateur enthusiasts, but failed in its endeavour.

A letter in the Spring Annual of the 1945 *Cricketer* magazine was to galvanise the very quiet and generally introverted statisticians, if not completely out of their back bedrooms, at least to the letter box. The letter began:

> 'Dear Sir, I have for a number of years now been struck by the fact that no reliable and accurate list is in existence showing the total batting and bowling figures of our leading cricketers, both past and present.
>
> 'I am by no means suggesting however that no such task has been attempted, for this, indeed, is far from being the case. There have in fact been a very large number of totals compiled for many batsmen and bowlers, but unfortunately few of them agree with each other.
>
> 'Of those published, there are the series of tremendous works by Sir Home Gordon entitled "Cricket Form at a Glance", which covered sixty years, and involved all cricketers who played in any two or more seasons during that period. Figures covering individual or more modest groups of cricketers and for smaller periods of time have been prepared at various times by F.S.Ashley-Cooper, R.O.Edwards, J.N.Pentelow, F.J.C.Gustard and E.L.Roberts, and in addition various cricket works have contained statistics such as Grace's "Cricket", Read's "Annals of Cricket" and of course the invaluable "Wisden's Almanac".
>
> In all these, however, there are a very large number of errors and inconsistencies, which make it impossible for

any of them to be accepted as trustworthy records.'

The author of this letter, Antony Weigall of Cheam in Surrey, goes on to suggest the formation of a society of statisticians, who could band together and systematically check seasonal figures for players, as well as agree a standard list of first-class matches. Weigall had been writing letters on statistical matters to *The Cricketer* since 1932 and the magazine had also published correspondence on the same subject from both Gustard and Roberts as well as other lesser lights.

In view of the criticism of previous statistical compilations noted by Weigall, it is rather ironic that *The Cricketer*, in its first summer edition following Weigall's letter, should commence Part One of a series detailing the career records of the principal players during the inter-war period. This new statistical series runs right through the 1946 issues of the magazine. The author was L.C.Fielding.

Tony Weigall was born in Rochester in 1902 and educated at Tonbridge – he was not in the XI, indeed his cricket playing ability was described as 'minimal'. However he had a very keen interest in the statistics and history of the game. A chartered accountant, being latterly a partner in the firm of Deloittes, Plender and Griffiths, his letter spurred similar minded enthusiasts to contact him. His dream of a statistical society was realised much more quickly than he might have hoped and he became the Editor of the society's statistical annual for its first six issues. Weigall died at his home in July 1977.

'The Society of Cricket Statisticians' was officially founded at a meeting in London on November 17, 1945. The initial membership was just under 60; the annual subscription was agreed at five shillings; the main objects were, as Weigall had sought, to compile complete and accurate records for first-class cricket from 1870 and the publication of a Year Book. S.Canynge Caple was elected as Hon Secretary. In June 1946 Weigall added to the new society's aim the publication of a cricket bibliography.

The monopoly of this new society was broken before anything concrete had been published. In May 1946, *The Cricketer* carried a letter from Roy Webber of Old Hunstanton in Norfolk. This letter proposed the formation of a 'Cricket Book Society', which would issue a series of booklets, each being between 32 and 64 pages in length. These publications would appear at roughly monthly intervals and cost about two shillings each. Webber stated that he already had six manuscripts in the pipeline. Two months later he officially formed the Society and announced that it required a membership of 500 to be viable. The major difference between Weigall's organisation and Webber's was that the former was purely amateur, with authors and officials being unpaid, whereas Webber was hoping to earn an income from his Society.

Webber's Society issued its first booklet in August 1946. *A Concise History of Cricket* was written by S.H.Butler. It was depressingly inaccurate, though only 40 pages in length. The booklet begins by stating that the first reference to the game of cricket occurred in the 15th century and the first overseas reference was in 1670 (in fact, 1676) in Antioch. William Clarke's All England Eleven was said to have toured the country for 'several' seasons, whereas in fact the team lasted over 30 years.

Research by Irving Rosenwater revealed many years later that S.H.Butler was just a pen name for Roy Webber and as Webber's subsequent efforts would make quite plain, his knowledge of cricket history was deficient. Roy Webber was born in Brighton in 1914; he trained as an accountant and served in the R.A.F. during the Second World War; he died in November 1962. Unlike Weigall, Canynge Caple and a number of the founding members of the Statisticians Society, there is no record of Webber contributing articles or letters to *The Cricketer* prior to 1945. This *Concise History* was his first venture into print and it seems obvious that he launched it without allowing for any known historians to check its veracity. In 1947 Webber took the post as scorer for the B.B.C. and his career as a major cricket statistician grew from that base, rather than from his Cricket Book Society.

In 1946 however Webber pressed on with his Society. The second booklet to appear was the first part of a revised version of Canynge Caple's *Cricketers' Who's Who*. There were to be four more parts which only took the cricketers to Trevor Every, after which the Society folded.

The third booklet introduced to the cricket book reading public a fresh face, Gerald Brodribb, though subscribers to *The Cricketer* would have noticed his name in the letters column from 1929 and under some articles from 1939. It was quite apparent that Brodribb was a cut above the usual compiler of cricket statistics.

Arthur Gerald Norcott Brodribb was born in St Leonard's on Sea, Sussex in 1915. He was educated at Eastbourne and University College, Oxford and although he did not obtain a place in either the school or university teams, he was a very useful club cricketer, playing for M.C.C. and the Jesters. He joined the teaching profession and was at Repton, Christ's Hospital and Canford before becoming headmaster of a Sussex Prep School. A keen archaeologist, Brodribb was a member of the Society of Antiquaries.

His first book for Webber's Society was *Some Memorable Innings*. Brodribb's Foreword has the note thanking county secretaries for permission to inspect county scorebooks. That point alone sets the author on a level not reached by the vast majority of cricket statisticians in 1946. He also includes a number of non-first-class innings, such as the one by D.K. Yarde for Central India v M.C.C. Yarde batted five hours 20 minutes for an innings of 24.

In 1951 Brodribb's *All Round The Wicket* was published by Sporting Handbooks. This is a collection of 36 essays by the author, some of which had previously been issued in *The Cricketer* or *The Field*. The essays cover a wide variety of subjects from Charles Dickens to an analysis of how often batsmen are dismissed by each of the modes of getting out. Brodribb followed this book with *Next Man In*, a survey of cricket laws and customs; the feast of incidents portrayed in the book demonstrate the depth of the author's researches into cricket literature. The book was later revised and re-issued as was another Brodribb title *Hit For Six*. This, as its name implies, is a book on the hitting of sixes and the author visited many cricket grounds in England in order to check the facts he had obtained from match reports. Brodribb later wrote biographies of Gilbert Jessop and Nicholas Felix. Stephen Green, the Lord's archivist, commented about Brodribb:

> 'One was always excited by the prospect of a visit from
> Gerald (he was such an engaging character) but one was
> also a trifle apprehensive. To be interrogated by him was
> like an extensive session of Mastermind. Questions were
> asked at an alarming speed on a vast range of topics. It
> was impossible to keep up with such a human dynamo.'

Brodribb's second booklet for the Cricket Book Society was *Some
Memorable Bowling*. It was a mirror of his book on Innings, with the
obvious and the obscure mingling. Webber used the back cover of this
book to print a piece which was headed in block capitals 'NOTICE!' and
began with, 'There is a great deal of controversy over the question of the
"ranking" of first-class matches prior to 1939.'

This point had exercised minds in the columns of *The Cricketer* in
the 1930s, when Gustard had some interesting comments to make. It
has already been noted that Webber's knowledge of cricket history was
superficial and the remainder of the remarks he makes in this 'Notice'
demonstrate exactly how naïve he was. He appears to consider all
matches played in the West Indies of doubtful first-class status, as well
as matches by Tasmania and Western Australia; on the other hand also of
supposedly doubtful status are matches played by Northants before 1905
and Worcestershire before 1899, when one cannot think of any other
'expert' who would remotely believe either county were deemed worthy
of first-class status before those seasons.

On the other hand, two months prior to Brodribb's book on bowling,
Webber had published *The Cricket Season of 1946. A Statistical Review*. It
is an excellent summary, with an alphabetical list of seasonal averages for
all first-class players, plus the figures given on a county by county basis
and other useful data – Mr Brodribb's help is acknowledged. It is however
worth noting that the Society of Cricket Statisticians also published an
alphabetical list of first-class seasonal averages for 1946 – Tony Weigall
being the principal compiler.

It would appear that the two organisations were on a collision course, but in 1946 Roy Webber was appointed Assistant Secretary of the Statisticians and the back page advert of his Cricket Book Society publication for May 1947 (*The M.C.C. in Australia 1946-47*) featured a quarterly magazine *The Field of Cricket* described as 'the official journal of The Society of Cricket Statisticians, due for publication on June 20th'. Webber was now trying to ride too many horses at once. He was the owner of 'The Cricket Book Society', the Assistant Secretary of the Statisticians and had just been appointed the scorer for the B.B.C.

The Field of Cricket was Webber's idea and the committee of the Statisticians seemingly allowed him full rein. He had the 48 page publication printed in Hunstanton, but when it appeared the Statisticians had no money to pay the bill, the printers sued Roy Webber; Webber claimed he was simply acting on behalf of the Statisticians' Committee. A court case ensued. The Statisticians lost and only a desperate appeal to the membership to loan the Society money paid off the printers and legal team's bills and allowed the Society to continue. Webber resigned from the Society.

While all this turmoil was being played out, Webber's Cricket Book Society folded. Eight booklets were published in 1947 and at the end of that year six of the booklets were re-issued bound as a single hardback book. By then Kenneth M.Arnott of Hunnington, Birmingham had assumed the role of Assistant Secretary to the Society. The Cricket Book Society Pamphlet no.1 was issued in the spring of 1948. It contained career records of all players likely to appear in first-class county cricket in England in 1948. (Padwick's Bibliography gives 1949 as the publication date – this is incorrect). A News Sheet issued with the pamphlet contains the following announcement:

> 'Programme Publications Ltd have published a Cricket
> Annual this summer under the name of Playfair Books,
> the editor being Mr Peter A.West, a member of the
> Society.'

It would seem that this pamphlet was almost the final booklet by the Cricket Book Society. The pamphlet does list five future publications

– one actually materialised, *The Graces* by A.G.Powell and S.Canynge Caple. Another had just appeared: *Glamorgan C.C.C. 1921-1947* by Roy Webber and Kenneth M.Arnott. This 176 page book was comprehensive, giving long descriptions of each first-class season and annual players' statistics. A second edition had six pages added when Glamorgan won the Championship in 1948. A record section gives career figures for all Glamorgan players and a fair selection of the county's records in general. The bowling averages for each season give columns for balls per wicket and runs per 100 balls.

C.M.Oliver is acknowledged for his help in checking the statistics and as he also was the compiler of the Pamphlet no.1 mentioned above, a brief biographical note is appropriate here. Charles Morley Oliver, born in Southport in 1923, was by profession a statistician specialising in economics. He was appointed Lancashire's official statistician in 1948 and contributed to the Lancashire Yearbook in that capacity until 1986. In addition he compiled season by season averages for many players and these figures were destined to appear regularly in publications of the Statisticians Society. Oliver moved from Lancashire to Hendon, Middlesex after the Second World War and played cricket for Hendon Buccaneers. He was an assiduous attender of meetings held by The Cricket Society and by The Association of Cricket Statisticians. He died in Mill Hill in May 2004.

Before describing the new *Playfair Annual*, which had been advertised by the Cricket Book Society, it is worth returning to 1946 and taking up the story of the pocket-size pre-war cricket annuals, which were revived. The 1939 *Athletic News Cricket Annual* was the 48th edition. It reappeared in 1946 (49th edition) but retitled *Athletic News Cricket and Golf Annual*. The editor remained Ivan Sharpe. It contained 85 cricket pages and 44 on golf. The cricket section was mostly first-class records, but the scores of the 1945 Victory Tests are given and the leading 1945 first-class averages. The fixtures for the major Northern Leagues are included as well as those for the leading Home Counties Clubs. In 1947 the annual became the *Sunday Chronicle Cricket and Golf Annual*, continuing as such until 1954. The final edition, in 1955, dropped the golf section. Ivan Sharpe continued as editor until the close, but in the post-war editions there is no acknowledgement for any specific person updating the record section.

The other national annual to be revived was the *News Chronicle Cricket Annual*. This reappeared very little changed, but Frank Thorogood had gone and the editor for 1946 was Percy Rudd. The following year he gave way to Crawford White, the newspaper's cricket correspondent and soon to become very well-known in cricketing circles. Crawford White was born in Glasgow in 1913, but moved to Lancashire as a journalist on a local paper, combining that job with being a cricket professional in the Lancashire Leagues. He was good enough to play for Lancashire Second Eleven though he declined a post on the playing staff at Old Trafford. Following war service with Bomber Command, he moved to Fleet Street and the *News Chronicle*. As their cricket correspondent he covered most of the major England Test Matches, home and abroad. He wrote brief accounts of four Ashes series, these being published in conjunction with Roy Webber's statistics. When the *News Chronicle* closed, White briefly joined the *Daily Mail*, before moving to the *Daily Express*. After retiring from journalism he worked in PR for Cornhill Insurance. An urbane man who seemed to attend every function on his overseas tours, he was ideal for the job. Crawford White died in November 2000.

It was for the third post-war summer that *The Playfair Books Cricket Annual* was launched. In essence it was a kind of cross between the old Red Lillywhite annual and Ayres before the latter was swallowed up with Public Schools data. The Editor was Peter West. Born in Addiscombe in 1920, Peter Anthony West was educated at Cranbrook, where he captained the cricket sides of 1938 and 1939. Invalided out of the Army, he joined Exchange Telegraph as a sports reporter and in 1947 began a second career commentating for B.B.C. Radio. It is most probably here where he first met Roy Webber, in the latter's capacity as scorer. Webber provided the statistics for the new annual.

At a higher price, it was a much glossier affair than the usual newspaper productions of the time. The first edition advertised the Cricket Book Society, as did the second in 1949, when Roy Webber retains the by-line

'Secretary, Cricket Book Society', though to all intents and purposes the Society was defunct. In retrospect the two best remembered features of the annual were the Who's Who of all current players and, separately, their career records. These features did not in fact appear until the 1950 edition. The Who's Who section commences ominously with the note 'To the best of our belief this Who's Who of English Cricketers is the most accurate and most complete record of its kind ever published.'

It is an interesting exercise to compare the *Playfair* Who's Who with that information in the 1950 *News Chronicle Annual*. The *News Chronicle* does not list University players, but tends to be more descriptive than *Playfair*. There's no clue as to the source of the *News Chronicle* data. In 1952 Roy Webber is credited as a contributor, though not until 1956 is he mentioned as Crawford White's assistant.

Another annual that covered the national English cricket scene in the early post-war period was *The Daily Worker Cricket Annual*, which almost copied the *News Chronicle* and was edited by A.A.Thomas. It lasted just three years 1948-1950. Thomas was also the author of *Test Form at a Glance*. Published in 1953 it ran in 188 pages and gave the statistics of every Test player rubber by rubber, together with the domestic team which each player represented and his dates of birth and, where relevant, death. An interesting section in the book gives wicketkeeping averages – a percentage of total victims against total wickets in fall. The major batsmen are listed with the bowlers to dismiss them most times and another section records most ducks and pairs. The volume was re-issued as a paperback, so sales must have been reasonable.

Findon's Cricket Annual, edited by Matty Watson was not so statistical as those others mentioned. No detailed county averages are printed; it gave recent Test Match scores and brief notes on each county, but also included sundry essays by well-known cricketing people. The annual lasted four years, 1947-1950.

Mention should be made of the pre-tour guides which accompanied the arrival of Test touring teams to England and in particular those edited by A.W.Simpson. The first came out for the Indian tourists in 1932 and the final one in 1953 for the Australian tourists. The brochures gave good pen pictures of the tourists and the possible candidates for the England Test side of the year, as well as photographs of each player.

One of the projected books by the Cricket Book Society which seemed destined to remain the author's pipe dream was entitled *The Blue Book of Cricket Records*. In 1951, under the Playfair banner, Webber's dream turned to reality. *The Playfair Book of Cricket Records* was published in the Spring. It ran to 320 pages, 9½" by 6", hardback bound on very good quality paper. The retail price was 25 shillings – an ordinary cricketing biography of 1951 cost half that amount, on the other hand Parker's new history of cricket (to be described in the next chapter) cost 30 shillings.

The Cricketer review of the new book was effusive:

> 'No doubt Mr Webber will receive letters from critics pointing out this and that; some of their suggestions may be of use, much of their criticism will arise from the unhappy feeling that this remarkable book has rendered all their private researches useless. Indeed, no one will henceforth dare to refer to any new record without a quick glance at one of those numerous pages; all disputes and arguments can be settled in a flash, and there will be no excuse for the publication of inaccurate statements.'

John Arlott in the 1952 edition of *Wisden* is more cautious:

> 'All books of statistics contain their errors and this one is not free from them. Thus, the eventual standing of the book must depend on the issue of further editions, which should correct the errors and keep the information up to date. In these circumstances the book's bulk and ambitious scope will make it both authoritative and unique.'

Under Webber's name in the Introduction appear two separate dates viz: Hunstanton, Norfolk, August 1946, and Finchley, Middlesex, September 1950. From other sources it seems clear that the bulk of the book was completed in 1946 and the next four years involved updating, with some corrections, mainly in overseas statistics. Webber claims to have begun his compilation in 1926 at the age of 12 and states that he had 'read and carefully noted over a long period of years', the following:

> Scores and Biographies, Volumes 1 to 15
>
> Wisden's Cricketers' Almanacs (*sic*), 1864 to 1949
>
> Lillywhite's Cricketers' Annuals, 1872 to 1900
>
> The Cricketer magazine 1921 to 1949
>
> And 'many other books and pamphlets on cricket too numerous to mention.'

The omission of the 33 volumes of the magazine 'Cricket' and the standard reference books containing detailed scores of games in South Africa and New Zealand is rather surprising. In hindsight what is rather strange is that if Webber was working industriously on compiling cricket statistics from 1926, his name is conspicuous by its absence from the correspondence columns of *The Cricketer*. Most of the cricket statisticians, from Ashley-Cooper in the 1890s, who later became well known for their published work, either raised queries by way of letters to the cricketing press, or sent in short articles, some of which were published, but there is no sign of Webber until the Cricket Book Society was mooted in 1946. In the absence of pre-war correspondence between Webber and the likes of Gustard or Roberts for example, one feels that Webber more or less completed his Record Book in 1946 single-handed. The launching of that Society brought him in contact, perhaps for the first time, with a number of important statistician-historians, such as Brodribb. Many of the notes which are attached to the tables in the book, plus the final part 'Miscellaneous Notes' have the ring of Brodribb about them.

Brodribb's assistance is acknowledged. Others whose help is noted are listed below:

- Edward Knight on India. Knight first provided some Indian statistics for *The Cricketer* in 1947 and continued to supply articles as well as writing letters to the magazine for the next twenty years. He also provided a great deal of data on India, Pakistan and Ceylon for Bowen's *The Cricket Quarterly* from 1963. Knight, who had lived in Formby, Lancashire, retired to a village near Grange-over-Sands and died in 1979. His only separate published cricketing work was an appreciation of V.M.Merchant, issued in 1950

- N.Stanley Curnow supplied the South African details. He was the official cricket statistician of the South African Cricket Union, and the South African correspondent for the *Wisden Almanack* until 1959. His first letter to *The Cricketer* had been published in 1933. He compiled a detailed score sheet for all Currie Cup matches.

- H.Haggarty supplied Sheffield Shield information. From 1939 to 1957 he had articles, mainly on Sheffield Shield matters, published in *The Cricketer*.

- J.D.Coldham, Webber noted, answered a special questionnaire – Coldham, who later became an esteemed Editor of *The Journal of The Cricket Society*, will feature in more detail later.

- John F.Griffiths checked the proofs. Griffiths was the compiler of the Record Section of the Kent C.C.C. Annual from 1954 to 1985.

The problems of Webber and the ranking of major cricket matches have been already noted and Rosenwater makes a meal of the fact that Webber did not investigate the thorny question of the status of 'borderline' matches. Webber does explain in a single page his criteria for first-class status, but such a bland remark as: 'South Africa, New Zealand and West Indies: There is no real difficulty in the assessment of these matches, all matches falling definitely into two categories', does not inspire much confidence in Webber's checking the score sheets of matches in those three Test Playing countries.

Having spent the last few paragraphs moaning that Webber was not Ashley-Cooper, it is vital to redress the balance and praise the positive side of the book.

Nothing approaching it had ever been published before. In effect Webber took the *Wisden* Record Section layout as a basic format and expanded it, as *The Cricketer* had stated in its review, 'no one will henceforth dare to refer to any new record without a quick glance at one of those numerous pages'. Of course the grey beards delighted in finding fault. Of course it was a pity that the status of matches wasn't cleared prior to publication, but one has to remember it took the Association of Cricket Statisticians (and Historians), ten years of arguing and countless hours of research to produce a list which was largely agreed by cricket statisticians. To compile a book as comprehensive as Webber's was a great achievement – just like Ashley-Cooper, Webber was a workaholic.

Chapter 10
Mainly County Histories and Overseas Annuals

If Webber's Record Book meant a new beginning for cricket statisticians, the same could not be said for the sumptuous new history of the game, *The History of Cricket* by Eric Parker, published by Seeley Service & Co, as part of the Lonsdale Library of Sports, Games & Pastimes, in 1950. It was the 30th volume in the series and Eric Parker was, with the Earl of Lonsdale, the joint editor of the whole series. In that capacity he had acted as Editor of *The Game of Cricket*, which had been issued twenty years before. This latter volume was a purely instructional work, in which the famous cricketers of the day explain how to bat, bowl, keep wicket and so on. It was a large work and competed with numerous other books of the sort; Parker's *History* had effectively only Altham-Swanton's *History* for competition; this had just appeared in its fourth edition.

Eric Parker was born in East Barnet, Hertfordshire, in 1870, educated at Eton and Merton College, Oxford. A prolific author, he started as a journalist on the *St James' Gazette*, but from 1911 worked for *The Field*, being editor-in-chief from 1930. For most of his adult life he lived in Hambledon – as he pointed out, not in Hampshire but in Surrey. His first book with any substantial cricketing content was *Highways and Byways in Surrey* published in 1908.

Parker's *History* lacks balance and appears to be a series of 41 chapters, each written in a vacuum. One hesitates to suggest the date at which Parker began writing the book, but it would seem that there were long intervals between each chapter and the inclusion of the chapter entitled

'Village Cricket' must baffle every reader. It amounts to little more than the author's memories of his own cricket at that level. (There was a similar chapter in Horace Hutchinson's Country Life book of 1903, but by C.F.Wood, rather than Hutchinson).

Like Altham, Parker ignores overseas cricket, except when English touring sides venture abroad. There are three chapters based on match series at Lord's, namely Gentlemen v Players, Oxford v Cambridge and Eton v Harrow, not perhaps so unusual, until one realises that the Eton v Harrow chapter is almost as long as the other two combined! Perhaps he was influenced by Taylor's *Annals of Lord's,* which has a similar bias? The more one dissects the book, the more it seems to be broadly based, not on Altham's work, but on Charles Box's History of 1877. One then remembers that Parker was born in 1870.

If these comments are rather caustic, there are some good pieces which deserve mention. The chapters relating to the early development of the game are well written. The 16th century document relating to John Derrick and Guildford is reproduced, as is a page from Davies' scorebook of 1832. There is a useful chapter on single wicket matches. The closing chapter, giving short histories of some 40 well-known English clubs, provides an extension to H.E.Powell-Jones' 1929 book *Famous Cricket Clubs,* itself being taken from a series of articles in *The Graphic*. One could however debate whether histories of local English clubs warrant a place in *The History of Cricket*. The sixty illustrations are well chosen and a worthwhile contribution to the whole. The book required a ruthless editor to weed out the irrelevant pieces, cut down the Eton v Harrow type sections and incorporate some meaningful essays on overseas affairs. Unfortunately the official editor was also the author.

Eric Parker, whilst his chapters gathered into one volume a collection of historical facts, did not add to the erudite historian's knowledge of the game's development, but one individual county history published just a year before most certainly did; this was Eric Snow's *A History of Leicestershire Cricket*. Edward Eric Snow was born in Leicester in 1910. He spent most of his life in his native county, unlike his two more famous brothers, C.P. (later Lord) Snow and Philip Snow. It is possibly heretical even to suggest that Eric's *History* will be studied and treasured long after the eleven volume saga *Strangers and Brothers* by Lord Snow has been forgotten, but Eric Snow set a new standard for county cricket histories

The first chapter of Eric's book treats cricket in the county up to 1824 and contains a wealth of information, hitherto unrecorded in cricket books, which the author gleaned from a detailed study of local Leicester newspapers. He has also researched the biographies of many personalities who do not feature in Haygarth's *Scores & Biographies*. Snow fills almost a hundred pages before he reaches the creation of the present Leicestershire County Cricket Club in 1879. Thereafter the book follows Leicestershire season by season with fresh biographies of many of the lesser known players – rather in the style of Ashley-Cooper's Nottinghamshire *History*, but with a lighter touch. Snow subsequently issued a second volume, taking the County Club's history up to 1977. He served on the Leicestershire Committee for 30 years and guarded the Club's archives for 40 years. Snow died in Evington, Leicester in 1998.

There could not be a greater contrast between two books on related subjects than Snow's Leicestershire history and *A History of Worcestershire County Cricket Club 1844-1950* by the Rev W.R.Chignell.

Born in Worcester in 1909 and educated at King's School, Worcester, Wilfred Roland Chignell was a slow left arm bowler, who was talented enough to have played in the Bradford League in 1934 for Lightcliffe, where he was serving as a curate. As Chaplain to the Parachute Regiment during the Second World War, he flew with the gliders into the fateful conflict at Arnhem. From 1952 to 1981 he was editor and principal statistician of the Worcestershire C.C.C. Year Book. He was a Vice-President of Worcestershire from the 1960s and also served a term as President from 1978 to 1980.

Chignell's *History*, with 443 pages, is longer than Snow's, but contains absolutely nothing fresh. It is a very dull plod through Worcestershire cricket, almost match by match, with the match descriptions often taken verbatim from *Wisden*. There are no biographies of players and no research

on Worcestershire cricket prior to the formation of the County Club –
for that, one had to wait until 1998, when *Three Black Pears*, by Bernard
Bridgewater, was published in association with the County Club. Chignell
actually issued, like Snow, a second volume, bringing the saga up to 1968.
The books are simply dreadful. The Rev Preb W.R.Chignell, a charming
companion and great cricket supporter, died in January 1995.

S.Canynge Caple was the author of *A History of Gloucestershire County
Cricket Club 1870-1948*. About a third of the 182 pages are statistical –
various tables of records and the detailed scores of 26 county matches.
There is almost nothing on cricket in the county prior to 1870 and
little relating to the biographical details of players, but the run through
the achievements by Gloucestershire on the field is much better than
Chignell's prose, even if there is a lack of fresh insight. It is the first book
on the subject.

In the same year, Louis Palgrave wrote *The Story of The Oval*. This is
a very misleading title, but the contents are explained in the author's
foreword. It was designed as a continuation of the great Surrey history
which was issued in 1902. Like Canynge Caple's book it does not tell
the reader anything that cannot be discovered via a set of *Wisden* for the
appropriate period.

Two more senior counties than Leicestershire and Worcestershire, the
second volumes of whose histories had appeared in the inter-war period,
had third volumes published in 1950.

J.M.Kilburn was the author of *History of Yorkshire County Cricket 1924-
1949*. Born in Sheffield in 1909 and educated at Holgate Grammar
School and Sheffield University, James (Jim) Maurice Kilburn was
appointed cricket correspondent of the *Yorkshire Post* in 1934, taking over
from A.W.Pullin. He remained in post until 1976 and has been described
as a rather austere presence in the press box – he had taken a degree in
economics and never had formal training as a journalist. On principle he
never attended press conferences or reported on cricketers' off-the-field
activities. He was a very useful cricketer. Like Chignell, he played in the
Bradford League and his first cricket reports were for the local paper

covering that league. His first major cricket book *In Search of Cricket* was published in 1937; it consisted of a series of essays, most of which first appeared in the *Yorkshire Post*. His style of writing was especially suited to the essay.

At the same time as Kilburn's 1924 to 1949 Yorkshire History appeared, a publishing firm, Convoy Publications, launched its series of 100 page county histories, beginning with, among others, another Kilburn book on Yorkshire. As John Arlott noted in his review of this brief Yorkshire history, Kilburn was much happier – his essay skills being more to the fore – than with the rather stilted longer book. Convoy published two other County Histories in the same year, Essex and Sussex. Author of the former was Charles (Charlie) Bray. He had represented Essex as a batsman from 1927 to 1937, though seemingly rather long in the tooth when he broke into first-class cricket, being born in Brighton in 1898. The reason for the delayed debut was that he worked in journalism in Bradford and then in Belfast, before moving South, on being appointed London editor of the Belfast newspaper, *Northern Whig*. He then joined the *Daily Herald* as its cricket correspondent, served in the R.A.F. during the war, returning to the *Herald* until it closed, after which he worked as a freelance on *The Sun* and *The Times*. His short history of Essex was the first attempt on telling the story of that county's cricket. It is a pleasant introduction and well written. The statistics are by John E.Clay. Clay, who lived in Wanstead, sent frequent letters to *The Cricketer*, mainly on matters related to Essex and from 1946 was, effectively the Essex official statistician. A founder member of the Society of Cricket Statisticians, he wrote a rather pedantic history of Essex cricket, which was serialised in the Society's News Letter in 1954. The Society also published season-by-season career records for many Essex players, compiled by Clay. He retired as Essex's statistician in 1971.

The third Convoy History of 1950 was written by Sir Home Gordon. He had been President of Sussex C.C.C. in 1948. He begins his book by announcing that he is in his 78th year. The book is a cheerful, if rather careless ramble, with Sir Home quite often pointing out what he thought and what he chose either to do, or not to do. The statistics consist of just two pages, which, considering all the figures he created through his long writing career, looks rather sparse. In 1939 Sir Home had written a 348 page volume entitled *Background of Cricket*. This comprises seventeen chapters of reminiscences and historical meanderings. Home Gordon died in Rottingdean, Sussex in 1956.

· Returning to more serious matters, the third volume of Middlesex's 'History' was also published in 1950. Nigel Esme Haig, nephew of Earl Haig and former captain of Middlesex, was the compiler of *Middlesex County Cricket Club Volume 3 1921-1947*. Born in Kensington in 1887, Haig was educated at Eton, but, surprisingly in view of his subsequent career, failed to make the College Eleven. He was later to achieve the 'Double' on three occasions. Haig's book echoed the pattern set by the two earlier volumes and is therefore basically statistical, containing the detailed scores of county matches during the period under review. Haig wrote occasional pieces for *The Cricketer*, and died in 1966.

As Sir Home Gordon was romping his way through Sussex's cricket history, Dr Henry Fremlin Squire had published his researches into cricket in the Sussex village of Henfield and thrown fresh light on some important aspects of the game's earliest recorded years. His book *Henfield Cricket and Its Sussex Cradle* remains an important source for historians. The book reproduces the 1727 Articles of Agreement between the Duke of Richmond and Mr Brodrick. Squire follows the course taken by P.F. Thomas in searching for the origins of the game and illustrates the way cricket, baseball, and other sports came from a common background. Another illustration is of the match score details for a game played a fortnight before the famous England v Kent match of 1744. He was assisted by his wife for the Henfield book and also for *Pre-Victorian Sussex Cricket*, which was an Index to early cricket matches played in Sussex, mainly matches which were published in local newspapers.

A quite remarkable man, H.F. Squire was studying medicine at Caius College, Cambridge at the outbreak of the First World War. He volunteered and served in the Mediterranean before being invalided home and resuming his studies. Although over age, he served in the same theatre during the Second World War and captured events of the time on camera.

Whether or not the Hon Terence Cornelius Farmer Prittie's cricketing books really belong in this work is open to question, but the titles invited inclusion, if the actual content does not. His first book *Mainly Middlesex* was published in 1946 and his second *Lancashire Hot-Pot* in 1949. The two were later combined as *Cricket North and South* in 1955. Educated at Stowe and Oxford, Prittie was taken prisoner in June 1940 and his book on Middlesex was written whilst he was a guest of the Germans. In 1946 he was appointed cricket correspondent of the *Manchester Guardian*, but the appointment only lasted a season. Both his books contain sketches of notable county players, written rather in the style of Robertson-Glasgow. Prittie died in London in 1985.

Of much greater importance than Prittie's cheerfully amusing essays is R.S.Rait Kerr's *The Laws of Cricket* published by Longmans, Green & Co in 1950. The book still stands as the major reference work on its subject. In 1944 Rait Kerr wrote a long letter to *The Cricketer* in response to an article by G.D.Martineau celebrating the 200th anniversary of the Laws of 1744. It was clear from Rait Kerr's letter that his knowledge of the history of the Laws was far superior to that of Martineau. In 1945, Rait Kerr was directed by the Committee of the M.C.C. to oversee a complete revision of the current Laws. After consultations with the overseas governing bodies and many other interested parties, the new Laws were agreed by the M.C.C. at their A.G.M. on May 7, 1947 and were to come into force for the 1948 season.

The enormous amount of work that Rait Kerr undertook in seeing the project through, allied to his knowledge of the Laws' history, made him the obvious person to write a detailed thesis on how the Laws developed and when and how new Laws were introduced. His book contains both Goldwin's poem of 1706 and Perry's translation of 1922, as well as the Articles of 1727, previously noted in Squire's book. A reproduction of the 1755 booklet containing the Laws, as well as the various versions of the Laws which were printed on the borders of early handkerchiefs are included in this thorough piece of research.

Rowan Scrope Rait Kerr was born in 1891; educated at Rugby he was in the XI in 1908, 1909 and 1910. He then went to R.M.A., Woolwich and joined the Royal Engineers. He played a great deal of cricket whilst in the Army and in India represented the Europeans in first-class matches. In 1925 he wrote a well-researched book, *A History of Royal Engineers Cricket 1862-1924*. In 1937 he had been appointed Secretary of M.C.C., but rejoined the Army at the outbreak of the Second World War. He retired from M.C.C. in 1952 and died in April 1961. His daughter was then in charge of the Lord's Library.

G.D.Martineau was mentioned in connexion with the history of the Laws. Between 1946 and 1957, Martineau wrote four books on various aspects of cricket history. He also toured the country giving lectures on the subject.

Gerard Durani Martineau was born in Lahore in 1897 and educated at Charterhouse and R.M.C., Sandhurst. He served as an officer in the Royal Sussex Regiment from 1915 to 1923, then retired to take up school teaching. From 1924 he had poems published in *The Cricketer* and from the mid-1930s many articles, some fictitious and others on historical subjects. His poems also appeared in *Punch, The Bystander, The Spectator, Country Life* and *The Morning Post.* He retired from school teaching in 1949.

Martineau's obituary included in the 1977 *Wisden Almanack* (he died after a long illness in Lyme Regis in 1976) sums up his cricketing prose: ... 'in general his books were not works of much original research. Pleasantly written, they were ideally calculated to arouse the interest of the novice and spur him on to try for himself the masterpieces of Nyren and Pycroft.' The four titles written by Martineau are *The Field is Full of Shades* (1946), *Bat, Ball, Wicket and All* (1950), *They Made Cricket* (1956) and *The Valiant Stumper* (1957).

1949 saw the publication of *Maiden Over* by Nancy Joy, a member of the 1948-9 England team in Australia. Primarily a diary of that tour, the book begins with a "Short History of Woman's Cricket" of some 60 pages, which remained the most accessible work on female cricket until 1976, when two more international cricketers, Rachel Heyhoe-Flint and Netta Rheinberg, brought out *Fair Play: the Story of Women's Cricket*.

In 1951 the well-known novelist, Laurence Meynell had published *Famous Cricket Grounds.* This concentrated on the English Test grounds, though noting a few others. It featured notable cricketers and their exploits at various venues and descriptions of famous matches played on the grounds described. John Arlott made some wry comments on the defects in the work – was it pure coincidence that a much slimmer, but more reliable book, *Homes of Sport : Cricket* was issued the following year, written by Norman Yardley in conjunction with J.M.Kilburn?

In contrast to Meynell's rather superficial effort the Kilburn-Yardley book described most of the grounds currently in use in first-class county cricket. It gave detailed descriptions of the facilities on each ground, with ground plans and photographs of all the county headquarters venues. It was a fresh concept and a fine guide to the general spectator. It would be more than thirty years before an updated version superseded this 1952 book. The plans of the grounds had in fact first been printed in the 1950 edition of *Wisden*, the editor stating that they had been included to assist readers who listened to wireless broadcasts from the specific ground.

Laurence Walter Meynell was born in Wolverhampton in 1899, educated at St Edmund's College, Ware and after serving in the H.A.C. he became a schoolmaster, then an estate agent and finally earned enough to become a full time author. His only other cricket book was a short biography of Pelham Warner, also published in 1951. Warner was the subject chosen by the publishers, Phoenix House, of a series entitled 'Cricketing Lives'. Although Meynell states that almost all the information for the book came from interviews he had with his subject, Warner had written so many books, including his autobiography that it was a difficult task for Meynell to bring much that was new. Having said that, the book, within the 20,000 words limit, is a delightful essay. The publishers selected equally competent writers for the other three books in the series issued that first year – Denzil Batchelor on C.B.Fry, Philip Lindsay on Don Bradman and John Arlott on M.W.Tate. The publishers advertised A.C.MacLaren by Neville Cardus, Hedley Verity by D.R.Jardine and W.G.Grace by Clifford Bax. The first two titles never appeared but in 1952, Bax's W.G.Grace was issued as well as Oliver Warner on Frank Woolley. Curiously Epworth Press published in an identical format in the same year, Hedley Verity by Sam Davis. At the present time the Association of Cricket Statisticians and Historians is revisiting the same format, but tackling players not so well remembered. Meynell died in 1989.

The mention of Warner as a subject in the above series requires a comment that he was still an active writer himself after the Second World War and in 1950 Harrap published Warner's *Gentlemen v Players 1806-1950*. This was to remain the standard reference work on that historic series of matches. All the match scores are printed with brief comments. The book also incorporates the Australians v Gentlemen and Australians v Players contests. There is a good statistical section compiled by Roy Webber and the volume runs to 516 pages – the previous book covering the matches had been by Ashley-Cooper in 1900.

The other major Warner title had been an updated version of Ashley-Cooper's Lord's History. Warner had this published in 1946. The first 170 pages cover Lord's up to the First World War and are little more than a summary of Ashley-Cooper's work. The period of 1919 to 1945 occupies 120 pages and therefore provides a useful history of that time. There are 52 plates, 12 of which are in colour.

Warner was appointed President of M.C.C. in 1950-51 and died in Sussex in 1963. He had remained connected with *The Cricketer* magazine to the end of his life.

Another author who continued to work after the Second World War was E.L.Roberts, but Roy Webber's statistical output and profile were soon placing Roberts in the shade. He had ceased to be in charge of the Records section in the *Wisden Almanack* after the 1940 edition, and his book *Cricket in England 1894-1939* issued in 1946 has been noted previously. The following year came *Test Match Cavalcade 1877-1946*, which gave potted scores of every Test and brief notes with Test career records and some other interesting statistical data. His last hardback book was issued by Edward Arnold & Co in 1949, its title being *Yorkshire's 22 Championships 1893-1946*. The book provides some six pages for each Championship title with, in most cases full scores of really significant matches, but, rather oddly, not the seasonal averages. J.M.Kilburn provides profiles of 30 of the best known players.

Most of the books compiled by Roberts had been published by E.F.Hudson Ltd of New Street, Birmingham, who were the best known retailers of cricket books in the 1930s and carried both new and secondhand titles. In their 1940 advertisement in *Wisden*, the firm put the following note 'A complimentary copy of Mr Roberts' new 'Cricket Records 1940' will be enclosed with each order'. It was a small 32 page paperback. Hudsons issued similar books for 1946, 1948, 1949 and 1951. According to J.S.Milner, Hudson's made a loss on all the books they published for Roberts. The bulk of his income derived from his statistical work for newspapers and magazines.

The Cricketer magazine continued almost unaltered in format through the 1940s and the 1950s – the page size reduced in 1940 compared to 1939, the only intrinsic change being a switch from full scores of first-class county matches to potted scores in 1952. H.H.Jarrett launched a rival magazine in 1948. Its initial title was *South Wales Cricketers' Magazine*, but in July 1950 it went national under the heading *The Cricketers' Magazine*. Harold Harvey Jarrett was born in Johannesburg in 1907. He emigrated to England, was educated at Highgate School and played 14 matches for Warwickshire in 1932 and 1933. He moved to South Wales and played one game for Glamorgan in 1938. The base for his magazine was Newport, Monmouth, his home town at that time. Unlike *The Cricketer*, which in the 1940s was fortnightly during the season, plus two annuals, Jarrett's publication was normally monthly May to September, plus one annual. Principal contributors to the magazine were John Arlott, Ian Peebles (usually fictional essays), G.D.Martineau, Gerald Brodribb, Roy Webber, Louis Duffus from South Africa, G.A.Brooking (on Lancashire Leagues) and Ron Yeomans. Women's cricket was well covered. In 1952 J.W.Speight took over as editor and then, for the final issue only (April-May 1953), Tim Saunders. When it switched to national distribution, it was published by Cricket Publications Ltd of 51 Mount St, Mayfair, London W.1.

Although this English magazine failed to attract sufficient subscribers, a very gratifying development in the 1940s was the first appearance of robust cricket annuals in overseas Test playing countries.

In India the rather amateur efforts of P.N.Polishwalla during the 1930s have been noted. In 1939-40, Muni Lal launched *The Crickinia* which ran until 1944-45 and provided scores and some data on the major matches played in India during the Second World War. In 1947 *Indian Cricket* edited by S.K.Gurunathan and published by Kasturi & Sons Ltd of Madras appeared for the first time. It was modelled largely on *Wisden* and for nearly 60 years was destined to be the standard work of reference for statisticians (though rivals attempted to take its place) The Record Section was the annual's weak point and it was never really satisfactory throughout the annual's life, despite several changes of editor. It began as just one section on Ranji Trophy performances, later came a separate section 'World Records' and brief sections on other Indian Competitions, each on its own. The editor did not tackle the problem of classification of matches in India head on, so, for example, performances by Indian players against overseas touring sides were in limbo, as were the famous Vizianagram matches of 1930-31.

Gurunathan was the sports editor of *The Hindu* and in 1946 compiled *Twelve Years of Ranji Trophy 1934-1945* which gave the detailed scores and thus linked to the first issue of his annual. He died in May 1966 aged 58.

A young enthusiast, G.C.Baker, compiled *The South African Cricket Almanac* for 1949-50. Graham Charsley Baker was a Rhodes Scholar at the time he produced his annual, which covered the season 1949-50, and was then aged 20. He died in February 1977. Although the annual made only a single appearance, its basic format was taken up by the South African Cricket Association, who published a *South African Cricket Annual* covering the 1951-52 season. The editor was Geoffrey Arthur Chettle, who had been born in Christiana, Transvaal in 1907. He left school to join the Merchant Navy and later developed a marine engineering business in Durban. In the 1920s he spent some time in England and was reputed to have had football trials with Manchester United and Doncaster Rovers. After the Second World War cricket reporting was only his spare time hobby – he was said to have required just four hours' sleep a night. From 1953 Chettle was South African correspondent to *The Cricketer* for several years, then from 1960 performed the same task for *Wisden* until his death. N.S.Curnow provided the Record Section for the South African Annual in the 1950s – he was also the *Wisden* correspondent but in about 1958 he lost interest in cricket and turned his attention to English literature. Under the editorship of Chettle the annual was not renowned for its accuracy, Chettle not being an enthusiastic proof-reader. Aside from the annual, he was the compiler of many cricketing brochures relating to cricket tours and Test series. He died in May 1976.

A third national annual founded around this time was *The Cricket Almanack of New Zealand*. Its first issue came out in 1948, covering the 1947-48 New Zealand season. The editors were Arthur H.Carman and Noel S.Macdonald. Published in Wellington it was undoubtedly the best of the three. From its initial edition, the New Zealand annual gave detailed scores, not only of first-class matches but also what they ranked as 'Second Class' with fall of wickets attached to each scorecard (*Wisden* did not add this detail until later). There were good biographies of the first-class players and, for this edition, very full coverage of the Fiji tour. The record section begins with a detailed list of what the editors regarded as qualifying as first-class matches in New Zealand. Prior to the Almanack's appearance the New Zealand Cricket Council had published the bare scores of matches played under their jurisdiction.

Macdonald retired from the joint editorship in 1957, but Carman continued until his death in November 1982. Born in 1902, Carman trained as a journalist, working on the *Wellington Evening Post* and specialised in reporting rugby. In 1924 he came over to England in that capacity with the All Blacks. In 1935 he created the *Rugby Almanack of New Zealand* and in addition to his journalistic work ran a business as a bookseller and stationer in Wellington. He was passionately interested in politics and stood successfully as an Independent on various local councils, as well as being an active member of the Wellington Hospital Board. As a pacifist he served a prison sentence during the Second World War. After his death, Walter Hadlee commented: 'Arthur Carman was not only respected for his ability – he was admired for what he was – a truly lovable person.' Carman's major cricket book was *Wellington Cricket Centenary 1875-1975*. As might be expected from the contents of his annual, this book is a sound work, giving summaries of each season and biographies of a good selection of the players. Career records for all the cricketers for Wellington from 1875 are included with a variety of other data. He wrote other books, mainly on rugby, but also one on the early history of Wellington.

A year after Carman's death came the news of the death of another long-serving overseas cricket journalist, Louis Duffus. Louis George Duffus was born in Melbourne, Australia, in 1904, but moved to South Africa, where he trained as an accountant. A talented cricketer, he made his debut as a wicketkeeper for Transvaal in 1923-24 and was on the short list for the squad to tour England in 1929. When he failed to be picked, he threw up his accountancy job and travelled to England, accompanying the South Africa team as a journalist. Whilst reporting free-lance he was engaged by the Argus Group of newspapers and continued as a journalist for the remainder of his life, covering not only cricket but most other sports. From 1930 he was the South African correspondent of *The Cricketer*. His major contribution to cricket literature and its history was the compilation of *South African Cricket 1927-1947*, published in 1948. It ran to 625 pages and was a worthy continuation of Luckin's two volumes. Duffus was sports editor of the *Johannesburg Star* for 17 years and died in Johannesburg in July 1984.

Two other publications appeared in the early 1950s, featuring cricket overseas, and merit especial attention. They are still standard text books in their particular field. *A Century of Philadelphia Cricket* edited by J.A.Lester, was issued by the University of Pennsylvania Press in 1951. Lester himself was a notable cricketer, captaining the Philadelphian teams to England in 1903 and 1908. He gathered several other well-known cricketers to contribute to his book, including J.Barton King and Percy H.Clark. The book relates the story of cricket in the city of Philadelphia and runs to 397 pages, not including a section of informative illustrations, which for some odd reason are bound into the volume at the end after the index. Lester died in 1969.

A book on Philadelphian cricket published in 1951 might seem rather obscure, but Philip Snow's subject was even more far-flung, the book's title being *Cricket in the Fiji Islands* published in New Zealand in 1949. Snow tells the detailed history of cricket in Fiji from its first recorded game in 1874. The book closes with the match scores and reports of the Fijian tour to New Zealand in 1948, when the team was captained by the author. Snow, a younger brother of Eric Snow the Leicestershire historian, was born in Leicester in 1915 and educated at Cambridge. He captained Leicestershire 2nd XI and was very disappointed not to have been given a decent trial whilst at University, being ignored because he went to a Grammar School. Leaving Cambridge in 1938 he immediately joined the Colonial Service and went to Fiji. After 14 years, he left to become the Bursar at Rugby School. Among Snow's other books are a biography of his brother Lord Snow, and two volumes of autobiography. From 1965 for 30 years he acted as Fiji's representative to the I.C.C.

Chapter 11
More County Histories and
The Cricket Society grows

After the Second World War came the arrival of a career policeman of relatively humble background, and he broke the standard pattern for the background of cricket journalist-cum-historian.

He left school to join the police force and by 1945 had risen to Detective Sergeant. Five years later he had transformed himself into perhaps the dominant figure in cricket journalism and broadcasting, whilst at the same time making an astute study of cricket's history. John Arlott moved from his safe job in the police force to join the B.B.C. as a literary programme producer directly after the Second World War

Almost by accident, he began commentating on county cricket and quickly became the most easily recognisable voice of the game. His career for the B.B.C. continued until his retirement in 1980. At the same time he reported cricket for a succession of newspapers, the London *Evening News*, *News Chronicle* and *The Guardian*. After retirement he described his life up to the year 1958 in an autobiography entitled *Basingstoke Boy*. His political ambitions, his poetry, and his work as a wine connoisseur are outside the confines of this book. His importance on our narrow stage is his intense interest in cricket and especially its history. Arlott built up a comprehensive cricket library and his collection was not merely decorative; he actually read the books he purchased. In 1950 he was appointed as book reviewer for the *Wisden Almanack* – the first time the annual devoted a section to 'Book Reviews'. He was to continue in this role until the 1978 edition and in some ways, from an historian's viewpoint, this long stint was the most valuable one which Arlott performed. Although his reviews were never over critical, he was able to pull out, from the many titles that flooded the post-war market, those works that merited a little more attention.

Although the majority of Arlott's cricket writing outside of newspapers or magazines were 'tour' books, (starting with the 1946 Indians) or vignettes for county cricketers' benefit brochures, two books during the 1950s comprise essays of wider scope and it is worth quoting *The Cricketer* review of the first, *The Echoing Green*. This was published by Longmans, Green & Co in 1952. The long review closes:

> 'Few writers understand at once the importance of cricket as a mirror of social history, of cricketers as a guild of craftsmen, or the game as an educational force, and can pass readily from the participants in the First Test Match ever played to such modern problems as lack of ground-staff apprenticeship and excessive pitch preparation. Mr Arlott examines all these as easily as he writes on bowling-machines and travelling conditions and concludes with a series of personal pen-portraits which challenge comparison with those of Mr Robertson-Glasgow. Again I find it impossible to say which I like best. This is a very good book indeed.'

By coincidence *Cricket All The Year* was reviewed on the same page. It was the first cricket book written by Neville Cardus in 17 years. The inter-war period had been the old master's time; the review did not quite match the one handed out to Arlott.

In 1953 Arlott wrote *Cricket* in a series called 'The Pleasures of Life' issued by Burke Publishing Co Ltd. The preceding volumes were on 'Drink', 'Food', 'Women', 'Gardens' and 'Clothes'. Arlott's was a more substantial volume. The Bibliography at the close of the book underlines the extent of the author's researches.

In 1957 came the first sizeable history of Hampshire County Cricket. No less than four authors are credited on the title page and that, despite the fact that the work is nothing like as substantial as Snow's Leicestershire volume. The book, discounting the statistical section, is divided into three parts of more or less equal length, yet the three periods covered are of vastly differing time scales. H.S.Altham's section 1756 to 1914 has 66 pages; Arlott's 21 seasons between the wars is given 59 pages and Desmond Eagar's 11 seasons (1946 to 1956) has 56 pages. In effect Altham waltzes through his piece more or less repeating the detail which appeared in his general history. Arlott provides very pleasant essays on six of his childhood favourites and then seasonal summaries. Eagar, as both captain and secretary of the County Club during the post-war period, provides the best section of the work though it was necessarily rather subjective. Roy Webber supplies 37 pages of records, but does not attempt to tackle the difficult problem of the status of Hampshire matches prior to 1895.

Edward Desmond Russell Eagar was born in 1917 and educated at Cheltenham. He played a few games for his native Gloucestershire and gained a cricket blue at Oxford in 1939. He joined Hampshire as captain-secretary in 1946, retired as player in 1957, but remained as County Secretary until his death in 1977. A keen cricket historian and bibliophile he edited the Hampshire C.C.C. Yearbook and wrote occasional cricket articles for the press, mostly on topics related to the County. It was a pity he had no time to research and write about early cricket history, since he had the knowledge and the ability to do so. The catalogue for the sale, in 2005, of his cricket library provides an insight into the study Eagar made of early cricket literature. His son, Patrick, became the best-known cricket photographer of his time (perhaps all time).

The mention of Roy Webber in connection with the Hampshire history provides the opportunity to review the very mixed bag of work that he had published following his ground-breaking *Playfair Record Book*. Webber compiled *The Playfair Book of Test Cricket* in two volumes, the first, covering matches up to 1939, was issued in 1952 and the second, bringing the record up to date in 1953. Like his *Record Book* it was a fresh concept (though it clearly owed something to Roberts' 1947 book) and the publishers again maintained a high quality in the production. Each scorecard – numbered in chronological order – had a 200 word match description. Fall of wickets, captains, wicketkeepers and umpires are shown as well as which side won the toss. Where a Test series comprised three or more matches, sets of averages for individual series are included. There is a section which contains the standard selection of record tables, also career records and a good index, both to players and the matches themselves. J.D.Coldham provides a bibliography of books which covered Test tours, a very useful appendix that was discarded when the volumes were later reprinted.

1952 also saw the appearance of Webber's *Who's Who in World Cricket*. This was an expanded version of the Who's Who that appeared in the 1952 *Playfair Cricket Annual*, plus the principal overseas cricketers and the main cricketing journalists and broadcasters. The last-mentioned was another feature that was never, we believe, repeated.

The players' career records were, rather surprisingly, very abbreviated and also no forenames were given, only initials. The *Playfair Annual* of the time was very patchy in its printing of forenames, so Webber , with only partial data to work with, omitted this detail.

All Roy Webber's industry over many years had now flowered into books that provided cricket followers with the basic statistics to be able to check new 'records' as they occurred. Further research in scorebooks and newspapers has unearthed pieces of information which to a limited extent adjusts the figures Webber laid down, but he built the foundations on which later statisticians could expand. With the increasing interest in statistical and other cricketing tables it is perhaps strange that some of the compilations included in Webber's early books have been omitted by later compilers and disappeared, although one could make the same remarks about some of Ashley-Cooper's work.

With this wealth of work behind him – he was, as has been mentioned, scoring for the B.B.C. and producing statistical data for the *News Chronicle* as well – Webber unfortunately launched himself from the statistical to the historical. In 1957 came *The County Cricket Championship : A History of the Competition from 1873 to the Present Day.* The Webber ship was caught on the hidden rocks that are the Championship's pre-1890 period. He failed to investigate the annuals and the press which published reports and notes on county cricket before that date, and instead published County Championship tables which were broadly speaking his own invention for the seasons 1873 to 1889.

In 1960 came Webber's *The Phoenix History of Cricket.* In 21 pages Webber describes the development of cricket in the British Isles from the beginning to 1859. In the next 13 pages he gives paragraphs on the development of cricket overseas, not only in the existing Test playing countries, but also North and South America, continental Europe and such places as Hong Kong, which paragraphs, perhaps not too accurate, do give the reader some basic detail which the Altham history omitted. From then on the book is largely devoted to Test cricket with occasional pieces on the County Championship. Webber does comment that the publishers cut 30,000 words from his original manuscript. It is therefore unfair to be too critical. Arlott in his review comments:

> 'Roy Webber wisely did not attempt to compete with the classical sweep of H.S.Altham's established – indeed classic – History. Rather he followed his own particular fact-recording bent.'

The year prior to Webber's history, the first comprehensive history of cricket in Australia was published. Alban George (Johnnie) Moyes, the author, was born in Gladstone, South Australia, in 1893. He played for South Australia before the First World War and, briefly, for Victoria after that war. Educated at St Peter's College, Adelaide and Adelaide University, he had served in the Australian Services in the war and represented the Dominions in matches at Lord's and The Oval in 1918. Taking up journalism he worked on various Australian newspapers, including the *Sydney Daily Telegraph.* After the Second World War, in which he served as a Lieutenant-Colonel, he began to work for ABC as a cricket commentator. He was to continue in that job until his death in 1963. His first cricket book had been a biography of Don Bradman, published in 1948. His book

Australian Bowlers was published in 1953 and its companion volume on batsmen the following year. The books, instead of an alphabetical listing of the 'Greats', treat almost all the Australian Test players in chronological sequence with a little background to the Tests played in their era. Both books were deservedly praised in the press and display Moyes' talent as an author and sound observer of the cricketing scene as well as being a knowledgeable historian.

It is no surprise that his Australian History, which runs to 615 pages, is a worthwhile textbook. Moyes traces cricket from its earliest roots in each of the six states. The history of the Sheffield Shield is portrayed in stages between international tours, both to and from Australia. There are many illustrations, quite a number of which had not been seen in any English publication.

Moyes acknowledges the help of historians from the various states, including the late Ernest Henry Hutcheon, whose book *History of Queensland* had first been published in 1946. Hutcheon died in Brisbane in June 1937 and his manuscript was eventually completed by Victor Gerald Honour. Honour, born in Bierton, Bucks, in 1910, emigrated to Australia in 1927 and played for Queensland in 1935-36 (Hutcheon had played for the state soon after the First World War). The book is crammed with information, but is a trifle pedestrian in the presentation, perhaps overwhelmed by the facts.

Reverting to the English county scene, the Convoy series saw four more titles issued in 1952, Glamorgan by J.H.Morgan, Lancashire by Rex Pogson, Middlesex by T.C.F.Prittie and Worcestershire by Roy Genders. They followed the identical pattern to those earlier described, which had been issued the previous year.

Rex Pogson was a solicitor and one time deputy Town Clerk of Lytham St Annes. He wrote regular pieces on league cricket in Lancashire for *The Cricketer* and also had cricket reports published in the *Manchester Guardian*, though considering his cricket writing as a hobby. In 1944 his Index to the *Wisden Almanack* had been published. His Convoy history was the first hardback book to relate the story of the County Club, but it would be soon superseded by Ledbroke's history.

Roy Genders played county cricket briefly for Derbyshire (his native county), Worcestershire and Somerset. Educated at King's School, Ely he went up to Cambridge, but failed to be awarded a blue. Like Chignell, Genders served on the Worcestershire Committee. His book, coming out just a year after Chignell's tome, was more entertaining. About half the book comprises essays on individual Worcestershire players and Genders is at his best with these.

In the same year, Genders' most notable cricket book, *League Cricket in England*, was issued by Laurie. It is the first attempt at an overview of the subject as a whole. William Roy Genders, born in Dore, Derbyshire, in 1913, became an expert horticulturist, writing many articles and some books on the subject. Another of his interests was the collecting of cigarette and trade cards. He died in Worthing in September 1985.

The author of the Glamorgan history was John (Jack) Hinds Morgan. Born in 1898, from 1921 he had reported on Glamorgan cricket for the Cricket Reporting Agency and then the Press Association, as well as the local newspapers. He was considered the leading sports journalist in South Wales. A keen local politician he had been made an Alderman and in 1957 was elected Lord Mayor of Cardiff. Morgan died in April 1978.

With a much shorter time span to cover the Glamorgan history gives more detail and includes the full scores with reports of eleven memorable matches. The author is in the fortunate position of having watched the county from its first first-class match and having known the players

Prittie's book on Middlesex is 50 pages longer than that for Glamorgan or Worcestershire and indeed substantially larger than Home Gordon's one on Sussex. Prittie provides reasonably long essays on the most famous cricketers, such as Warner, Hendren, Compton and Bill Edrich, but little if anything on the lesser lights. He begins with the formation of the present County Club and makes no reference at all to the ground problems Middlesex had before they finally settled at Lord's.

The Convoy County series, which gave readers a useful first taste of their county's cricket past, ceased, after having published the seven titles which have been featured. Four, more substantial, county histories were published between 1952 and 1959. The first, in 1952, was Ron Roberts' *Sixty Years of Somerset Cricket*. As the title implies it deals with the County Club since first-class status was restored in 1891. Anything prior to that date is bundled into four pages, one of which is solely devoted to the actual founding of the present County Club in 1875. The whole book runs to 208 pages including 13 pages of records provided by R.F.Trump and S.J.H.King, Reg Trump was the current County scorer, whilst King, described as a wizard with figures, resided in North Wembley, Middlesex.

The book is pleasantly written with interesting comments on the principal personalities from Sammy Woods onwards. Ronald Arthur Roberts was born in Liverpool in 1925 and began his journalistic career with the *Somerset County Herald*, before moving up to the *Bristol Evening World*. From 1954 to 1956 he was a member of the Executive Committee of the County Club. Then he moved to London, joining the Hayter's Sports Agency. During the winter he accompanied a number of England touring sides abroad and reported freelance for the *Daily* and *Sunday Telegraph*. In addition he organised and managed several tours, which included well-known cricketers, to lesser cricket playing countries including the United States, Canada and a number of African former British colonies. Roberts died in August 1965 after a long illness.

Another journalist who wrote a history of his County was Archibald 'Archie' William Ledbroke – he was tragically killed in the Munich air crash of February 1958 along with members of the Manchester United team. Born in Woking in 1905 and educated at Leamington College, Ledbroke represented his school at cricket, rugby and lawn tennis. Leaving school for journalism he rose to become the Sports Editor of the *Manchester Evening News* and in 1934 was appointed principal sports writer to the *Daily Dispatch*. He was elected Chairman of the Cricket Writers Club in 1951 and was also Chairman of the Football Writers' Association. His book, *Lancashire County Cricket 1864-1953* came out in 1954. The idea and general format for the work had been the brain-child of John Arthur

Brierley, a Preston journalist, who had reported on cricket for various Lancashire papers since 1895. He had previously written the Jubilee History of the Football League. In September 1951 Brierley died aged 79 in St Annes-on-Sea.

Ledbroke took over the rough manuscript from Brierley's widow and with the help of the extensive notebooks that Brierley had kept, he developed the final work.

The book comprised 500 word descriptions of each season, with separate chapters on the various notable personalities, both players and officials. Unlike Snow's Leicestershire history there is virtually no detail prior to the formation of the County Club in 1864, only a note on the matches v Yorkshire before that date and nothing on the historic Manchester v Liverpool contests.

Northamptonshire Cricket, published in 1959, is a much better researched book than either Roberts' or Ledbroke's. The author, James 'Jim' Desmond Bowden Coldham, has been mentioned briefly before. Born in January 1924 and educated at King's School, Harrow, he was conscripted in 1942 and served in India and Burma as part of the 14th Army. In 1947 he joined the Crown Agents Office of the Civil Service and remained there until forced to retire early due to ill-health in 1979. During the war he was a frequent letter-writer to *The Cricketer* on many subjects – Dickens being one, lob bowling another and of course Northants. Although he was a founder member of the Society of Cricket Statisticians, his interest lay in the history of cricket rather than its statistics. In time he built up a rather specialised library of cricket material tending to bypass the heavyweight volumes in favour of the shorter booklets written by Ashley-Cooper and others of that ilk.

Although he is now best-known for his history of Northamptonshire, which is a very soundly based work, perhaps not quite in Snow's class, but worthy of great merit, his short essays which appeared in *The Cricketer* and *The Journal of The Cricket Society* must really be his monument.

He was editor of that Journal from March 1970 to April 1984 and his overall knowledge of cricket's history made him the ideal man for the job. He was capable of evaluating the diverse material which members submitted for publication, a lot of it was of a poor quality, but he keenly encouraged the more timid souls who produced pieces that were worthy of the magazine. At the same time his own contributions were always of a high standard. He also in the Society's early days made a start on one of the founder's principal ambitions, a bibliography of cricket, though John Everitt was the first member to be officially put in charge of the project.

In 1983 his biography of Lord Harris was published. It was a trifle disappointing and lacked the depth of this complex character (see later comments on Guha's book on Indian cricket, for example). Coldham was responsible for the research which went into the *Complete Who's Who of Test Cricketers*, published under Martin-Jenkins' name in 1980. From 1981 to his death, which occurred in Tooting, South London, in January 1987, Coldham was responsible for many of the items in the obituary section of *The Cricketer* and he also contributed to the *Wisden Almanack*.

Jim Coldham is linked historically with Geoffrey Copinger and a paragraph on the latter would seem to be appropriate at this point and indeed on The Society of Cricket Statisticians. This Society was left, in Chapter 9, recovering from its law-suit against Roy Webber. Copinger took over as the Society's Chairman in 1947 and by the time he retired, six years later, the Society was beginning to grow from its nucleus of 200 or so members. The name was changed in 1950 from The Society of Cricket Statisticians to The Cricket Society in order to broaden its appeal. Copinger is thanked for his assistance with the compilation of the complete player by player first-class averages which were published in the Society's first Yearbook covering the 1946 season. He worked in his spare time for the Cricket Reporting Agency compiling the averages which appeared in many newspapers on a weekly basis during the English season. The Society also launched a Newsletter, edited by Ayton Whitaker, who, in 1947, was the Society's vice-chairman.

Geoffrey Arthur Copinger was born at Buxhall, near Stowmarket in December 1910. Educated at Haberdashers Aske's, Hampstead, he left school for a career in banking. In 1947 he was appointed as editor of the

Cricket Records section of the *Wisden Almanack*. He continued in this post until 1963. His weekly, then bi-weekly compilation of English first-class averages continued to 1982, a quite formidable record. From a schoolboy he collected cricket books. The collection expanded as the years went by until, at its peak, he housed some 12,000 titles in his Hampstead house. He died in Hampstead, after a long illness, in May 1998.

William Stanley Conder took over the editing of the Society's Yearbook from Tony Weigall and was a major contributor to the Society's Newsletter, as well as assisting with the compilation of the *Wisden Almanack* from 1950. He was employed in the City and died at his home in Kew in May 1979, aged 69.

One of the quiet men behind the scenes for the Society was Leslie Edward Stephen Gutteridge, who helped to save the Society during the brouhaha of 1959. He ran the Epworth Press and its bookshop in City Road, London. The Press was the publishing arm of the Methodist Church. He joined the society in 1949 and soon afterwards housed the Society's library at the Epworth Press, being appointed the Society's Hon Librarian. The Epworth Press building also contained the best secondhand cricket book shop in the country and became a mecca for collectors. Gutteridge's own cricket writings were confined to the occasional article in *The Cricketer* and some book reviews for the *Playfair Cricket Monthly*. He emigrated to Canada to take up an appointment at the University of Alberta, retiring in 1979. He died in Edmonton, Canada in July 2000, having curiously been born in Edmonton, Middlesex, in 1914.

A founder member of the Society who contributed many articles to its publications was Harold 'Tod' Stratton Scales. He began writing letters to *The Cricketer* in 1935 and became a great friend of Gustard. Educated at The Leys School, Scales took up a business career in the City with Messrs McDonald, Scales & Co. His overwhelming cricket interest was researching biographical details of players from the mid 18th century onwards. He was fortunate to inherit manuscript notebooks compiled by Ashley-Cooper. The notebooks listed every player of any consequence and where references to those players could be found amongst cricket's literature. Scales also possessed a splendid collection of county yearbooks, including most of those issued by Minor Counties. He delighted in composing lists of players with given characteristics, such as bespectacled cricketers, bearded cricketers, left-handers and many other more esoteric categories. He compiled an exhaustive list of 18th century players, which was published in instalments by The Cricket Society. His final articles for *The Cricketer* were printed in 1962 after which he suffered increasingly from ill-health. He died at his home in West Byfleet, Surrey in January 1974 aged 67.

Another early stalwart of the Society was Leslie Charles Fielding, whose major published work 'Batting, Bowling and Fielding Figures Between the Wars' printed in 11 parts in *The Cricketer* through 1945 has already been mentioned. A P.E. teacher from Manor Park in Essex, he contributed regularly to the early Society publications, chiefly with season-by-season figures of notable cricketers. He died in Manor Park in February 1981, aged 78.

A more original statistician than Fielding was his near neighbour, A.H.Wagg. A maths teacher in London he scoured the British Museum Newspaper Library in Colindale for match scores of overseas games and built up an unrivalled collection, becoming the authority on the subject, especially in relation to matches in the Indian sub-continent and the West Indies. It was through his researches that the detailed scores of the 1930-31 Vizianagram Indian tour matches were eventually published. He wrote many letters to *The Cricketer* between 1937 and 1953 and later contributed articles to *Playfair Cricket Monthly*, as well as the Society Newsletter. He resigned from The Cricket Society when he felt the Society had drifted away from its core aims. Alfred H.Wagg died in Wanstead in April 1980, having been born in February 1903.

Returning to the subject of county histories, in the same year as Coldham's book was published, *Sussex: A History* was issued. Although the author was a well-known journalist, in contrast to too many histories by that tribe, where the seasons fondly remembered by the author swallow a large portion of the work, half the Sussex history is devoted to pre-1914 cricket, with the work and research carried out by Dr Squire acknowledged and constructively employed.

The author was John Norman Marshall. Born in Surrey in 1906, he moved to Sussex as a boy, was educated at Brighton College and then began a career in journalism, working mainly for Associated Newspapers. He was on the London *Evening News* for many years, being the editor from 1950 to 1954. Following some years overseas, Marshall was appointed an Executive of Associated Newspapers. His first cricket book, *The Weaving Willow* (published by Hodder & Stoughton in 1953), was little more than a series of amusing essays, most of which were related to his own cricketing experience. John Arlott provided a pleasing Foreword. His book on Sussex is much more serious and a textbook for history students on the development of the game in the county. There is a statistical appendix supplied by the Sussex scorer, George Washer. The question of whether Sussex were County Champions in 1875 was supported by Washer, but glossed over by Marshall (this point will be returned to). Washer, who the previous year had published *A Complete Record of Sussex County Cricket 1728-1957*, died in February 1975, having been the county scorer for 21 years.

After his book on Sussex, Marshall published the following year *The Duke Who Was Cricket* The subject was the 2nd Duke of Richmond, who resided at Goodwood, and organised major cricket matches in the 1720s and 1730s. Marshall undertook a great deal of research in the Goodwood archives and presents a rounded picture of the family and of cricket at the time. Marshall was later the author of short histories of three Test Match Grounds – Lord's, Headingley and Old Trafford. He died in Worthing in March 1985.

Fresh avenues were explored by W.P.Hone with the publication, in 1955, of his book *Cricket in Ireland*. It was the first comprehensive history of the game in that country, though the author stresses in his Acknowledgement that the work falls short of his original intentions. In particular he states that cricket in Northern Ireland was not properly covered and he fears that his personal family history intrudes more than it should. His father played for Ireland from 1861 to 1878 and his uncle also represented the country. The author himself had 20 years of international cricket. Despite Hone's concerns, the book has become the standard work of reference on the subject. William Patrick Hone was born in Monkstown, co.Dublin in August 1886. He was educated at Wellington and then Trinity College, Dublin. By profession a railway engineer, he worked in both Canada and India. He fought in France in the First World War, being awarded the MC at Verdun. Hone died in Clondalkin, Dublin in February 1976. His brother, Joseph, a well-known historian and novelist, assisted him in writing the book, providing the political background, while Derek Scott, the leading Irish cricket statistician and later Hon Secretary of the Irish Cricket Union, is thanked for the record section. Derek Scott was a very early member of The Society of Cricket Statisticians and a founding member of the ACS. Although he is now retired from office, he was for many years editor of the Irish Cricket Union Yearbook.

Two biographies issued in the latter half of the 1950s demand attention. They are opposite ends of a pole, one being purely statistical, the other verging on the romantic.

Bradman The Great by Bertram Wakley was the ultimate analysis of every first-class innings played by Bradman. Each innings is detailed with a description of the match and Bradman's part in it – in some cases 1,200 words. After these matches, which occupy the bulk of the book come over 60 pages of tables and analysis – even a section on Bradman's batting performances on rain-affected wickets occupy three pages. Wakley has discovered that Bradman survived 93 dropped catches, but 269 of his innings were chanceless. His average time to reach the milestones of 50, 100 and 200 are presented in another table. The book is very well produced and runs to 317 pages in hardback. It is still the template for any one wishing to complete such a work on a cricketer's statistics. Bertram 'Bertie' Joseph Wakley was born in July 1917, shortly after his father had been killed in action in France. Educated at Wellington and Christ Church, Oxford, he served in the Mediterranean theatre during the Second World War and was called to the Bar in 1948. From 1973 to 1992 he was a Judge dealing mainly in family matters. His first-class brain was allied to a keen sense of humour. In 1964 he was the author of a second book of statistics, *Classic Centuries*. This details every hundred scored in the England v Australia series of Tests. It is treated very much along the lines of his Bradman work with many similar tables. Wakley, who was a very useful cricketer, opened the batting for Wimbledon C.C. and wrote a history of that club, published in 1954. He was also a founder member of The Society of Cricket Statisticians. He died in September 2001.

The second biography, published in 1957, also involved one of cricket's greatest players and was appropriately titled *The Great Cricketer – W.G.Grace*. H.S.Altham comments 'A fresh and sparkling biography of the immortal WG. Never before has the whole story been told with such compelling intimacy and charm'. The book certainly made pleasant reading, but with over a dozen books already featuring WG, the author did not provide any additional data and several further biographies have placed this work in the shadows. The author, Arthur Alexander Thomson, was born in Harrogate in April 1894. Educated at Harrogate Grammar School and King's College, London, he served in France and Mesopotamia during the First World War. After the war he became a full time writer with a reputation for humorous fiction and travel pieces. His work included novels, verse, stage plays and radio comedies. Among his total of some sixty books are 24, some of which have cricket connexions, others are solely devoted to the game. His first of the latter was *Cricket My Pleasure* issued in 1953 and comprising a dozen essays. His Yorkshire roots are demonstrated by the fact that the Introduction is by Len Hutton and the Foreword by George Hirst. He wrote a joint biography of Hirst and Rhodes in 1959 and then another on Hutton and Washbrook in 1963. His books proved a popular success and several were re-issued by the Sportsman's Book Club. In 1963 he was elected President of The Cricket Society and remained in office until his death in June 1968.

Chapter 12
Rowland Bowen causes Ripples

Jerry Desmonde's television programme 'The 64,000 Question' would appear an unlikely catalyst for a fundamental change in the interpretation of cricket's history, but so it proved. The programme ran for three years, from 1956 to 1958. Despite much research it seems impossible to pinpoint the exact date of the specific programme, which brought about this sea change, but a letter written by Roy Webber and dated May 29, 1958 refers to the broadcast being 'last winter'. Be that as it may, the question which was asked concerned the naming of the counties which had *never* won the County Championship. The contestant did not include Sussex among those counties and his answer was ruled incorrect. The list of winners published in the 1957 edition of *Wisden* did not include Sussex, however the book by Roy Webber on the history of the County Championship gave Sussex as joint Champions in 1875. It was not until the 1958 edition of the *Playfair Cricket Annual* that Webber changed the champions list there to feature Sussex, as joint winners in 1875.

The question setter had clearly followed *Wisden*. However the cricket world was split between the *Wisden* version and Webber's 'discovery'. Sussex of course were delighted, as has been pointed out in the previous chapter's comment on George Washer and the Honours Board in the Hove pavilion was altered to record the Sussex success. An appeal by the author for the youthful competitor of the 64,000 Question to come forward produced some replies, but not from the person himself. Whether the organizers came to an amicable arrangement with him after the programme is still unknown. One man even more incensed than the contestant that Sussex belonged in the list of County Champions was a certain Major Rowland Bowen.

In 1952 Webber had begun a regular feature on cricket statistics in *The Cricketer*. In June 1953 he broaches the subject of the County Championship competition of the 1870s and subsequent articles regarding the history of the Championship in general appear through 1954. At the foot of one article Webber had noted:

> 'Several readers have written to me about this series of articles on the early days of the County Championship. Regular readers of *The Cricketer* will remember the article by "Senex" last year and my reply. This provoked a considerable amount of correspondence, including a lengthy letter from Major R.Bowen....'

In hindsight, perhaps it was a pity that Bowen's letter was not published. So far as the public was concerned the controversial subject of the 1870s Champions then lay dormant until the fateful TV programme. Norman Preston, the editor of *Wisden*, was affronted that Webber had the temerity to challenge the long established cricket facts as published in the *Almanack*. When Rowland Bowen appeared on his white charger to confront and try to flatten the upstart Webber, Preston was delighted to offer space in the 1959 edition of *Wisden*, so that Bowen could uphold the proud position *Wisden* held in cricketing circles. At that moment, it must be a matter of conjecture how well acquainted Preston was with Rowland Bowen, when he agreed to print Bowen's essay on the subject of the 1875 County Champions. Bowen never did things by half. Instead of merely checking out the controversial season of 1875, he cast his net much wider and did thirty years of digging into contemporary accounts of county cricket each season from 1860 to 1889.

The resultant essay, running to 5,000 words, explained in detail the views of the various contemporary publications and this duly appeared in the 1959 *Wisden*. It served Preston's purpose of demolishing Webber's 1875 Sussex theory, by the simple method of demonstrating that Webber had done virtually no research into the press reports of 1875. However Bowen discovered that though the *Wisden* list was correct for 1875, it was incorrect for two other seasons and Bowen also argued vehemently that the champions list ought to commence in 1865 and not in 1873 (the start date given in the *Wisden* list of champions). Preston diplomatically added a footnote to Bowen's essay:

> "Editor's Note: Without in any way disputing the conclusions reached by the author, I do not think we can alter the accepted list as regularly published in *Wisden* for over forty years, even where there are good grounds for disagreeing with it."

After a lapse of some years however, Bowen wore Preston down and the 1963 edition of *Wisden* finally switches from Preston's 'traditional' list to Bowen's – by an odd coincidence Bowen's list moves back one season to 1864 (the 1963 edition of *Wisden* was its 100th).

The reactionaries waited until after Bowen's death to make their move. The popular *Playfair Cricket Annual*, which was Webber's baby, changed from Webber's list to Bowen's in 1979, but in 1986 chopped out all the early Champions and from then began its list in 1890. In 1997 *Wisden* copied this new *Playfair* format.

Rowland Francis Bowen, born in London in 1916, was educated at Westminster, then spent much of his adult life working in the Middle East and in India, as a surveyor, policeman and soldier. He returned to England in the 1950s and living at the parental home in Eastbourne worked at the War Office, with the rank of Major. As far as is known he was never an active cricketer of any standing.

The protracted debate on the early County Champions with its necessary research and resultant findings, not only forced Bowen to build up a library of books dealing with cricket history but sparked him into action regarding many other historical 'facts' which appeared on a regular basis in cricket literature. Too many writers seemed to have been swayed, not by the scholarship of works on cricket history, but on the literary quality, which is not necessarily the same thing. It became apparent that no one had conducted any serious research into the broad basis of cricket history for some thirty years – since the deaths of F.S.Ashley-Cooper and of P.F.Thomas – except Buckley, whose published findings had rather gathered dust, and the narrow diggings of the Squires.

In Bowen's mind the only way to tackle the subject was not just to burrow for new material, but just as important to test to the limit all and every piece of information already in the public arena. The whole sorry muddle of cricket history had begun with the myths and half-truths published (along with much valuable material) by Nyren and Pycroft and then regurgitated by many writers who had never looked beyond those sources, save for the information given in Altham's history. Bowen's forthright attitude was not going to make for a happy relationship with many long established 'historians-statisticians' of the Webber ilk.

Whilst Bowen had been working on his Championship researches he had gained some allies, especially Gutteridge (of Epworth Books), John Arlott, the now elderly G.B.Buckley and H.S.Scales. Bowen joined The Cricket Society. In 1958-59 as a result of contact with Gutteridge Bowen initially hoped The Cricket Society might aid his endeavours to untangle cricket's history. In the event he found the Society in disarray. The causes for this disagreement are not part of this present work, but it hardly needs adding that Bowen threw himself into the fray. With some like-minded members, namely P.A.L.Barling, G.Brodribb, H.A.Cohen, E.D.R.Eagar, J.D.Lane, C.Nichols, A.A.Thomson, A.Cureton, E.Grayson, A.W.T.Langford, I.Rosenwater and B.J.Wakley, he first forced a postal ballot and then two Extraordinary General Meetings, after which the whole of The Cricket Society Committee was replaced.

Bowen urged that the Society become more pro-active and that the rather dated *Newsletter*, ought to be replaced by an authoritative *Journal*, which would give the Society a more influential voice in the cricketing world as a whole. The new Committee appointed Bowen as Editor, but in reality he was not the person to produce a publication under the overall aegis of a committee. Cracks soon appeared in the new structure and Bowen resigned before the first issue of the *Journal* was even assembled. The

Journal was to be issued twice a year and the first issue appeared in April 1961, with the Committee turning to a man nearly twenty years younger than Bowen – a man who at first glance seemed to be a reincarnation of Ashley-Cooper. This young man had from boyhood hidden himself away in the darkest corners of Somerset House, the British Museum, Colindale and other repositories of ancient documents and moved on to devour the library at Lord's, all the time building up his own cricket library.

Irving Rosenwater, initially registered as 'Isidore', was born in Mile End, East London in September 1932. His parents worked in the 'rag' trade and he was educated at Parmenter's Grammar School before becoming an articled clerk in a legal firm. Like Bowen his prowess on the cricket field was minimal. His first letter published in *The Cricketer* and dated June 1949, commences:

> "Allow me to correct an error which appears in the current issue of your fine paper…"

Rosenwater is writing from his parents' home in Diggon St, Stepney. A year later his second letter to The Cricketer begins:

> "May I be permitted to point out one or two omissions which have occurred in the recent publications of Minor Counties Records…"

His letter of April 1955 provides a good example of the depth to which his researches had gone:

> "Mr Roy Webber's note in the *Spring Annual*….requires considerable emendation as it is based on a wholly erroneous assumption…"

The subject was Endean's hundred before lunch for Transvaal.

Rosenwater's first signed article in *The Cricketer* was published in 1956. Entitled 'The Hazards of Cricket', the piece describes many injuries suffered by cricketers, spectators and innocent passers-by, beginning with Mr Legat in 1731. In 1960 he was commissioned to write a regular column 'Feats, Facts and Figures' – it was hardly a coincidence that Ashley-Cooper ran a feature with precisely that title in the *Athletic News Annual*, from 1914 to 1931. In 1962 *The Cricketer* provided space both for Rosenwater's column and 'At The Sign of The Wicket' (another Ashley-Cooper title) by Rowland Bowen.

Would the wildly enthusiastic amateur (Bowen) be able to work in conjunction with the dedicated professionalism of Rosenwater? In the first issue of *The Journal of The Cricket Society* no articles by Bowen appeared. The two principal pieces were J.D.Coldham's 'Northamptonshire v Yorkshire At The Wicket' which consumed 12 of the 64 pages and 'Index to The Cricketer' Part One by H.A.Cohen (also 12 pages). Five pages were given to The Society's Winter Lunch. Rosenwater himself provided a short essay on 'Throwing'.

In July 1961, a few months after the launch of the *Journal*, Rosenwater organised and managed Stuart Surridge's team's tour of Bermuda. This would seem to indicate that he had left the legal profession in favour of cricket, and at the same time progressively strengthened his links with *The Cricketer*. In August 1965 The Cricket Society announced:

> 'Due to business pressure, Irving Rosenwater is giving up
> his post as Editor of the *Journal* (of The Cricket Society),
> as he has been appointed to the staff of *The Cricketer*'.

Bowen severed his links with that magazine, his final article being in late 1962. The hackneyed phrase 'he didn't suffer fools gladly' summed up the reason for his departure. In 1963 he launched and financed his own magazine *The Cricket Quarterly*.

Bowen's Introduction to the new publication begins:

> 'Nature abhors a vacuum and that, perhaps, is why fools
> rush in where angels fear to tread. It now appears that
> there is a very real and pressing need for a publication to
> deal with the more serious aspects of cricket's past as well
> as to chronicle, as a matter of record, some of the more
> interesting and worth-while facts about cricket below its
> top level.
>
> 'It has always been a feature of cricket writing, apart from
> topical events, that the best, as well as the most valuable,
> research has been produced by those who regard it as a

hobby, and who have wide-ranging other interests; by the amateur in the best eighteenth century sense of the term. If Ashley-Cooper was an exception in these, since he relied on his writings for his living, yet his approach was that of the scholar, not of the day-to-day writer for the popular newspapers. In this modern age, what is now needed is a Nuffield Chair of Cricket History and Research but till that is founded, there are plenty of people up and down the country who have something worth while to say, and we believe, to read...'

The first issue was largely written by Bowen, the other signed articles being by two or three well-known cricket historians. An unidentified hand writes about a forthcoming encyclopedia of cricket which is stated to be appearing in 1964 edited by a well-known journalist. The work is more or less condemned unseen and a comparison drawn with Golesworthy's little tome – not the most sane of comments. The magazine did in fact grow to become the best historical vehicle on cricket and quite a number of excellent researchers and historians contributed to it over its eight-year life. It was unfortunate that Bowen first persuaded worthwhile contributors to write for the magazine and then, in too many cases, fell out with them.

The example of Rosenwater was perhaps the most notorious of these. Ironically the subject which caused the split was none other than Ashley-Cooper. Rosenwater submitted his essay on the famous cricket historian to Bowen in 1964. He could just as easily had it published in *The Journal of The Cricket Society*, so the question of why Rosenwater chose Bowen's magazine is open to debate. It ought perhaps to be mentioned here that Rosenwater was heavily involved in the forthcoming cricket encyclopedia, which *The Cricket Quarterly* had condemned the previous year.

Bowen decided that Rosenwater's piece on Ashley-Cooper required some editorial adjustment. Rosenwater refused, as indeed he always did, to have his work altered. One version of the story then claims, Bowen rejected the piece, the other that Rosenwater withdrew it. Be that as it may, Rosenwater published his work in *The Journal of The Cricket Society*;

Bowen wrote his own essay on Ashley-Cooper and printed it in his own magazine. Bowen was out to prove that not only did Ashley-Cooper make mistakes, but that he showed a distinct reluctance to acknowledge and correct any errors he made.

Whilst these two historical leviathans were jousting with one another, lesser mortals were plotting to create another English cricket magazine. It will be recalled that the *Playfair Cricket Annual* had been originally the work of Peter West and Roy Webber. In 1954, Peter West left the annual for his blossoming broadcasting career and the editorship was taken over by Gordon Ross.

Gordon John Ross, born in 1918, had served in the R.A.F. during the Second World War and after being demobilized had sought a place in sports publishing. In 1949 he was appointed editor of the *Playfair Rugby Annual*, which also entailed the editing and production of Rugby Union match programmes as well as the match programmes for Arsenal F.C. At the same time he wrote articles for the press on both codes of football and on cricket. Ross in 1954 also took over from Peter West as editor of the pre-tour brochures for Test Teams to England (Pakistan 1954 being Ross's first). As with the Playfair annuals, Webber provided the statistics.

Ross was the stereotypical marketing man – he was later to become the cricketing person for Gillette and very good in the role – but in 1957 he decided to launch himself as a cricket historian with a hardback book *The Surrey Story*, cashing in on Surrey's brilliant run of County Championship honours. The book is very lightweight and merely an updated version of Palgrave's work

In May 1960 in harness with Roy Webber, Ross launched *Playfair Cricket Monthly*. It was the first serious rival to *The Cricketer* since the demise of *The Cricketers' Magazine* in 1953. As one might expect from the Playfair stable, the new periodical was far slicker than *The Cricketer*. The page layout was more attractive, the paper quality better, the larger picture content was better reproduced. The page size was larger. The new magazine was monthly throughout the year, whereas *The Cricketer*, which had been weekly before the war was now fortnightly through the season only and then had two much larger annuals (usually 96 pages as against 36) – in November and March-April.

The old magazine was still issued from Langford's home address – it looked cottagey and was. The annual subscription was 25 shillings; the *Playfair* cost 28 shillings. Gordon Ross commissioned John Arlott for the Test Match reports and Neville Cardus as a features writer. *The Cricketer* used W.E.Bowes, the former England fast bowler, to describe the Tests and in 1960 was serialising Henry Grierson's 'History of the Forty Club'. *The Cricketer* continued its extensive coverage of Public Schools cricket, London Club cricket and the major Northern Leagues, whilst the new magazine was very much centred on Tests and County cricket, though initially it did give some space to cricket at a lower level. In the winter issues the *Playfair* published full scores of many overseas first-class matches – the influence of Roy Webber clearly showing through. *The Cricketer*, with only its two annuals during the winter months, concentrated on England teams touring overseas and more general articles.

It took *The Cricketer* three seasons to realise that it was losing ground to its new rival. On September 1, 1962 the magazine carried a full page declaration, which opened with:

'The Cricketer – An Important Announcement
From its next issue (on sale November 15) The Cricketer will appear in a greatly enlarged and improved form. Expanded, The Cricketer will contain fascinating new features that will appeal to all lovers of the game, whether they be players or spectators. There will be many more pictures too.'

The new format had John Warner as Managing Editor, Peter Morris as Editor; Club Cricket Editor was Arthur Langford and Tom Ward the Advertisement Manager – the last named produced 19 full pages of adverts out of a total of 64, a vast increase, which no doubt improved the finances. The new editor did not survive, Langford resumed his old post, but the more powerful figure behind the scenes was E.W.Swanton, who was Chairman of the 'Editorial Board', which in 1964 became the

'Editorial Committee'. It was no doubt that through his connections with Swanton that Rosenwater was appointed 'Manager' in 1965. In some quarters Rosenwater was thought of as Swanton's cricket secretary. For the few who cared about such things, the fact that Rosenwater was an integral part of *The Cricketer* set-up, meant that historical matters in the magazine had an authoritative eye cast upon them.

It is doubtful whether Sir Pelham Warner had much say in this fundamental change. Some two months after the format hit the bookstalls, the founder of the magazine died. In an editorial obituary, John Warner comments:

> 'Lately, he (Pelham Warner) has been unable to take much part in the running of *The Cricketer*, but his encouragement was most valuable and he often said how happy he was that the magazine was to continue.'

Back in 1950, his elder son, Esmond, had criticized the way the magazine was run (by Langford) and urged his father to take over the reins again. As a result, Warner sought the advice of the aged C.B.Fry In a sealed letter written some years earlier, but to be opened on his death Pelham Warner had asked that his son, Esmond, be given a post at *The Cricketer*, though in the same letter Warner asks that Langford take over as Editor on Warner's death. Things did not turn out quite like that.

The day before (in November 1962) the revamped *Cricketer* magazine hit the bookstalls, Roy Webber was attending a meeting at the offices of the *Playfair Cricket Monthly*. He then left the premises to drive home, but collapsed and was taken to St Bart's Hospital, where he was pronounced dead. He was only 48, but had for years been very overweight. Webber was the one cricket statistician known to the general cricketing public, through his work for the B.B.C., for the *News Chronicle* and of course through the various Playfair publications. He was a workaholic and in that sense followed the footsteps of Alcock, Pentelow and Ashley-Cooper. The additional work load created by the demise of the *News Chronicle* possibly proved too much for him. Webber had provided the statistics for both the *News Chronicle Cricket Annual* and the *Playfair Cricket Annual*. The first was edited by Crawford White and the second by Gordon Ross, as has been mentioned, but the *News Chronicle* collapsed in 1961. Webber then decided to run the paper's cricket annual on his own – it appeared in 1962 purely as *The Cricket Annual* – the proverbial straw and camel's back come immediately to mind. His ability to set cricket statistics out in a manner that was easily comprehensible to the ordinary reader was quite admirable, his major flaw as has been commented upon, was his terrible lack of historical understanding.

Two men took over Webber's great statistical mountain. Arthur Wrigley, who had been Webber's scoring colleague with the B.B.C., was handed the task of updating Webber's books on Test Matches. Wrigley, born in Heaton Moor, Lancashire, in 1912 and educated at Heaton Moor College, was, like Webber, an accountant by profession. He began scoring for the B.B.C. in 1934 and, after war service as a bomber navigator with the RAF, he resumed his B.B.C. work. Unlike the two volume work on Tests which Webber had compiled, Wrigley fitted all the Tests into a single volume. This was published by Epworth Press in 1965. Wrigley changed the Webber format, in that he arranged the Tests as a set of series, rather than simply running them from 1877 in straight chronological order. There is an extensive record section of 176 pages. It was to prove Wrigley's only cricket book – he died in Stockport on October 30, 1965 aged 53.

Webber's mantle in so far as the Playfair publications were concerned, was taken over by Michael Fordham. A local government officer from Maidstone, though born in Faversham, Fordham had only just taken on the role of principal statistician to The Cricket Society from W.S.Condor, when Webber died; Fordham resigned his new post in October 1963 in order to allow time for his work with Playfair. A modest man, he did not possess Webber's ebullience and preferred to keep in the background. Gordon Ross and Roy Webber had been joint editors of most of the current Playfair cricket titles: in future Gordon Ross took sole charge, just crediting the statistical work to Fordham. In historical matters, Fordham proceeded with extreme caution. His only cricket title was to be a brief book on the Gillette Cup – this appeared in 1976. He married Daphne, the widow of Roy Webber.

In the first half of the 1960s, whilst the *Playfair Cricket Monthly* and *The Cricketer* fought out the contest for readership of the general cricketing public, the two new more serious magazines, *The Journal of The Cricket Society* and *The Cricket Quarterly* competed for the niche market of cricket statisticians and historians, Rosenwater v Bowen.

Bowen brought on board a number of prominent cricket historians, several of whom have been previously noted. Eric Snow, the Leicestershire historian, serialised his history of Sir Julien Cahn's Team (with statistics by Keith Warsop); Gerald Brodribb wrote about big hitting; the extensive cricketing notes left by G.B.Buckley were combed by Bowen and the edited results published; H.S.Scales, though now suffering ill-health, sent in pieces; J.D.Coldham and B.J.Wakley were other early supporters of the magazine who contributed essays. All these were well-known and respected figures in the small world of cricket historical research. There were some new faces. The most important contributor on early cricketing history was John Goulstone, who was born in 1940 and spent much of his time researching archives in Kent for early cricket references. In August 1959, in his first published correspondence to *The Cricketer*, the opening paragraph provides the sine qua non of what would become a lifetime of research into sports history:

> "I have been looking through the registers of gamekeeper
> deputations for Kent and a number of hitherto unknown
> facts concerning Kent cricketers have come to light, some
> of which may be of interest to those of your contributors
> who write on 18th century cricket."

Goulstone's initial piece in the *Quarterly* was to reveal the discovery of William Bedle, described at his death in 1768 as 'the most expert cricket player in England'. Goulstone also wrote about the Dartford cricket side of the 1750s. Goulstone's researches were to add great stature to Bowen's magazine. Later Goulstone published his own magazine, as well as separate booklets on specific aspects of the game.

The Cricket Quarterly also made a name for itself for its trenchant book reviews, almost all written by the Editor. It has been noted that Golesworthy's *The Encyclopedia of Cricket* came in for criticism in the first issue of *The Cricket Quarterly*. A further comment on this book is necessary, if only because it became the most popular book of its type through the 1960s and 1970s, six editions being issued.

Maurice Golesworthy, a West Country sports journalist, living in Devon, was principally concerned with soccer and wrote encyclopedias on football and boxing prior to turning his mind to cricket. The standard of his cricket book can best be judged by John Arlott's comments in the 1963 *Wisden*:

> "This book, however, has many errors which are not matters of opinion nor mere 'literals', but major inaccuracies and cardinal omissions."

Golesworthy acknowledges as his main helper G.D.Martineau, though in later editions John E.Price comes to his aid. Price is credited with providing questions for the TV programme 'Sporting Chance' and producing statistical data for B.B.C. TV Test broadcasts, since the death of Roy Webber.

In 1962, George Allen & Unwin decided to reissue Altham and Swanton's *History of Cricket* in two volumes. Volume Two is 1919 to date, solely by Swanton. Bowen fills five pages of his magazine with comments on this revised work. Bowen's main concern centres on the Hambledon period, which aspect was to grow into a typical Bowen obsession and like too many of his obsessions it gradually became increasingly irrational.

Meanwhile, how was Rosenwater coping with his editorial role within The Cricket Society?' His editorship covered eight issues – about 500 pages – before he left for *The Cricketer*.

In each issue there was one, sometimes two, articles by Rosenwater and these always commanded respect. The *Index to The Cricketer* by H.A.Cohen was to outlive Rosenwater's time, but its entries were flawed – entries under 'A' for example included: 'Accent on Youth', 'After the War', 'Against the Fathers', and 'All in the Game'. Commander H.Emmet had his reminiscences serialised. The statisticians, Messrs Weigall, Fielding, Conder and Oliver etc, are given plenty of space. Donald King, the

Canadian Secretary, reports regularly on matters from his country, women's cricket gets a fair airing, Frank Crompton's 'History of Bedfordshire' is also serialised. Martineau and A.A.Thomson produce their light pieces. David Kelly writes two worthwhile essays on overseas cricket and Marder writes on the United States. The book reviews are very limited; Golesworthy's effort and even the new Altham-Swanton history are not mentioned. One wonders at the long review given to Rosenwater's own *A Portfolio of Cricket Prints*, especially when his notes are singled out as the best part of the book. There is nothing wrong with the work, but...

R.G.Ingelse wrote one article for the magazine. Ray G.Ingelse was the mainstay of the Dutch cricket club, 'Still Going Strong'. The club, similar to England's Forty Club, was formed in 1929 for older cricketers. Ingelse was a major publicist for Dutch cricket who was in addition a most knowledgeable historian on the subject. From 1936 he had contributed Dutch notes to *The Cricketer*. He died in May 1976 aged 78.

Passing reference has already been made to John Marder, the United States equivalent of Ingelse. Marder's initial notes in *The Cricketer* concerning United States cricket appeared in 1932. Born in Nottingham in 1908 he had emigrated in 1927 to Canada and then moved on to the United States, law being his profession. He had served on the Western Front in the Second World War and was injured in Belgium. Based after the war in California he determined to revive cricket in that state and having been instrumental in the reformation of the United States Cricket Association, revived, in 1963, the United States v Canada annual match. In 1967 he published *The International Series : The Story of the United States v Canada at Cricket*. The book brought together for the first time the detailed scores of all the matches in this long series and just as vitally gave notes on most, if not all the players who had taken part. Marder died in London in August 1976.

Chapter 13
The World of Cricket

In terms of size and scope, one book commands centre stage in the 1960s: *The World of Cricket*, General Editor E.W.Swanton, Associate Editor Michael Melford, Assistant Editors Irving Rosenwater and A.S.R.Winlaw. The publishers were Michael Joseph and the book lists no less than 68 'Chief Contributors'. The volume contains 1,165 pages, 9½" by 8" ; in addition there are 20 pages of coloured plates. Black and white photographs and illustrations are scattered throughout the general text. The closest precedent to this new work was Warner's *Imperial Cricket.*

The entries in the work are arranged in a strict alphabetical order, so, for example, 'Big Hits (an essay by Gerald Brodribb) slots in between 'Bexhill CC' and 'Birkett, Lord', who is followed by 'Bishop's Stortford College' and then 'Bite, to' the last being the dictionary definition of the verb as related to cricket.

Two points need to be made immediately, though both are obvious. Firstly, a book with 68 main contributors is clearly as strong as those authors and a check through the list shows they vary in quality from the best to the second rate. Secondly, a key issue was the decision on what entries (there are some 2,000) were to be included. One possible fault with the book is the amount of space given to public schools and amateur clubs, at the expense of the professional game, which today makes the book appear very old-fashioned.

With 68 presumably notable cricket scholars enrolled, who could be found to give the finished work an objective review? The personnel running *The Cricketer* magazine are heavily involved in the work; John Arlott, who reviews books for *Wisden*, is a contributor; Gordon Ross acts as reviewer for the *Playfair Cricket Monthly*; also contributing were most, if not all the broadsheet cricket journalists.

As a disinterested party, Rowland Bowen had the reviewing field to himself. Given that he had condemned the book, unseen, two or three years prior to publication, it is scarcely surprising that his comments are caustic. It is rather curious though that the book's section on the County Championship follows the Webber path – although no author is given for this section. What is equally blatant is that the foundation dates for the various counties, researched so diligently by Bowen and published mainly in *The Cricketer*, have been ignored completely. Whether these two rather odd aberrations can be placed at Rosenwater's door, designed just to annoy Bowen, seems to stretch the enmity a little too far.

A brief biographical note on Swanton has been given in Chapter 8. By 1966 he was perhaps the most authoritative voice in English cricket, but, for his knowledge of cricket prior to the First World War, he had to lean heavily on Rosenwater. Second in command of the book was Michael Melford. Melford, born in London in November 1916, was educated at Charterhouse and Christ Church, Oxford, where he achieved sporting prowess as an athlete. He served in the Royal Artillery in the Second World War, then joined the *Daily Telegraph* as a sports journalist; in 1961 he was appointed senior cricket and rugby correspondent of the newly founded *Sunday Telegraph*. He had had a column in *The Cricketer* magazine in 1954 and continued to submit articles on mainly topical matters for the magazine. He was a popular journalist of sound judgment who wrote well, but his only major cricket books were Peter May's ghosted autobiography and a book on post-1945 cricket. His ability to ferret out historical errors in the work of the other contributors was minimal. He was later editor of the *Daily Telegraph Cricket Year Book*, which ran for nine years from 1982, giving a pleasant, but relatively superficial overview of the preceding English season, with statistics provided at different times by Bill Frindall and Wendy Wimbush.

The third major figure in the compilation of the book was Tony Winlaw. Antony Sebastian Roger de Winton Winlaw was born in Harrow, Middlesex in March 1938, and educated at Harrow, where he was in the XI in 1955 and 1956. Like both Swanton and Melford, he was a sports journalist with the *Daily Telegraph* and *The Cricketer*. His value as a checker of historical facts was on a par with Melford. How far Rosenwater could alter the copy sent in by the 'experts' is not known. In later years he might well have declined to assist in such a flawed project. Rosenwater was, ten years later, to upbraid the Association of Cricket Statisticians for rushing their publications into print! When the second edition appeared in 1980 Rosenwater was no longer the Assistant Editor.

During the 1960s, Rosenwater published four other works which show him in an entirely different light. Three are slim volumes of meticulous scholarship – *F.S.Ashley-Cooper* (1964); *The Story of a Cricket Playbill* (1968), and *J.N.Pentelow* (1969). Each demonstrates the depth to which the author went to get his facts right as well as the care with which he assembled the facts His major work of the 1960s was *England v Australia: A compendium of Test Cricket betweeen the Countries 1877-1968*. His co-author was Ralph Barker. Barker had a rather unorthodox career; his working life began in journalism in 1934, drafted in the RAF during the Second World War, he was not demobbed in 1945, but continued to serve until 1961. He then set himself up as a free-lance writer. He was the author of several books on flying, including *The Schneider Trophy Races* and a biography of F.Spencer Chapman. In 1964 his first cricket book appeared, *Ten Geat Innings*. This was well received; Bowen comments:

> "We understand that this is the author's first book on cricket though he has written several others on widely different topics. We hope it may be the first of many for the author shows clearly he has the stuff of cricket in him, and he can write."

John Arlott is equally laudatory when Barker's second cricket book, *Ten Great Bowlers* was published in 1967:

> "These are satisfying biographies, obviously the result

of patient research, and told with considerable narrative skill."

In the case of Rosenwater's book on England v Australia, Barker wrote the descriptive passages for each Test, but the overwhelming part of the book is statistical. Rosenwater undertook a major piece of research in discovering the second innings batting order for each match – commonplace now, but never previously published in any of the numerous volumes which had featured the detailed Test Match scorecards. At the time the book appeared *Wisden* of the day did not give such data for the matches which it printed.

In complete contrast to *The World of Cricket* was *The Story of Cricket* by Vera Southgate in the "Ladybird" series for children. As superficial as one would expect for a juvenile item, one should not underestimate its influence in propagating, to a generation of children, myths such as the 'popping hole' and the female invention of round-arm bowling.

In 1902, the *History of Cambridge University Cricket* had been published, with W.J.Ford as author (see Chapter 6); sixty years later a volume on Oxford University Cricket, in the same depth, finally made its appearance. The author was Geoffrey Bolton, who had been born in London in July 1893, educated at Repton and University College, Oxford. He served in France and Italy in the First World War, after which he became a Prep School master and eventually a headmaster, retiring in 1960. A slow left arm bowler, he failed to get into the XI at either Repton or Oxford, but played cricket for Sussex Martlets (being President from 1950 to 1964), Cryptics and Repton Pilgrims. Bolton died in Cuckfield, Sussex in April 1964.

He had written and published a modest 16 page history of Sussex Martlets in 1956, but his book on Oxford, with 374 pages, was much more ambitious. The detailed score of each University match is printed and the first-class averages in all Oxford matches on a season by season basis. Each season has a two page review. There is a chapter on Oxford cricket prior to the first University match – Ford published the scores of all major Cambridge games, going back in 1821 – but Bolton only gives brief mentions of these early games; possibly lack of space precluded their publication. There are no biographies of blues, but the early ones are in J.D.Betham's very comprehensive book (see Chapter 5) and the *Three Great Schools* volume (see Chapter 8) covers many others The author states that the illustrations are severely limited due to cost.

Another addition to cricket's history published in the 60s was *The Paddock That Grew,* the author being the *Melbourne Sun-Herald* journalist, Keith Dunstan. At 304 large pages it is possibly the most ambitious volume yet to appear on Australia cricket and certainly on a single aspect of the game on that continent – Melbourne Cricket Club. The work is well illustrated. The author explores the pre-Melbourne Cricket Ground history in a thorough manner before launching into the detailed history of the present ground and many of the major matches played there. The book was revised and enlarged in 1974 and again in 1988. Dunstan acknowledges the expertise of Hugh Field, who had over many years researched the subject.

Dunstan's book was first published in 1962, the same year as *Felix on the Bat*. This title was briefly mentioned in Chapter 9, but deserves more than a passing reference. It is the most attractive of all the works written by Gerald Brodribb and the final 58 pages are a reproduction of Felix's original book (issued in 1845). The first 145 pages are Brodribb's biography of the remarkable Felix. It is a model for such a work. The author details not only Felix on the cricket field, but his life as a schoolmaster, artist and writer, thus providing a rounded portrait of his subject. There are some splendid illustrations.

Was it a coincidence that within 12 months of Brodribb's book appearing, the same publishers, Eyre and Spottiswoode, issued Patrick Morrah's work, *Alfred Mynn and the Cricketers of His Time*? He acknowledges Brodribb's work. However, Morrah did investigate the Mynn family in depth and adds quite a number of points not found in previous works in which Mynn features. Rosenwater was employed to provide a workmanlike index and, perhaps, provided some small pieces to the jigsaw. The book was certainly favourably reviewed.

These books on Felix and Mynn were important milestones in the writing of cricket biography. They were the first two hardback volumes on historical cricketing figures in which the author did extensive research into the player's life outside cricket. The few other earlier works, such as Darwin's life of W.G.Grace, merely regurgitated the facts already printed in other cricketing publications. Rosenwater's extended essay on Ashley-Cooper was another example of this new trend for in-depth research.

Patrick Arthur Macgregor Morrah, born in 1907, was a journalist connected in the main with the *Daily Telegraph*. His chief historical interest centred on the Restoration and he wrote several books on that period. A wine buff and bon viveur he died in February 1991. In 1967 his book *The Golden Age of Cricket* was issued. This is a theme ploughed by several other hands and his work added little to the general information known of the era.

Moving from the biographical to the statistical, it is worthwhile looking at the development of the county yearbooks in the 1960s on a county-by-county basis:

Derbyshire

The 1961 Yearbook and that of 1969 are almost identical (the 1970 edition is not used as a sample, since it is a special edition to mark the county club's centenary). The Births and Deaths section lists all the first-class county players and is very comprehensive – where gaps occur the editor is actively researching players' biographies to fill those gaps. The Record Section is reasonable. Local clubs and leagues are featured (some counties published a separate yearbook for local club cricket). The First XI matches are headed by good match reports and in 1961 Derbyshire was the only county to provide second innings batting orders. There were 176 pages in 1961 and 172 in 1969 – the price rose from one shilling to two shillings. The joint editors are F.G.Peach and A.F.Dawn. Francis 'Frank' George Peach was born in April 1911; he was a founder member of both the Cricket Society and the ACS. Educated at Derby School, he was employed as a chemist with the Spondon company, Celanese. The two editors had founded the Yearbook in 1954 with the same basic format that was still in use in the 1960s and indeed until very recently.

Peach remained editor until 1982 – he also served as an official of the Derbyshire's Supporters' Club and on the County Club Committee. Very meticulous, Peach preferred to delay publication of the Yearbook by a week or two, rather than rush any final proof-reading or checking. He was later the author of *Derbyshire Cricketers* in the ACS series. He died in Derby in February 1996.

Frank Dawn, who compiled the local club section of the Yearbook, was educated at Bemrose School in Derby. He was a useful club cricketer, but better known as an administrator both in Derbyshire and at a national level. Alfred Frank Dawn died at his home in Derby in May 1983, aged 74. The yearbook created by Peach and Dawn was a model which many other counties strove to emulate but few, if any achieved.

Essex

The 1961 Handbook was produced as a commercial venture by M.L.Pepper (Publicity) Ltd of Harrow. The firm also published handbooks for Gloucestershire, Hampshire and Sussex. Essex's book, edited by the England all-rounder (and County Secretary) Trevor Bailey was 152 pages long and cost two shillings. There was a very abbreviated Record Section of seven pages by John E Clay (see Chapter 10), plus season-by-season figures for two or three notable Essex players. The handbook did however publish full scores of both First and Second XI matches. By 1970 the handbook had shrunk to 124 pages costing 2s 6d, and the record section and the full Second XI scores had gone. The editor was C.A.Brown, who had also taken over from Trevor Bailey as Club Secretary – he was appointed in 1967 and retired in 1972. M.L.Pepper remained as publishers.

Glamorgan

The 1961 Yearbook was a very modest affair of 112 pages, costing two shillings. It listed all members, but without addresses. There were full first-class county scorecards with short reports and a three page Record Section. One assumes that the Club Secretary, Wilf Wooller, was the editor. He is listed as such in the 1970 edition, when the contents remained as in 1961, but the price had risen to three shillings.

Gloucestershire

This yearbook is another Pepper production, but it is 52 pages longer than the Glamorgan book and costs only one shilling. The list of members and their addresses occupy 50 pages, but there is a comprehensive Record Section of 36 pages which had originally been compiled in the 1930s by D.C.Moore. No one is credited with updating the Section in 1961 – presumably it was done by the scorer?

Hampshire

Another handbook from the Pepper stable. In 1961, Desmond Eagar, though retired as County captain, was still the Club Secretary and, one assumes, the handbook's editor. Unlike many of the other 1961 handbooks, Hampshire's includes quite a number of articles by writers outside the county – Rowland Bowen, Gordon Ross, Diana Rait Kerr and Ron Roberts. There is no Record Section, but full First XI match scores and good, lengthy match reports. The price is two shillings and the number of pages 128. In 1968's edition a Record Section by Roy Webber was introduced (culled from the 1950s county history – Webber had died in 1962). The Records had been updated by Norman Drake, a retired police officer, who was appointed county scorer in 1955 and remained in post until his death in January 1973 – aged 68. Apart from the records, the 1970 yearbook remained much as in 1961.

Kent

The famous Kent 'Blue Book', which had remained largely unchanged since its inception, changed in style but scarcely in content in 1947. The President's Message states: 'This year we are unable to follow our usual custom in publishing the Kent County Cricket Club "Blue Book", but thanks to our editor Mr Armitage and the publishers, Messrs Geerings of Ashford, who have come to our help, we are presenting a record in a somewhat different form.' However the format that was in use in 1961 was introduced in 1953, when, for example, a comprehensive Record Section of 27 pages was compiled by John F.Griffiths (see Chapter 9). The full scores for both First XI and Second XI matches were printed. There were articles by E.W.Swanton and H.W.Warner – in 1960 Warner had published 'The Story of Canterbury Cricket Week, an 80 page book which follows a rather familiar path. R.L.Arrowsmith had written a very long essay in the 1948 Yearbook, commemorating the Centenary of Canterbury Week and back in 1892, E.Milton Small had published *The Canterbury Cricket Week: Its Origins, Career and Jubilee.* Indeed, the first book on the Canterbury Festival came out in 1865, and is valued today primarily for its inclusion of real photographs of contemporary players – believed to be a 'first' in cricket publishing.

Warner had previously published a history of Beverley Cricket Club. He had been a Kent member since 1930 and made a regular appearance in the correspondence columns of *The Cricketer*, as well as helping Langford by providing club cricket details from Kent. Warner died in 1991.

Commencing in 1954, the Association of Kent Cricket Clubs published an excellent handbook, entitled *Cricket in Kent*. Compiled and edited by H.A.W.Daniels the book gave a comprehensive coverage of clubs based in Kent and at the time without equal. The Kent County yearbook continued through the 1960s unchanged.

Lancashire

The Lancashire Yearbook at 200 pages in 1961 was second in size only to Yorkshire's. The Record Section by C.M.Oliver (see Chapter 9) ran to 56 pages; he also provided season-by-season statistics. It is most informative to compare the records in the Derbyshire, Lancashire and Yorkshire books of 1961. Derbyshire provide, as has been noted, a good Births & Deaths section, but no career records; Lancashire combine years of birth and death with a career record, but there are many more 'gaps' in the B&D than in Derbyshire. Yorkshire has two separate sections, but rather ominously the career records are by Sir Home Gordon.

The Lancashire first-class match scorecards have no reports and the Second XI matches are only very briefly summarised. The editor of the 1961 Lancashire Yearbook is the County Secretary, C.G.Howard. By 1970 the price has dropped from two shillings to 1s 6d; the format is unchanged and the editor is Robert 'Bob' Warburton, the County's Assistant Secretary.

Leicestershire

The Yearbook for 1961 was priced at one shilling and contained 108 pages. The editors were Eric Snow (see Chapter 10) and F.M.Turner, the County Club Secretary. Detailed scorecards of First XI matches were included with good reports; there was a Who's Who of current playing staff and a 24 page Record Section with an alphabetical list of all players, though no birth or death data, no career records, but simply date of debut. The 1970 edition saw little change – sadly the County ceased to publish a Yearbook after 1975 and it was more than a decade before one reappeared.

Middlesex

In 1961 Middlesex County Cricket Club simply published an annual report of 26 pages. It had no historical content and the very briefest summary of the county's matches in 1960, plus the seasonal averages. Padwick only lists this modest publication as starting in 1951, but surely members ought to have received an annual report in earlier years?

Northamptonshire

The yearbook broadly followed the format set by V.W.C.Jupp, who edited the first modern Northants yearbook in 1925. A records section first appeared in 1947, running to fourteen pages, compiled by the Secretary, W.C.Brown. W.C. 'Beau' Brown was born on November 13, 1900 and died on January 20, 1986 in Brighton. Born in Wellingborough and educated at both Wellingborough and Charterhouse, he became a solicitor. He played for Northants from 1925 to 1937, was captain from 1932 to 1935 and Hon Secretary from 1937 to 1942. In 1948, Cyril Smith of Wellingborough added season-by-season partnership records – his first contribution to the yearbook. Records were omitted from the 1950 yearbook, being published as a separate booklet compiled by W.C.Brown and Cyril Smith – 32 pages selling for one shilling. The booklet was republished in 1952. Whilst lacking any records section, the 1950s yearbooks did contain a series of historical articles by Jim Coldham.

Records only reappeared in the yearbook for 1960. This cost 2s 6d and was 191 pages in length. Cyril Smith had compiled records for

J.D.Coldham's book on the County's history, which appeared in 1959 and these were transferred to the yearbook for 1960. They comprised 39 pages, including career records of all first-class players. Missing for two years, they reappeared in condensed form (14 pages) in 1963; amendments running to nine pages were published in 1965, then records disappeared from the yearbook until 1984, which included 47 pages compiled by L.T.Newell. Cyril Smith died in Wellingborough on January 12, 1994, aged 92. Working for British Railways, he compiled statistics not only on Northants (to whom he presented a complete set of *Wisden*), but also on Northampton's football and rugby clubs, and on Tottenham Hotspur.

Detailed scores for both First and Second XI matches were included and the whole was edited by the County Club Secretary, K.C.Turner. Financial problems which bedevilled Northants, meant that the yearbook perished after the 1966 edition (when the cost had doubled to five shillings) and after this the County just issued an annual report along the Middlesex lines, until 1988, when a full yearbook was resurrected.

Nottinghamshire

The yearbook for 1961 followed the pattern introduced in 1948. The cost was one shilling and the length 100 pages. Detailed First XI scorecards with good match reports were included, but for Second XI matches, the scores were given with no bowling analyses or report. A seven page Record Section was compiled by Roy Webber, but there was no list of past and present county players. The annual also contained details of the local leagues in the county.

In 1970 there was a radical change. The editor from 1948 had been a serving member of the County Club's Committee and in 1969 that was Harry Richards, who was also Sports Editor of the local daily paper, the *Nottingham Evening Post*. Harry Evers Richards, who had been a useful cricketer in the South Lancs League, died in 1979, having retired the previous year. Mike Carey, born 1936 and a journalist, originally with the *Derby Evening Telegraph* and then with the *Daily Telegraph*, the *Observer* and the *Guardian*, took over as Editor. Local club cricket disappeared from the annual (there was a separate Notts Cricket Association Handbook);

the Second XI match details were reduced to potted scores and the reports disappeared from the First XI scores. There were one or two articles by national figures.

Mike Carey ghosted Dennis Amiss's autobiography *In Search of Runs* and in 1997 he wrote the biography of the Derbyshire and England cricketer, Les Jackson, but Carey retired from cricket journalism in the 1980s.

Somerset

The yearbook covering the season 1960 is given as 'Year Book 1960-61'. It is 92 pages in length, but no price is shown. Ominously the Foreword begins:

> 'The absence of photographs, other than the usual team
> photograph, in this year's publication is due entirely to
> the lack of suitable material'.

However the First XI scorecards are accompanied by good match reports and although the Second XI scores are only potted, there are brief reports of each match. There is no Record Section. One assumes the County Club Secretary is the editor – Ron Roberts provides a short essay on the 1961 Australians. Later in the 1960s appeared *Cricket in Somerset* which was a combination of county and local club data and *The Somerset Dragon* which annual appeared in 1969. The County Club issued an Annual Report, but what might described as a 'proper' annual did not reappear until 1979, when Michael Hill started to develop what is still the county annual.

Surrey

The 1961 yearbook continued the long line of Surrey annuals which began in 1884. There are full scorecards for all matches involving the County Club including Club & Ground, Colts and Young Cricketers of Surrey. Unlike the Yorkshire annual there was no tradition of listing every Surrey cricketer, either with dates of birth and death or just career records. In the 1960 edition, Roy Webber had introduced some very basic Surrey batting records, culled straight from his Record Book; in 1961 four pages or so were given to bowling and fielding records. The cost of the annual was 2s 6d and it contained 176 pages. In 1970 the number of pages is reduced to 136, though with a slight increase in page size. The Record Section, now by Michael Fordham, remains very slim. Season-by-season figures are shown for all current players and full scores of the Surrey Young Cricketers matches are still featured.

Sussex

The yearbook is produced by the Pepper organisation and it is very feeble. Even the First XI matches only shown as potted scores; no record section appears. However local clubs and leagues are listed and this is undoubtedly the best section in the publication. With 108 pages the cost is one shilling. Through the decade there is little material change in this state of affairs. The book is compiled by the 'Handbook sub-committee' – curiously the list of officials divides into seven sub-committees, but not one headed 'Handbook'!

Warwickshire

The 1961 annual, 112 pages in length, no price given, is edited and compiled by W.G.Wanklyn and E.A.Davies. The First XI scorecards are printed with reports, but only potted Second XI scores. There is an extensive Record Section of 19 pages. This publication ceased in 1963 and the County Club then reverted to an enlarged Annual Report with Leslie Deakins, the County Club Secretary, as editor. There were no full match scores, but a remarkable feature was the obituary section which included many personalities with only a passing affiliation to Warwickshire cricket.

William G.Wanklyn was born in Worcestershire in 1916. He was appointed Cricket Correspondent of the *Birmingham Evening Mail* in 1947, retiring in 1978. In 1980 he suffered a severe stroke and he died in Milford Haven in August 1982.

Worcestershire

From 1958 Worcestershire created a yearbook sub-committee, the leading light of which was the Rev W.R.Chignell (see Chapter 10). This yearbook contained the full First XI match scores with reports – it was enlarged in the County Club's centenary year of 1965 and the Record Section included a feature unique among yearbooks of the 1960s. Each of Worcestershire's county opponents has a page devoted solely to Worcestershire performances against that county – such items as batsmen who have hit 1,000 runs for Worcestershire v that county, or bowlers to take 100 wickets etc. This all in addition to the usual records found in a yearbook. Assisting with the yearbook was A. Ross-Slater, who, unlike most others in his position, was the county's Hon Scorer. He began with the County Second XI in 1961, but quickly moved to the First XI. Educated at Uppingham and Cambridge, he had spent his working life as a prep school master. He died in February 1981 aged 79.

Yorkshire

Edited by the County Club Secretary, J.H.Nash, the Yorkshire Yearbook, unusually was hardback. It ran in 1961 to 424 pages, dwarfing all its 16 rivals. However 208 pages of the book contained the names and addresses of the members. The cost was five shillings to members or 7s 6d to non-members. A comprehensive Record Section is 60 pages in length. Full scores of both First XI and Second XI matches are given, but no match reports – the yearbook retained the page size it had been since it began in the 1890s (i.e. the same size as *Wisden*) As has been mentioned the birth and death dates of all Yorkshire players are given, as well as career records – no one is credited with keeping the Record Section up to date.

To describe the annuals issued by the Minor Counties, the various Leagues and some major clubs is clearly beyond the scope of this book. Some do contain statistical Record Sections and on occasion historical essays.

However the progress of a national annual for Scotland is deserving of note. In 1962 *The Scottish Cricket Annual*, edited by James Cowe, with Assistant Editors A.M.C.Thorburn and Bill Heeps, was published for the first time. This annual succeeded the tiny (3 ½" x 2 ¼") *Scottish Cricket Record*, published by R.W.Forsyth Ltd, the Scottish clothing retailers. This had printed a complete list of Scottish International players, but the new annual added to that data, the list of all major matches played by Scotland since 1865, with potted scores.

James Cowe died in 1964 with Thorburn and George G.Lawrie taking over the reins. The new annual, in fact, only lasted to 1968, but in 1971 Thorburn revived it under the title *Aitken & Niven Scottish Cricket Guide*.

The 'modern' *Irish Cricket Union Yearbook* was created in 1979. This gave detailed scores of current Ireland matches, but a Record Section did not emerge for some years. Derek Scott, the then Hon Secretary of the Union, was the editor. The leading historian-statistician in Ireland he was born in Ireland in 1929 and from 1955 had provided a column on Irish cricket for *The Cricketer* magazine.

A survey of the major overseas annuals issued between 1961 and 1970 shows little change from the previous decade. *The Cricket Almanack of New Zealand*, perhaps the leader in this field, was still edited by A.H.Carman, though by 1970 it was sponsored by Shell and the 1970 edition had grown to 188 pages (148 in 1961) – the Record Section ran to 12 pages.

South African Cricket Annual continued under the editorship of Geoffrey Chettle. The Who's Who of current players and the Record Section remained unchanged in format through the decade. The latter ran to 13 pages in 1970.

Indian Cricket saw a change of editorship in 1966, with P.N.Sundaresan taking over. The content remained the same with the Records concentrating on Ranji Trophy matches, and other major competitions, rather than all first-class matches, which state of affairs gave rise to some criticism.

Dicky Rutnagur launched a rival annual in 1957-58. It had a larger page size – *Indian Cricket* remained *Wisden* size. The one major feature in the new annual, which the long-running annual did not contain, was a Who's Who of current players in Indian first-class cricket. The editor, rather nicely, thanks Gordon Ross when Rutnagur states that the Who's Who is set out in a similar fashion to that in the *Playfair Annual*. In reality Rutnagur's Who's Who is vastly more comprehensive, including such notes as players' occupations outside cricket. Anandji Dossa is responsible for the Record Section, which only includes Ranji Trophy matches. Rutnagur has compiled the Test records. He was born in 1931 and was the cricket correspondent of the *Hindustan Times*, though better known in India for his radio broadcasts on cricket. He later moved in England and reported on various sports for the *Daily Telegraph*.

Tony Cozier established the *West Indian Cricket Annual* in 1970, breaking new ground; it will be dealt with in a later chapter. There was no established national Australian cricket annual in the 1960s. Each State continued to publish its own 'Yearbook'.

Chapter 14
Bowen Bows Out

For a decade, Rowland Bowen's personality enlivened the small world of cricket historians. 1970 saw the finale of his endeavours. His book *Cricket: A History of its Growth and Development Throughout the World* was published by Eyre & Spottiswoode; in December 1970 the final issue of *The Cricket Quarterly* was dispatched to subscribers. Judging by the final sentences in his signing off piece, when the magazine closed he was not sanguine as to the effects all his scholarship had had on the cricket world:

> "Some time ago, we recall the late N.S.Curnow saying that it was wrong to try and correct mistaken or non-existent facts and figures held by cricket enthusiasts: such people were best left to their pleasures, for fear they would come to a greater ill without them. Perhaps he is right? When is man going to get away from his nursery and beliefs and illusions acquired in his youth?"

It is impossible to try and compare Bowen's history with its immediate predecessors – those of Altham/Swanton and Parker. To attempt to do so would be like comparing the virtues of the elephant against those of the lion. They are different animals. As has previously been commented upon, Altham/Swanton and Parker, after some early historical chapters, were both writing of cricket at the top level and of cricket largely based in England or England teams touring overseas. Bowen, in the same space, surveyed the game at all levels in every country, in which he believed the inhabitants took cricket seriously. One third of his book comprises a chronology of the game divided into separate countries or continents. It is a vastly extended and learned extension of the 'Dates in Cricket History', which has erratically appeared in the post-1945 editions of *Wisden*. The Index to Bowen's book is a masterpiece of its kind, which encompasses both the main body of the work and the chronology.

Bowen had spent a decade trying to demolish a myriad cricketing myths. In his early chapters however he creates his own theory on cricket's origins. The idea he puts forward is that cricket began in northern France. It's an interesting idea, but Bowen presents it as a definite fact, which is, to say the least, very misleading. The Cromwellian extermination of 17th century cricket in Ireland, based on a single unsubstantiated quotation, is also no more than a tentative suggestion. Bowen ought to have made quite transparent that these are his thoughts and no more.

As with *The World of Cricket* (see Chapter 13) it is very difficult to read the reviews of Bowen's book as being objective. By 1970, through his magazine, he had split the handful of erudite cricket statisticians into two camps – pro or anti-Bowen. Perhaps the most amusing 'review' of Bowen's book was in *Playfair Cricket Monthly*. There wasn't one! Gordon Ross had suffered enough at the hands of Bowen, though the magazine did accept a half page advertisement for it. Neither the South African nor the New Zealand annuals reviewed the book. The new *Australian Cricket Yearbook* which was a magazine style production devoted a double page spread to books of the year, but merely gave a brief summary of each book's content, with no editorial comments – the magazine's publishers also acted as book retailers.

Indian Cricket however is not so reticent. The two page review by N.S.Ramaswami commences:

> "This is an unusual book of a type which only a writer with encyclopaedic knowledge, enormous patience for research and certain personal beliefs could have written. It is nothing less than a history of cricket in every country in the world where a ball might have been bowled and of

all classes of cricket, not first-class alone. Those who have attempted to chronicle the history of a segment of this vast whole will be the first to salute Mr Bowen's gifts."

The review concludes:

"This is a hard hitting book in addition to its supreme value as a work of statistical and sociological history. It provides food for thought as well as entries for one's record book. Mr Bowen disclaims the literary qualities of Altham's history. But there can be no better model for a historian of Indian cricket than a combination of Altham and Bowen."

Irving Rosenwater reviewed Bowen's book for *The Cricketer* and was not complimentary, save in his opinion on the *Index* and the idea of the *Chronology*. Rosenwater listed a stream of factual errors. What is rather irritating in the circumstances is that Rosenwater was also given the job of reviewing the book for *The Journal of The Cricket Society*. In this review, Rosenwater ends with:

"This book needed a keen editorial hand before it was let loose on the market. H.S.Altham's work still stands unchallenged."

Rather hypocritical when one considers that Rosenwater was presumably the 'keen editorial hand' on *The World of Cricket*.

Turning to Bowen's acknowledgements in his volume, three names are singled out, R.L.Arrowsmith, John Goulstone (see Chapter 12) and C.L.R.James.

Robert Langford Arrowsmith was born in Canterbury in April 1906. Educated at Charterhouse and Oriel, Oxford, he was in the XI at school as a left-hand batsman, but failed to get a blue at Oxford. He was a master at Lancing for ten years, before moving back to Charterhouse, where he stayed for the rest of his teaching career. His adult cricket was for M.C.C., Free Foresters, I Zingari, Charterhouse Friars and a number of similar wandering teams. He died in October 1988. Arrowsmith had letters published in *The Cricketer* from the 1940s onwards, often on biographical matters. He also had a number of articles in the magazine, with wandering clubs a particular interest. He was co-author of a short history of the Butterflies C.C. in 1962 and from 1964 is listed as a contributor to *Wisden*. He later took charge of the obituaries section of that work and was still in command at his death. As can be understood his knowledge of biographical matters, especially relating to Public School and University cricketers was extensive. He had decided opinions on a variety of subjects, but was always loyal to his friends. The fact that the strong personalities of Arrowsmith and Bowen managed to work in harmony was somewhat astonishing.

Cyril Lionel Robert James, born in Chaguanas, Trinidad in January 1901, and was educated at Queen's Royal College, Port-of-Spain. He came to England in the 1930s, reporting cricket for the *Manchester Guardian* from 1933 (he arrived to cover the West Indian tour of that summer) to 1938 and the *Glasgow Herald*. He then moved to the United States, before a brief spell back in England and a return to his home island, where he edited *The Nation*. Later in life he came to live in South London, where he died in May 1989. He fought for the cause of racial equality in the West Indies, as well as that of independence from colonial rule of the islands, though as a Federation rather than separate states. James was a friend of Learie Constantine and a useful cricketer in his own right. His major cricketing work was *Beyond A Boundary* published in 1963. John Arlott begins his *Wisden* review of this book with:

> '1963 has been marked by the publication of a cricket book so outstanding as to compel any reviewer to check his adjectives several times before he describes it and, since he is likely to be dealing with superlatives, to measure them carefully to avoid over-praise – which this book does not need.'

Arlott goes on to describe it as the finest cricket book ever written. James inter-weaves the history of West Indies cricket with some superb portraits of notable cricketers, but more essentially the whole ethos of West Indian life and of the attitudes of writers and thinkers in general. It is a book that must be studied in depth to be fully appreciated.

In addition to these three major figures, Bowen thanks another 27 for their help in various ways; many of them were, in 1971, the experts in a particular aspect of cricket history and had contributed to the pages of *The Cricket Quarterly*. Among these were Kenneth Erskine Bridger, who was born in Buenos Aires in March 1920. His major contribution to cricket's literature is *North v South,* the history of the major annual match played in Argentina. He also wrote a weekly cricket column for the English language *Buenos Aires Herald*. A second name to note is Professor John Ferguson, who died in Birmingham in May 1989 aged 68. An educational specialist, his particular cricketing interest was the etymology of words and phrases used in the game. The results of his scholarship appeared in *The Cricket Quarterly* and other magazines – it was a great pity he did not live to edit an updated version of Lewis's *The Language of Cricket*.

Diana Rait Kerr, the librarian at Lord's from 1945 to 1968, had a profound knowledge of the books kept there and, just as important, knew the contents of many of them. She assisted Bowen in the same way as she helped any who sought her guidance. Her major cricketing book, written in conjunction with I.A.R.Peebles, was *Lord's 1946-1970*, being a continuation of Warner's book on the ground. She was the daughter of the M.C.C. Secretary. Born in Dublin in 1918, she was educated at Perse High School.

Donald King was Bowen's Canadian expert, born in Naramata, British Columbia in October 1916 of American parents. However he was educated in England and, during the Second World War, worked for the Admiralty. He returned to Canada in 1947 and resurrected the Canadian Cricket Association, based in Ontario, in 1950. In 1961 he was described as 'the organiser around which the (Canadian) national wheel of cricket revolves'. In the course of his work he became well-versed in the history of the game in Canada. King died in Toronto in October 1977.

Edward Knight, who wrote articles on Pakistani and Indian cricket for both *The Cricket Quarterly* and *The Cricketer*, provided Bowen with data relating to those countries.

S.J.Reddy was one of a well-known family of journalists who reported on non-European cricket in South Africa from the 1950s. His father, J.J.Reddy, edited *Cricket Souvenir* which appeared in 1950 and 1951, whilst S.J.Reddy edited its successor, the *South African Non-European Cricket Almanack* from 1953. S.J.Reddy was also Secretary of the Eastern Province Cricket Federation. He provided Bowen with information on cricket in South Africa. The leading historian on Danish cricket was Douglas G Steptoe, born of English parents in Copenhagen in 1923. He had served in the Royal Navy during the Second World War. After the war he returned to Denmark and played an active part in cricket there. He died in Copenhagen in June 1994.

This might be an appropriate moment to mention the publication of *The Story of Continental Cricket* which was published in 1969. The three authors, Piet Labouchere, Tom Provis and Peter Hargreaves, the last two based in Denmark, are absolutely castigated by Bowen in a two page review in *The Cricket Quarterly*. The authors quoted and mis-quoted the magazine extensively, but declined Bowen's offer to check the finished manuscript. It is unnecessary to add that Douglas Steptoe does not receive a mention!

Roger Page and S.S.Perera, two most valuable members of Bowen's 'team' will be mentioned later; A.M.C.Thornburn and A.H.Wagg have been noted earlier. Keith Warsop, born in Nottingham in 1935, was a journalist on a number of provincial newspapers, finally with the *Yorkshire Evening Post*. His cricket research for *The Cricket Quarterly* covered detailed statistics for Sir Julien Cahn's Team and much on pre-1864 English cricket. He is also a notable football historian, in particular on Notts County F.C., having several historical works on soccer published. He compiled *E.G.Wynyard* in the ACS *Famous Cricketers* series. More recently he has been engaged in extensive research into major 18th century cricket matches and the players involved.

In 1968 and again in 1969, Bowen had indicated that he wished to close *The Cricket Quarterly*, but admirers pushed him to continue. In 1968 he made the newspaper headlines in a story that claimed he had tried to sever his own leg. I received a letter from him dated September 24, 1968, in which he notes:

> "I came back home yesterday – feeling a trifle weak, but otherwise OK. The papers made a ghastly story out of it and where they got it all from I do not at all know."

He left his family home in Eastbourne and retired to Mullion in Cornwall, marrying a year or two later. He died suddenly at home in Buckfastleigh, Devon in September 1978. Despite the immense influence Bowen had on cricket historians of his day and indeed succeeding generations of historians, the fact that *The Cricketer* magazine confined Bowen's obituary to just 38 words, is indicative of the feathers he had ruffled.

Returning to *The Cricketer*, as has been mentioned its format was drastically altered in November 1962, but this was just the beginning of a major upheaval. According to E.W.Swanton it was apparently on a whim that Noel Holland and R.A.A.Holt of the book publishers, Hutchinson, decided to take over the publication. Richard Anthony Appleby Holt, born in Kensington in 1920, had captained the Harrow side of 1938. He played a few games for Sussex that year and in 1939. After Cambridge and war service he qualified as a solicitor and was appointed Chairman of Hutchinson's in 1959.

The magazine publishers, Mercury House, took over the reins from Hutchinson's in 1970, but soon discovered that the magazine was not viable and thought the only option was to close it down.

Ben Brocklehurst, the former Somerset captain, who was at Mercury House, decided to resign from the company, buy *The Cricketer* and in effect run it from the back garden of his house in Ashurst, Kent. He was destined to remain the owner of the title until it merged with *Wisden Cricket Monthly* in October 2003. Benjamin Gilbert Brocklehurst died in June 2007 aged 85.

So much for the tale of *The Cricketer*'s financial control, but of more importance to the cricket reading public and historians is the editorial staff and the actual content. It has already been noted (when the rival *Playfair Cricket Monthly* was launched) that E.W.Swanton became the

Editorial Director with Irving Rosenwater as the Assistant Editor. The latter resigned in 1967-68 and the new 'workhorse' brought in was C.D.A.Martin-Jenkins. Born in January 1945, Christopher Dennis Alexander Martin-Jenkins captained Marlborough in 1963 and then went up to Cambridge, where he failed to get a blue. After three years with *The Cricketer*, Martin-Jenkins moved to the B.B.C., where he remains as a member of the 'Test Match Special' team. He has also reported on cricket for the *Daily Telegraph* and *The Times*. Over the course of forty years Martin-Jenkins has been the editor or compiler of numerous cricket books, some of which will feature later.

Following the departure of Martin-Jenkins various journalists came and went in rapid succession. T.R.P.Scanlon was Martin-Jenkins' immediate successor – he lasted less than a year. In January 1971, Alan Ross is described as 'Acting Editor', then in March Robin Brooke-Smith becomes 'Assistant Editor'. By September H.A.Pawson, the former Kent cricketer, was labelled 'Deputy Editor'. – he was not the sort of person who wanted to run the magazine on a day-to-day basis.

Swanton and Brocklehurst needed a keen young enthusiast to do the hard work. Such a person, in search of a post in cricket journalism, had just landed from Australia. David Edward John Frith, born London in March 1937, had written a few articles for *The Cricketer* in the 1960s and in 1970 had published *My Dear Victorious Stod*, the biography of A.E.Stoddart of Middlesex and England. The book won the newly designated Cricket Society Literary Award.

In November 1972, Frith took over as Deputy Editor, with Pawson confined to 'Club News'. In less than six months Frith was upgraded to Editor, though Swanton remained as Editorial Director. What Frith did not immediately foresee was that Dickens Press, the owners of the *Playfair Cricket Monthly*, were keen to be shot of all their magazine titles, including the *Playfair*. Brocklehurst jumped at the opportunity to swallow *The Cricketer*'s only national rival. The two magazines merged in May 1973. Roy Webber had really been the initial powerhouse behind the *Playfair* and after his death, the magazine, still edited by Gordon Ross, had cruised. Part of the deal in taking over the *Playfair* title was that Gordon Ross was appointed Executive Editor of the new combined magazine; in addition a new quarterly magazine was launched titled *The Cricketer Quarterly*, which featured the detailed overseas first-class match scores that had always appeared in the *Playfair* magazine.

Sub-titled 'Facts and Figures', the new *Quarterly* in no way resembled Bowen's creation. In page size it was the same as the county annuals of the 1960s and ran to 80 pages. Gordon Ross was the editor and the statistical team was led by Michael Fordham. The first edition contained articles by such diverse figures as Neville Cardus, Irving Rosenwater interviewing E.W.Swanton, Ian Peebles and Mike Denness. Exactly half the magazine's pages had full scorecards or averages; in addition the first-class County scores and Currie Cup scores were potted. The fourth edition had a Who's Who of current county players by Michael Fordham, though Bill Frindall ran a 'Meet The Newcomers' piece in the three earlier editions.

Bill Frindall was the B.B.C. radio scorer, who had taken that job when Arthur Wrigley died unexpectedly in 1965. Born in Epsom, Surrey in March 1939, William Howard Frindall was educated at Reigate Grammar School and after briefly studying architecture joined the R.A.F. He left the service, by chance, just before the scoring vacancy appeared. He was to continue as B.B.C. scorer until his death in February 2009. His first article in *The Journal of The Cricket Society* appeared in November 1967; his first in *The Cricketer* in 1968. In 1970 he provided the Sunday League statistics for *Playfair Monthly* and in the same year his book *The Kaye Book of Cricket Records* was issued. This was in effect an update of Roy Webber's Record Book (this had been re-set and updated in 1961). Frindall would also update Webber's book containing all the Test match scorecards, but his most innovative publication was 'Frindall's Score Book', which reproduced his 'vertical' scoring system in book form for Test Matches, commencing with the 1975 England v Australia series. The previous Test scorer to use this format had been Bill Ferguson, who acted as scorer and baggage man for many Test touring sides, beginning with the 1905 Australians. He went on no less than 42 tours, ending in 1953-54.

Another statistician who joined the new *Quarterly* magazine was Barry Desmond Anselm McCaully. Born in 1933 he was a solicitor by profession. His name first appears in *Playfair Monthly* in 1967, when he provided the end of season statistics. He remained with *The Cricketer Quarterly* until 1985 and for three years(1983-85) was in charge of the Record Section of *Wisden*. Latterly he suffered ill-health and died in Poole, Dorset in November 1998.

Playfair Cricket Monthly ceased, as has been noted, in April 1973. Before passing on, a brief survey of its life is worthy of comment. The two feature writers who wrote articles throughout its existence were Rex Alston and Neville Cardus – the latter's essays were also reproduced in book form. Following Webber's death, Michael Fordham compiled most of the statistics. Gordon Ross, aided by other well-known journalists, wrote the Test Match reports. Serious historical essays came from Diana Rait Kerr from 1966 to 1971, and her successor at Lord's, Stephen Green, provided regular pieces from July 1970 to the closure.

The principal overseas correspondents were Frank Tyson from Australia (the former England fast bowler had taken a teaching post there), Rusi Modi from India and Geoffrey Chettle from South Africa. The Leagues in Lancashire were covered by Arnold Whipp, the B.B.C. scorer, who drowned whilst on a bird watching expedition in March 1968. From the statistical viewpoint, A.H.Wagg caused a fair rumpus when the full scores, which he had dug out of the Indian papers, of the 1930-31 Vizianagram matches, were printed in the magazine in December 1962. These games featured not only the leading Indian players of the day, but also J.B.Hobbs and H.Sutcliffe. The arguments as to whether these matches rank as first-class or not has rumbled on ever since.

Many of the letter-writers to the magazine were the same familiar names, also found in *The Cricketer* – Irving Rosenwater, Jack Burrell, Rob Brooke, Leslie Newnham, Tony Woodhouse, H.S.Scales and Gordon Tratalos are examples. Some of these have been noted previously, some will appear later, but a word about Jack Burrell; he first came to the notice of the cricket reading public with his column 'In The West'. This began in *The*

Cricketer in 1957 and ran until 1963. It concentrated on club cricket in the Bristol area. In 1960, Burrell launched *Who's Who in the Minor Counties*, a typed and duplicated annual which gave brief biographies of many current Minor Counties cricketers. It continued until 1976 when it merged with the ACS *Minor Counties Cricket Annual*. Another project he founded was 'Find-a-Pro' designed to assist local clubs in search of a professional. His letter writing to *The Cricketer* began in 1957 and continued until 1999. Burrell's only hardback book *Sides & Squares*, a history of Clifton C.C., published in 1983, is a typical example of the detailed research which he really enjoyed. Employed by the Bristol Parks Department through his working life, he died in Bristol in September 2001, aged 79.

Like *Playfair Cricket Monthly*, the annual issued under the same banner saw fundamental changes in the period under review. Through the 1950s the two principal English 'pocket' cricket annuals were *Playfair Cricket Annual* and *News Chronicle Cricket Annual*.

In the 1950s the full title of the latter was *News Chronicle & Daily Dispatch Cricket Annual*, but the *Dispatch* piece was removed in 1960. As has been noted it was edited by Crawford White and Roy Webber, ran to 192 pages (or thereabouts) and 4" by 5 ¼" in size. The *Playfair* from 1955 was edited by Gordon Ross, with statistics by Roy Webber, had 176 pages and was 5" by 7". In 1960 the *News Chronicle* publication cost 1/6d, the *Playfair* 6/-. The *Playfair* was a much superior production with good quality pictures, but the actual factual difference in terms of information given differed very little between the two books.

As has previously been mentioned, the *News Chronicle* folded in 1960 and for two years Webber edited *The Cricket Annual* using the *News Chronicle* format. The *Playfair Annual* continued for those two years unaltered. However for 1963, the Dickens Press took over the Playfair titles. The large format *Playfair Cricket Annual* disappeared and the *Playfair* name was attached to the former *News Chronicle Cricket Annual*. Gordon Ross, the editor, explains in his Introduction:

> "Since the two cricket annuals were published for the
> 1962 season, the Playfair titles have been taken over by

> The Dickens Press, the publishing branch of The Daily
> News Ltd, which owned the News Chronicle and The
> Star (the London Evening newspaper) until their closure
> in 1960."

It will be recalled that Roy Webber had died in November 1962. The only person credited with assisting Ross with the hybrid 1963 annual is Michael Fordham, but it is quite a hunt to discover where his name is mentioned.

Whilst these 'pocket' cricket annuals were changing and also the cricket magazines, there was no change for *Wisden*. The editor between 1960 and 1973 was Norman Preston; the compilation of the Record Section did change hands, though not the layout or content, other than updates. Copinger retired in 1963, Leslie Smith acted as 'updater' from 1964 to 1969, Irving Rosenwater took over for 1970 and then resigned as a matter of principle. He did not agree that the England v Rest of The World matches (played in lieu of England v South Africa) in 1970 should be considered as Test Matches.

Bill Frindall took over for 1971. To many cricket statisticians the job of updating the record section in *Wisden* was the pinnacle of a statistical career – the first port of call for anyone seeking to confirm a major cricket record was the section in *Wisden* and had been since Ashley-Cooper conceived the present basic layout prior to the First World War. It is curious that Frindall in his 2006 autobiography does not mention his appointment and indeed Rosenwater's name is searched for in vain in Frindall's book, very odd! Leslie Smith, mentioned above, worked for the Cricket Reporting Agency and from 1935 was drafted in to assist in the compilation of *Wisden*. He retired after the 1969 edition.

In the period 1970 to 1972 another attempt was made to publish popular histories of the first-class county clubs. The publishers were Arthur Barker and the books, hardback, between 160 and 200 pages in length, also had a variable picture section on art paper. It cannot be said that any of them contained much original research, the concentration tending to be 20th century cricket.

The books which were published were:

- Glamorgan by Wilf Wooller
- Kent by R.L.Arrowsmith
- Lancashire by John Kay
- Middlesex by E.M.Wellings
- Surrey by Gordon Ross
- Yorkshire by Mike Stevenson

Warwickshire by John Solan was advertised, but was never actually published.. Of the authors, Arrowsmith and Ross have been commented upon. John Kay, born in Middleton, Lancashire in January 1910, was educated at Durford School, joined the *Manchester Evening News* in 1926 and remained on that paper until 1975 when he retired. He contributed to *The Cricketer* notes and articles on league cricket in Lancashire from the 1950s to 1979. He went to Australia with the England touring side several times and published books on two of those tours. His most important book from the historical standpoint was *Cricket in the Leagues*, published in 1970. The work covered not only the Lancashire leagues but most of the other major leagues in the north of England. He remained as the *Wisden* correspondent for Lancashire until 1982. John Kay, who had been a very useful club cricketer in his younger days, died in February 1999.

Evelyn Maitland Wellings was born in Alexandria, Egypt in April 1909. Educated at Cheltenham and Oxford, he was awarded his cricket blue as an off-break bowler and appeared fleetingly for Surrey in 1931. Taking up journalism he was much feared in some quarters. It was noted that he 'reported more than 200 Tests with a trenchancy that has never been matched'. His principal work was for the London *Evening News*, which he joined in 1938 and retired from in 1973, going to live in Spain. He wrote a column, in his retirement, for *Wisden Cricket Monthly* in its early years. He wrote books on several Test series, but his only book of an historical nature was the one mentioned on Middlesex – it goes without saying that his Middlesex work was the liveliest of the Arthur Barker series.

Mike Stevenson was born in Chinley, Derbyshire in June 1927. Educated at Rydal and Cambridge, he appeared occasionally for Derbyshire. Initially he was a schoolmaster, but switched to journalism, reporting cricket and rugby for the *Daily Telegraph*. His articles for *The Cricketer* began on a regular basis in 1969. A great companion and brilliant cricket coach, he was a complete contrast to Wellings.

As a balance to these 'popular' county histories the more serious students of the game could purchase John Shawcroft's definitive history of Derbyshire, which was published to celebrate that county club's centenary in 1970. The book was well researched and the details clearly laid out – Frank Peach had whetted Shawcroft's appetite when the former gave a series of lectures on cricket in Derbyshire and then encouraged his 'pupil' to undertake the writing of the history. John Shawcroft was born in Derbyshire and, a journalist by profession, he was for twenty years the editor of the local weekly newspaper, *Ripley and Heanor News*. He wrote the historical essay on the Derbyshire County Cricket League for its 75th anniversary and the ACS book on *Derbyshire County Cricket Grounds*, published in 2008.

In the early 1970s John Goulstone published a series of typescript works which added considerably to knowledge of the history of the game. The most extensive of these was *Early Village and Club Cricket*, 126 pages in length. This was a catalogue of the first known references to cricket in many of the towns and villages of England and Wales. It was laid out alphabetically, county by county. In broad terms, it contained every reference known at that time, up to 1800, but some references after that date are included. This most valuable work remains the first source for anyone doing research on local cricket.

Two of Goulstone's books of this period are directly connected with Kent – *Early Kent Cricketers*(1971) fills in some of the voids in the biographies contained in Lord Harris's 1907 Kent History, but adds many new earlier Kent cricketers, whose details were hitherto unknown. *Cricket in Kent* (1972) includes several new match scores, biographies and cricket notices. *The 1789 Tour* (1972) is an oddity, in that it purports to add a great deal to the bare bones of this famous trip which is briefly noted by Haygarth in *Scores & Biographies*. However, unusually for Goulstone, the work is almost entirely speculative, rather than based on hard facts.

John Ford, a lecturer in English history at the United States International University, wrote *Cricket: A Social History 1700-1835* published in 1972. Although this work adds nothing to the known cricketing data, Ford has worked largely from Bowen's history and the standard reference books such as Buckley and Waghorn. He thereby builds a picture of cricket in the context of the general pattern of English life at the time.

In Australia another academic, Professor John Mulvaney, researched a cricketing subject not previously investigated, the story of the 1868 Aborigines Tour to England, *Cricket Walkabout*. This was published for the centenary of the tour. As a result of its publication much new source material, including the original account books of the tour, came to light. A second edition under the joint authorship of Mulvaney and Rex Harcourt was issued in 1988 – almost double the length of the initial edition, with the number of plates increasing from 12 to 39. It proved the famous Warsopian edict, 'never publish the first edition of an historical book'.

Professor Mulvaney had specialised in studying the history of the Aborigines. He was Professor of Prehistory in the Faculty of Arts at the Australian National University, having originally graduated from Melbourne University. Rex Harcourt also graduated from Melbourne University and was involved in Civil Aviation until he retired in 1980 when he became the Research Librarian to Melbourne Cricket Club.

In 1958, Roger Page published *A History of Tasmanian Cricket*. This broke new ground and remains the standard work on the subject. There are 28 illustrations, many not previously seen in publications.

Finally, in South Africa, Stewart E.L.West and W.John Luker celebrated the centenary of the Western Province Cricket Club. *Century of Newlands* was published in 1965. The authors regret that due to costs, the original manuscript had to receive a number of cuts.

Chapter 15
The Formation of the Association of Cricket Statisticians

The Cricket Society Newsletter for 1972 contained a note stating that R.W.Brooke and D.A.Lambert wished to form a statistical group within the Society's Midland Branch – this branch organised Society meetings at Edgbaston during the winter months (the main society meetings were held in London). The editor of the Newsletter suggested that Brooke and Lambert liaise with the Society's Statistical Officer, E.K.Gross.

An accountant and for 25 years the Chairman of the Council of the Institute of Administrative Accountants, Ernest Kingsley Gross was born in 1902 and in the 1920s was a useful club cricketer with Acton Town C.C. He had moved to St Ives in Huntingdonshire after the Second World War and had for many years been compiling lists of cricketing feats below first-class level. In the 1960s he had embarked on a 'statistical history of cricket'. Some of his work had been published by Bowen in *The Cricket Quarterly* and other pieces had appeared in the Cricket Society's own Journal. He had been appointed Statistical Officer of the Society by default. To explain how this state of affairs occurred, one has to return to the beginnings of the Society.

The Society's main publication from its foundation had been the detailed seasonal averages for English first-class cricket. However the Annual providing the season's statistics had ceased in 1960, because the *Playfair Cricket Annual* printed the identical information. The Society then decided to publish the detailed averages season by season for the inter-war years commencing with 1919. This had been one of the Society's original ambitions back in 1946, as the Chairman's Report for that year had noted:

> "Statistics. It is particularly unfortunate that it has still been found impossible to issue the first-class figures for the period 1919-1939 since so much painstaking work has been done by so many members. It was hoped that it would be possible to have these figures printed so that with financial support from the Society's current finances a very small contribution would be required from members. It would appear however that the cost of type-setting for such a mass of statistics is so high that the cost of printing is quite prohibitive."

On inspection however compiling statistics for 1919 was not straightforward, due to the numerous errors in the *Wisden* printed match scores of that season, so the Society decided to begin with the 1920 season. W.S.Conder had retired as the man in charge of the Society's statistical output in 1961. He was succeeded by Michael Fordham, who retired due to taking on extra work when Roy Webber died suddenly. For a year or two the statistical arm of the Society was almost in abeyance – members sent in compilations for publication in the Journal, but on an ad hoc basis. In 1965 Eddie Solomon was appointed 'Statistical Chairman'. He dusted off the files and appealed for members who specialised in a specific county to compile that county's player-by-player record for 1920. The resultant booklet was issued in 1966, unfortunately incorrectly laid out; Solomon resigned in haste and Gross reluctantly filled the vacancy.

Solomon's first published material had been a modest four page pamphlet containing the Gillette Cup Statistics for 1965. He had acted as scorer for Middlesex on odd occasions and in 1968 scored the Test Matches. For about 20 years Solomon served on the Middlesex C.C.C. committee, retiring in 1996. He also wrote a short history of Edmonton Cricket Club. He died in 2006.

Returning to Brooke and Lambert, they received little response to their suggestion of a statistical group within The Cricket Society, but undeterred they inserted the following advert in *The Cricketer* of October 1972:

"STATISTICIANS. Anyone interested in formation of 'Cricket Statisticians Association' contact Box No.226"

Several years before C.J.Fuke had asked readers (in *Playfair Cricket Monthly*) whether there was anyone who might be interested in such an organisation and asking them to contact him. Fuke cited the example of the National Union of Track Statisticians (founded in 1958) as the kind of group he wished to create. Seemingly he had no response. Christopher Fuke was the statistician for the Surrey Cricket Clubs Championship Association and collected all the match scores as well as providing the statistics for the annual handbook (founded in 1973) of the Association. He joined the ACS soon after its founding.

Brooke and Lambert provoked sufficient reaction to call for a meeting of possible members. Between 20 and 30 interested parties turned up at Edgbaston in April 1973. Among those present was Irving Rosenwater, who spoke eloquently against the formation of a Statisticians' Association, stating that those who were in attendance should work within the confines of The Cricket Society. He failed, but only by a single vote, to scupper the proposed new organization. The new society was formed and it was resolved by the meeting that it should be called 'The Association of Cricket Statisticians'.

Robert William Brooke was born in Solihull in 1940 and educated at Yardley Grammar School. His first publication, at the age of 19, was an eleven page statistical survey of the match series, Warwickshire v Worcestershire. He had his first letter printed in *Playfair Cricket Monthly* in March 1969, in *The Cricketer* in October 1971 and, a particular interest of his, contributed a first obituary notice to *The Cricketer* in December 1971 (that of I.W.Smith). Brooke is a Warwickshire man and he also was to become that county's statistician and librarian. His devotion to the history and statistics of cricket is absolute – a flaw has therefore been a difficulty in comprehending that not all members possessed his fanaticism. His career as a cricket historian will unfold as this narrative continues

Dennis A.Lambert was born in August 1934 and educated at Skinners'

School, Tunbridge Wells. An accountant by profession he was a very useful club cricketer and in 1973 he was living in Bulkington on the Leicestershire-Warwickshire borders. His principal cricket interest rests in Leicestershire – he was later became the official statistician for that County Club – and in overseas first-class cricket.

Having voted for formation, the meeting then elected a five-man Committee, viz Brooke (Chairman), Lambert (Secretary), Peter Wynne-Thomas (Treasurer), Philip R.Thorn and David Gallagher. It is perhaps worth noting that no one on this committee had reached the age of 40; quite a contrast to the first Cricket Society Committee all of whom were over 40 – the first President was actually 97!

It was not long before the newly formed ACS Committee realised that progress on 'First-class Cricket Records' could not be made until a definitive list of First-class Matches had been debated by the membership, agreed by the membership and published so that everyone interested in these matters could understand any figures which might emerge from the ACS. The lack of such a published list had bedevilled the compilation of understandable statistics since such figures had first been published.

The Committee began by looking at matches in the British Isles. The following major obstacles required examination of resolution:

- The status of Somerset and Hampshire before 1890
- From what dates should Ireland and Scotland rank as first-class
- Whether any odds matches should rank as first-class (there were members who doubted even the first-class status of 12-a-side games)
- The date from which first-class cricket should start.

In addition there were a number of specific matches whose status needed clarification. Lists of matches were printed in *The Cricket Statistician*, a quarterly journal which the ACS set up almost immediately and of which Brooke was the Editor. Members' comments on 'borderline' matches were received and there were heated debates at more than one General Meeting. In late 1976 *The Guide to First-Class Matches in the British Isles 1864-1946* was finally published. Perhaps the most important feature of this guide and one which was sustained through the subsequent guides was that there were notes on all 'borderline' matches explaining why the ACS either included or excluded them from its final first-class list. John Arlott reviewed the book in the 1977 *Wisden*:

> "It would be well, in the absence of any further evidence, and in the important cause of uniformity, if statisticians accepted this classification which, if not watertight – what such list could be? – is the product of careful study by as many dedicated researchers as might reasonably be wished."

It would take the Association another 13 years before guides to all the other countries playing first-class cricket were published, or 16 years since the first Committee embarked on the project. There would be even more heated discussion on some of the very tricky decisions required for some overseas matches, but such was the nature of the beast. Much later the ACS would define what was the first-class equivalent in terms of major limited overs matches. This latter exercise scarcely caused a ripple and was principally the work of Philip Bailey. These matches are 'List A'. The ACS as yet has not published a book detailing 'List A' matches with suitable notes explaining why borderline games are included or excluded.

Looking back in 2010 it seems almost ridiculous that the brotherhood of cricket statisticians, who had been arguing over the status of matches for sixty years, had not solved the problems of first-class status earlier.

Running parallel with the task of listing first-class matches was the project of trying to identify every first-class cricketer – obtaining basic biographical data and in some cases discovering whether two players, were in fact one man, whose surname had been mis-spelt, or initials incorrectly recorded, also the converse, where one man was in fact two separate individuals.

As an initial start, the Committee decided to tackle English players on a county-by-county basis. Warwickshire was chosen as the first county to be tackled since Brooke had been researching the biographical data of players for several years and had prepared the career records. The fact that Warwickshire first-class cricket began in 1894 avoided many of the problems of debatable first-class status in English matches and, in comparison with many counties Warwickshire had comparatively few players involved in overseas first-class cricket. Due to expense these county booklets contained only very basic biographical notes, though the players' career records were given both for the individual county and in all first-class cricket. Statistics in limited overs matches (already the most popular form of the game among spectators) were not shown, but the handful of players who had appeared for the county in only limited overs matches were listed separately. Matters however did not run as smoothly as was anticipated. Leslie Duckworth, a local journalist, had been commissioned by the county club to write a comprehensive history of Warwickshire C.C.C. Duckworth, born in Bradford in 1904, had been until retirement in 1970 the News Editor of the *Birmingham Post*; he was awarded the M.B.E. for his services to journalism. Writing this Warwickshire history was his retirement job. A personal friend of the Warwickshire Secretary, Leslie Deakins, he had followed Warwickshire since the 1920s. He was relying on the two semi-official County Club statisticians, Ted Hampton and Philip Pike (the Warwickshire First Eleven scorer) for the statistical 'facts' for the book. Hampton and Pike had done little or no historical research into Warwickshire. They accepted the statistics handed down by their predecessors and merely updated them.

Bowen had discovered the so-called facts 'handed down' were too often faulty. As Duckworth, aided by Hampton and Pike, prepared his manuscript, Brooke, inspired by Bowen's call for original sources to be researched, was correcting long established 'facts'. He then began to bombard Duckworth with his 'discoveries'. Duckworth was in a no win situation. He chose to stay with the data as handed down, so the official Warwickshire history differed from the first County book published by the ACS, causing quite a furore at the time. It was clear to the committee of the Association that established statisticians would not be persuaded overnight that the entire body of published 'first-class' statistics needed re-checking, where possible from original scorebooks or contemporary newspapers, and as result altering in many cases.

Duckworth died in Codsall, Staffordshire in July 1983; Ted Hampton, a good club wicketkeeper, died in Birmingham in 1980 aged 78. He had been supplying statistics to the County Club for insertion in the Annual Report for more than 30 years.

The principal organ of the new ACS, *The Cricket Statistician* was a much more lively publication than the more staid Journal of the Cricket Society and it quickly attracted contributors. Gordon Tratalos was appointed Brooke's Assistant Editor from Issue 15 and he contributed a regular column 'Records At Random' which featured a wide variety of topics. Tratalos, who suffered health problems throughout his life, died following a stroke in March 1985 aged 52.

The magazine seemed to open the floodgates for both historians and statisticians. After only twenty issues it had attracted nearly a hundred contributors – to give a sense of scale, the 156 issues of *Playfair Cricket Monthly* attracted about 250 correspondents in total and *The Journal of The Cricket Society* seemed to have the same 20 or so writers over 20 years.

Brooke published a potpourri of information from all over the world and compiled numerous articles and short pieces himself. His personality shines through every issue. The trenchant book reviews, for which he later became notorious, did not appear in earnest for several years. Brooke wrote personally to every new member of the ACS and almost shamed them into sending some article in for publication.

Many of the contributors to *The Cricket Statistician* have previously been mentioned – Rowland Bowen, Jack Burrell, John Ferguson, Leslie Fielding, John Goulstone, John Griffiths, Henry Holmes, John Marder, J.S.Milner, Leslie Newnham, Frank Peach, Irving Rosenwater, A.H.Wagg and Ernest Gross (he sent material on minor cricket for almost every edition and had resigned as Statistical Officer of The Cricket Society, since the act of forming the ACS had demonstrated how poorly the Society had treated statisticians in recent times).

One contributor to *The Cricket Quarterly* and founder member of the ACS, not mentioned so far in any detail, is Philip Thorn, who was born in

Surrey in 1937 and educated at Banstead Grammar School. He specialised in tracing biographical details of cricketers and his first letter to *The Cricketer* on that subject was published in 1951. Soon after that he began forwarding obituary notices to *Wisden*. In 1955 he informed the editor of the death of F.L.Fane. Unfortunately after it had been printed, it was discovered that the person who died was not the England Test cricketer, but his cousin. Wisden's editor, Norman Preston, declined to accept any further information from Thorn. Thorn continued his researches and in 1970, Bowen published in *The Cricket Quarterly* a very long list of cricketers' deaths that *Wisden* had missed, including many missed since Preston declined Thorn's help. Thorn tended to see everything in black or white – there were no shades of grey and therefore if he fell out with an individual, the falling out was absolute. An insurance consultant, Thorn was to continue to ferret out players' biographical details for the ACS until his death, which occurred in Colsterworth in May 2006. He built up a large collection of reference books such as public schools' registers and Army and Navy lists, as well as extensive telephone directories for both the U.K. and Australia as well as some West Indian islands and South Africa. His knowledge on biographical matters was formidable, but a softer approach to some of his fellow researchers might have made the ACS a more comfortable band.

Another original member of the ACS Committee was David Gallagher. He contributed to *The Cricket Quarterly* almost from its inception and had a particular interest in West Indian cricket. Due to his family commitments he was unable to devote sufficient time to the ACS and therefore resigned from the Committee in its first year. He resides in Whitchurch, where he is employed in the printing industry.

A regular contributor to *The Cricket Statistician* from August 1974 was Brian Hunt, born in Bishop Auckland in 1947. His initial article was on wicketkeepers, but in 1975 he provided biographical data for many Minor County cricketers and this area of expertise was to remain his principal interest, the emphasis being on Durham's players. Since 1976 he has been the scorer for Durham, initially jointly, but from 1991 solely. He also scored for Bishop Auckland and in 1978 published an excellent history of that club. He is the official statistician and historian for Durham C.C.C.

From the viewpoint of general credibility, the ACS was fortune to have the immediate co-operation of Roger Page. Born in London in June 1936, he had emigrated to Tasmania with his parents and had attended the University of Tasmania, qualifying as an English teacher. He played cricket for the University and indeed helped to revive its cricket club. As has been earlier noted, Page wrote the first serious history of Tasmanian cricket in 1957. In 1964 he made his first contribution to *The Cricket Quarterly* and the following year became Bowen's main contact in Australia. He moved to Victoria in the 1960s and was a founding member of the Australian Cricket Society; later he joined that Society's committee. This new Society began by issuing a quarterly typed newsletter and from 1968 a Journal which would appear at irregular intervals through the 1970s. It was centred in Melbourne, but branches sprang up in other states and in Canberra.

Through Roger Page the Association of Cricket Statisticians began research on biographical data for Australian first-class cricketers using the same format as in the U.K., i.e. on a state by state basis. Again due to Roger Page the Australian membership of the ACS rose to over 100.

During 1974, the ACS published its second book on county players – Worcestershire by Timothy John Neilson, who was not long out of Worcester Royal Grammar School, having been born in Nigeria in 1957. He had organized an cricket exhibition in Worcester Library, containing many items that had gathered dust in the nooks and crannies of the County Ground for years. Worcestershire had only been raised to first-class status in 1899 and therefore, like Warwickshire, the difficult problems of match classification affected very few of their players. Soon after the Worcestershire book appeared, Neilson went off to pursue other non-cricketing matters.

The ACS had decided that one county book would appear every year and in 1975 Somerset was published (the classification of early Somerset matches had recently, after some blood-letting, been decided).

Whilst this flurry of activity was emerging from the ACS, The Cricket Society, in August 1974, appointed Derek Lodge as its new Statistical Officer. Regular statistical notes by him began to appear in the monthly Newsletter. Lodge had joined the Society in 1970 and in the Spring of 1974 won the inter-society quiz. Aside from The Cricket Society he sent a number of articles for publication in *The Cricket Statistician*. Derek Harry Alan Lodge, born in Lewisham in January 1929 and educated at KCS, Wimbledon, was a civil servant throughout his working life, latterly with the Office of Arts and Libraries. He was also a Lib-Dem local councillor and was later elected Deputy Mayor of Amersham. By the cricketing public he was probably best known for his column 'For The Record' printed as a regular feature in *Wisden Cricket Monthly* from the establishment of that magazine in 1979. In addition he provided regular quiz questions for the magazine. His various cricketing publications will be noted later. Derek Lodge died in Amersham in July 1996.

At the same time as the ACS was being founded, a new English cricket annual was launched, the *John Player Cricket Yearbook*. The editor was the England Test cricketer, Trevor Bailey – he was by 1973 a well-known cricket journalist and broadcaster – and the statistics were provided by Bill Frindall. The new production could best be described as a deluxe version of the original *Playfair Cricket Annual*. The first edition was 352 pages in length, cost £1.80 and had many black and white photographs, plus several colour sections. England Test Matches were given in fair detail; there were reviews and averages for each county; potted Championship and one-day county scores; reports from some overseas countries and minor counties and public schools.

The Who's Who of current County players was perhaps the most informative section. This gave the basic 'Playfair' style data and then several lines of comment. In 1977 the annual's title was changed to *World of Cricket*. The last edition appeared in 1980, by which time the price had increased to £4.95 and Graeme Wright was described as editing and designing it, though Bailey was still the main Editor. In the final years one of the faults was that the informative biographical comments on players had become very dated. The picture content throughout was provided by Patrick Eagar.

Leaving the English scene and reviewing early 1970s cricket publications overseas, in Australia another attempt to establish a national cricket annual, the *Australian Cricket Yearbook,* was attempted in 1970 with Eric Beecher as editor. He had founded *Australian Cricket* in November 1968, which was published six times a year. Magazine in style, the first edition of the annual had 138 pages. There were full Sheffield Shield match scores and full coverage of Australian major overseas tours as well as a good coverage of club cricket throughout the country. David Roylance was the principal statistician. The second edition included a Who's Who of current Australian players. Phil Tressider took over as editor in 1974 (he also took over editorship of the magazine *Australian Cricket*) – Phillip Lyle Tressider was born in Kensington, New South Wales in September 1928. He was a sporting journalist based in Sydney and had been educated at the Boys High School there. He died at Randwick on October 19, 2003. The publication changed its title to the *Australian Cricket Annual* in 1979.

An Australian journalist who was to publish a number of hardback books on cricket history was Jack Ernest Pollard, born Campsie, New South Wales in July 1926. He was the editor of *Cricket: The Australian Way* in 1961, but a much revised second edition appeared in 1968. This was broadly a coaching book, though Arthur Mailey provided some biographical sketches. Pollard had also written or edited books on tennis, rugby league, surfing and shooting, as well as a novel. In 1964 he edited *Six and Out* which was a collection of essays on many aspects of cricket by mainly notable Test cricketers. In 1971 came *Bumpers, Bosey, Brickbats*, which described controversies and oddities in the game. He had been based in London from 1947 to 1956, but then moved back to Australia, working for the *Sydney Telegraph*. His series of books on the history of Australian cricket appeared in the 1980s and will be noted later. Pollard died in May 2002.

An Illustrated History of Australian Cricket written by R.S.Whitington was published in 1974. A talented first-class cricketer, he was a journalist

Brian Croudy

William Powell

Brian Heald

Tony Woodhouse

Rex Harcourt

Irving Rosenwater

F.G.Peach on left with Derbyshire C.C.C. Supporters.

John Marder seated in centre.

Roger Page

Keith Sandiford

Ken Williams

Robert Brooke

"MR. JONES, WITHOUT YOUR GREAT UNCLE'S SURNAME, IT'LL BE DIFFICULT TO DECIDE WHETHER OR NOT HE PLAYED FOR US!"

Author at work.

B. G. Brocklehurst

Jack Pollard

John Arlott

E. W. Swanton

Ken Trushell

P.J.Bailey

Les Hatton

Peter Griffiths

David Lemmon   *D.R.Allen*

Ian Maun, Roger Heavens and Martin Wilson.

David Harvey

Derek Lodge

Jim Ledbetter

Dennis Lambert

by profession and had written a number of books in conjunction with Keith Miller, dealing with various Test series in which Miller took part. Whitington's History was a jump too far and was described at the time as 'slipshod'.

A broadcaster and journalist who takes more care and worries more about the nitty-gritty of cricketing data is Tony Cozier from the West Indies. Born in Barbados in 1943, he is the son of Edward Lloyd Cozier, who also was a journalist by profession. In 1970 he created *The West Indian Cricket Annual*. From the age of 20, Cozier junior was a regular West Indian correspondent for *The Cricketer* and like his father a well-known broadcaster. He published in 1978 *The West Indies: Fifty Years of Test Cricket*. This gave potted scores of Test Matches on a series by series basis and brief data on all the West Indian Test cricketers. Gordon Ross had published in 1976 *A History of West Indies Cricket* – a misnomer; the book really dealt with the same ground as Cozier's. The pre-1928 'history' occupied just nine pages.

The idea of books devoted to a single country's Test cricket seems to have been a fad of the 1970s. A.H.Carman, in 1975, compiled *New Zealand International Cricket 1894-1974* which covered much the same ground as Canynge Caple's *The All Blacks at Cricket 1860-1958*. Both used summaries of Reese's two volume history to cover the early years. In 1975 came two Indian books, *Indian Test Cricket 1932-1974* by Vijayan Bala (this appeared in several updated editions, the last in 1979) and *From Porbander to Wadekar* by N.S.Ramaswami which gives a little more space to first-class cricket, but not a great deal. In 1976 came Edward Docker's *History of Indian Cricket*. This neglects any deep analysis of the development of the game on the sub-continent and begins with the 1926-27 M.C.C. Tour to India. However Docker had done a considerable amount of research into such matters as the creation of the Indian Board of Control and the background to each Test series is well described. Edward 'Ted' Wybergh Docker is the son of the New South Wales cricketer, P.W.Docker (1886-1978); other members of the family also appeared in first-class cricket. In 1978 Ted Docker wrote a second cricket book *Bradman and the Bodyline*

Series – this was one of the better assessments of that notorious Ashes rubber.

Staying with Test cricket, David Frith was the compiler of *England v Australia: A Pictorial History* published in 1978. This was a volume which would be updated and reissued on several occasions. Frith is a fanatical collector of cricket memorabilia and the illustrations in the book demonstrate the depth of his interest and knowledge. Each Test Match is briefly described and in most cases has several photographs attached – there are about 1,000 illustrations, many of them appearing a book publication for the first time.

Frith was busy writing other less extensive volumes – *Archie Jackson* (1974), *The Fast Men*(1975), *Cricket Gallery* (1976). His book *The Golden Age of Cricket* has previously been noted. Despite this prodigious output (including his editorial work for *The Cricketer*) Frith maintained a very high standard of historical accuracy.

The other author renowned for his attention to detail, Irving Rosenwater, wrote three more short, but carefully studied, works in the later 1970s – *A.J.Gaston* (1975), *Cricket Books – The Great Collectors* (1976) and *Arthur Langford* (1977), then in 1978 came his magnum opus, *Sir Donald Bradman*. It is worth quoting Alan Gibson's review:

> "There is also a good deal of repetition in the book and, although it was in the nature of the exercise that we should have heaps of statistics, some of those in the text could have been switched to the appendix. Mr Rosenwater's style, though lucid, is prolix. I recommend to him one of Orwell's Rules for Writers: 'If it is possible to cut a word out, always cut it out.' This is curious because Mr Rosenwater is capable of writing a graceful essay, and is also a pleasant poet, and poetry is a disciple which should teach economy in words".

Despite this rather barbed review, Rosenwater's biography still remains pre-eminent. Later works have not improved upon it.

For bibliophiles, the standard work of reference was published in

1977 – *A Bibliography of Cricket* compiled by E.W.Padwick. The idea of a cricket bibliography had been mooted in the earliest days of The Cricket Society. J.D.Coldham had begun the initial work on the project; J.P.Everitt of Chingford then continued, but progress was very slow. Geoffrey K.Whitelock, who had written brief bibliographies of various county clubs for *The Cricketer* in the 1950s, took charge of the project in 1957 and the work gained some momentum. He was succcccded in 1966 by Michael L.Pearce, who had joined The Cricket Society in 1961. Born in Margate in May 1930 he was educated at KCS, Wimbledon and was an actuary by profession. In 1970 the decision was made to employ the expertise of a professional librarian, E.W.'Ted' Padwick, Deputy Librarian of the Guildhall Library. His most important research was undertaken at the library of Geoffrey Copinger, but also using the libraries of Tony Woodhouse, Hal Cohen, Alan McKay, Bob Jones and Jim Coldham, as well as the Lord's Library and its librarian, Stephen Green. A second expanded edition appeared in 1982, which included many more publications from outside the British Isles. As a result the number of items included grew from 7,000 to 10,000. For those who want more detail on how the work on the bibliography progressed, Irving Rosenwater published a short treatise on the subject entitled *The Padwick Bibliography* – this was issued in 2002.

One of cricket's most long-running and curious adventures began in 1975. Designed to run to 26 volumes *Hambledon's Cricket Glory* was researched and written by Ronald D.Knight. It tells the story of Hambledon village and its inhabitants, but centring on its famous cricketers. The individual volumes vary in quality and size. Not all the planned volumes were in fact issued. Those published were volumes 2 to 19, together with index volumes 26 to 28.

Two books dealing with first-class counties were published in 1977. Volume Two of Eric Snow's Leicestershire history followed very much the pattern of his first excellent work. Less ambitious than Snow's book was L.F.Newnham's *Essex County Cricket 1876 to1975*. Running to 93 pages it is sub-titled 'A Brief History'. Newnham's pride and joy in his book is the register of all Essex players, though the brief biographical details lack statistical records. Newnham was an ultra-cautious researcher, famous for his frequently stated remark, 'Wisden has yet to publish an error-free Essex match scorecard in its almanack.' He was loathe to provide any data unless he was absolutely sure of its authenticity, which is an excellent ideal, but carried to extreme means that little ever would appear in print. A local Government Housing Officer from Malden, he had joined The Cricket Society in 1959 and the ACS at its foundation. He wrote occasional critical letters to both *The Cricketer* and *Playfair Cricket Monthly* in the 1960s, but his principal cricket work was for the Essex Yearbook. He was the county's official statistician for 15 years, prior to his death, which occurred in Chelmsford in June 1987 – he was aged 67.

Robert Brooke, on behalf of the ACS, took over the *Minor Counties' Who's Who* (founded by Burrell in 1960) in 1976. After several changes of format, the ACS went into partnership with the Minor Counties Cricket Association in 1984 to publish the annual under the title *Minor Counties Cricket Annual and Official Handbook*. This was edited by the M.C.C.A. Secretary David Armstrong, but the current players' biographies were compiled by Brian Hunt, the averages and potted scores by Robert Brooke and career records by Richard Holdridge. David Armstrong was born at Thorpe St Andrew Rectory, Norwich in August 1936. He was educated at St John's, Leatherhead and Selwyn College, Cambridge. He took up teaching as a career, with 20 years spent at Beeston Hall School in Norfolk. In 1967 he was appointed Hon Secretary to Norfolk C.C.C., before becoming Secretary to the M.C.C.A. In 1958 he wrote a brief history of Norfolk C.C.C. – this reappeared in an expanded and revised version in 1990.

Richard Holdridge studied at Durham University before qualifying as a Chartered Accountant, then founding his own professional training business. He is now the official historian to Leicestershire C.C.C.

In 1988 Ken Trushell took over as the biographical researcher for the Minor Counties Annual. As Hon Treasurer of the ACS and Assistant Secretary to Lincolnshire C.C.C., Trushell had been instrumental in linking the ACS Minor Counties publication to the M.C.C.A. Annual. Kenneth Scott Charles Trushell was born in Grimsby in 1926 and resided in that part of Lincolnshire all his life, being employed in the Courtaulds factory there. He had joined The Cricket Society in 1956 and soon afterwards became the de facto statistician for Lincolnshire. He had joined the ACS in its first year and from 1974 contributed articles to *The Cricket Statistician*. Developing out of his interest in his own county's cricketers, he created his own Who's Who of all cricketers to appear in the Minor Counties Competition. He was editor of the Lincolnshire C.C.C. Yearbook from 1980 and in 1993 was largely responsible for the ACS book , *Lincolnshire Cricketers* He also was heavily involved in the *ACS Guide to First-Class Matches in Pakistan*. A methodical researcher, Trushell had been a very useful cricketer at club level and later was noted both as a ballroom dancer and table tennis player; he always looked on the sunny side of life. He died in Grimsby in April 2001.

In 1990 a rival Minor Counties yearbook – *The 1990 Guide to Minor County Cricket* – appeared edited by Mike Berry. A full time journalist, Berry was born in Leamington Spa, but was based in Northampton – he had been a semi-professional footballer and had written for *The Times* for six years before moving to the *Daily Telegraph*. In the winter he reported on Northampton Town FC. This new annual printed the detailed scores of all Minor County matches, but only survived for two issues. In 1996 Mike Berry, now the Publicity Officer for the M.C.C.A., was appointed editor of the Minor Counties Annual, though it was still produced by the ACS with Ken Trushall and Rob Brooke as the main contributors. This marriage proved unsatisfactory and the 1997 issue was the sole production of the M.C.C.A., with Berry as Editor. He left the post in 2001 and Philip August took over the compilation.

In April 1977, Robert Brooke and Peter Wynne-Thomas launched *Cricket News*: a weekly review of the game. The magazine aimed to publish full scores of all first-class and county limited overs matches, as well as Minor County matches and County Second Eleven matches, plus weekly comments on the major leagues. There were monthly issues during the winter, in which a similar coverage of cricket overseas was attempted. The magazine really harked back to the magazine *Cricket* of pre-First World War days. The new publication survived two full years plus the 1978-79 winter, but folded in May 1979. The clock could not be turned back!

Unknown to the two founders, a new monthly English cricket magazine was to appear in book shops in June 1979.

Chapter 16
A Rival for The Cricketer

While the brief life of *Cricket News* flickered and died, there were quite substantial changes among larger English commercial cricket publications. The 1979 *Wisden* announced on its title page, 'Published for the proprietors John Wisden and Co Ltd by the Queen Anne Press Division, MacDonald and Jane's Publishers Ltd, Paulton House, 8, Shepherdess Walk, London N1 7LW.' Since 1938 the almanack had been published by Sporting Handbooks Ltd, a part of J.Whitakers of Bedford Square, London W1.

The new publishers retained Norman Preston as the Editor, but brought in Gordon Ross as Associate Editor and Graeme Wright as House Editor. Preston describes Ross as his old friend and his pedigree has previously been detailed. Graeme Wright has been mentioned in passing as an editor of the *John Player Cricket Yearbook* (another work published by Queen Anne Press), he originally trained as a banker in his native New Zealand, but arrived in England in 1968. The author of a number of general sports books, mainly related to football, but also the Olympic Games, he ghosted several biographies of sportsmen. Later he was appointed Deputy Editor of *Wisden Cricket Monthly*, but retired after nine months and somewhat later moved back to the *Wisden Almanack* as Editor.

Aside from the minor changes of personnel, the one alteration which readers noticed when the 1979 *Wisden* appeared was the disappearance of John Arlott as book reviewer, replaced by Gordon Ross. Whilst Arlott had commented on all the books which were sent for review, Ross surveyed a mere handful. This met with fierce criticism and Arlott was reinstated for the 1981 edition.

On the magazine front, David Frith was 'sacked' as editor of *The Cricketer* in July 1978 – those who knew Frith's personality had been surprised that he survived so long. He is too much of a free spirit for such an establishment posting. In his place Brocklehurst and Swanton opted for a safe pair of hands and appointed Reg Hayter, famous for never turning down the offer of a job. A sporting journalist, he was a non-stop worker, and whilst he had a reputation for producing readable copy on time and making certain the end product was in the bookstalls on time, he was not really the person to check and cross-check the cricketing minutiae on which *The Cricketer* had built its foundations. Reginald James Hayter was born in Paddington in December 1913, educated at St Marylebone Grammar School and, at the age of 18, joined the Cricket Reporting Agency. He moved on to become the principal cricket reporter for the Press Association. After the Second World War, Hayter, working for Reuter's, travelled overseas with several England Test sides. In 1955 he set up the independent Hayter's Agency. This was to become the largest sports agency in England and was to be a training ground for many a tyro sports reporter. Hayter, through knowing many sportsmen, then became an agent for sporting stars, notably, in the early days, Denis Compton. He is credited with writing several cricket books, but undoubtedly ghosted many more. Before the war he had been an active cricketer, playing chiefly for Stanmore. Hayter died in Northwood, Middlesex, in March 1994.

Whilst Hayter and his assistant, Alan Hughes, kept *The Cricketer* going, David Frith was not idle. He found financial backing to float a new magazine, *Wisden Cricket Monthly*, and persuaded a number of high profile cricketing figures to man the Editorial Board – John Arlott, Ted Dexter, David Gower, Jim Laker and Bob Willis. Patrick Eagar, the photographer, was poached from *The Cricketer*. All the new Board initially wrote columns, or pieces for the new publication, which, whilst concentrating on Test and first-class cricket, also had a leaning towards the history of the game; its obituaries and book reviews being a major feature, the latter mainly written by Frith. The first issue appeared in June 1979 – Frith had spent much of the 1978-79 winter in Australia covering the Ashes series. He was one of ten authors to have his account of the rubber published in book form. The general printing and layout quality of the new *Wisden Cricket Monthly* was more akin to the old *Playfair Monthly*, than to *The Cricketer*. Frith was also keen on the good reproduction of photographs. Historic photographs, not previously seen by the ordinary cricket reader, were to become a valuable addition as the magazine gathered momentum. It should be noted that Frith's venture was not a partnership with the *Wisden Almanack*. The two were entirely separate.

The ACS was also expanding its horizons and in 1978 published the first of its Australian state booklets – on Victoria. The researcher and author was Roger Page and his effort broke new ground for Australian cricket literature.

ACS members, now numbering over 1,000, were being increasingly frustrated in their personal researches by the continuing rise in price on the second-hand market of the standard research tools – *Wisden Almanacks* pre-1900 and copies of both Haygarth's *Scores & Biographies* and the magazine *Cricket*. The committee therefore decided to launch a series of first-class match score books, beginning with the season of 1864. The easy option would have been to simply copy the scores from the three sources named, but it was decided that newspapers and, where possible, original scorebooks should be scoured in order to add data not given in the standard cricket publications. So Robert Brooke volunteered to dig out such information as fall of wickets, close of play, toss, captains, wicketkeepers and as far as possible the correct identity of the 22 players – the lesser-known ones were often given incorrect initials, or indeed no initials in *Wisden*. The project was a new venture in cricket publishing – previous books had covered simply the scores of a specific club, or, of course, Test Matches. The ACS quickly discovered there was a demand for these scores (the books also included overseas match scores, some of which were very obscure). Over time the project was expanded, first, to include matches from 1801 to 1863 and then 1901 to 1914. Philip Bailey took over the research from Robert Brooke, and by 2008 the whole period from 1801 to 1914 had been completed. Major 18th century scores were published in 2010, edited by John Bryant and incorporating a good deal of new information unearthed by Keith Warsop and Martin Wilson.

With the demise of *Cricket News*, Robert Brooke moved to *The Cricketer* and beginning in October 1979 created a column 'Milestones'. which each month dealt with a topical statistical item and put it in its historical context. It was destined to run for over 25 years and be 'spun off' in book form. It might be assumed that Brooke's column was a response to 'For The Record', Derek Lodge's *Wisden Cricket Monthly* column (see Chapter 15).

1979 not only saw the breaking of *The Cricketer* monopoly, it also saw a rival to the *Wisden Almanack*. The last attempt at a comprehensive hardback cricket annual to vie with the venerable *Wisden* had been Dewar's in 1892. The new title was *Pelham Cricket Year* and it surprised the cricketing public by being in the bookshops before Christmas 1979, yet covering the 1979 English season in great detail. The price was £5.75 as against *Wisden* at £6.75. The English first-class season was treated chronologically with a report on matches played in a three day period, followed by the potted scores, except for Tests, when the full score was printed. A similar layout was used for the county one-dayers. Every player's record was given with innings, or bowling analysis in chronological order and then the columns totalled up and balanced with extras to the team total. The same treatment was given to the Australian and New Zealand domestic seasons, but the remaining countries were confined to internationals, except the 1978-79 England tour to Australia which is published in detail.

The editor of this volume was David Lemmon. A teacher of English, he decided to abandon his profession three years after *Pelham Cricket Year* was established and take the risky option of earning a living by writing cricket books – as a full-time occupation, with no other income, it was an option that no other cricket-minded person had tried, or if they had then they had failed. (Lemmon did write a book or two on theatrical subjects, but the great majority of his post-teaching career was in hardback cricket books). Most cricket books were written by journalists, the income from the books being a nice 'extra'. Even Ashley-Cooper had a regular cricket column and Rosenwater was for some years a scorer for radio or television.

Checking the credits for the information in the first *Pelham Cricket Year* it would seem that Lemmon compiled most of it. Frank Tyson, the old England cricketer, now domiciled in Australia contributed an essay on the Australian season and Don Cameron seems to have written the small New Zealand section. If Lemmon did in fact compile the rest, it was a mammoth undertaking and relatively error-free. The one area of *Wisden* into which Lemmon's book did not trespass was 'Cricket Records', nor did it tread on the toes of the *Playfair Annual's* staple diet of potted biographies for current players.

After three years, sponsorship from Benson & Hedges was secured, the page size increased, the number of photographs, including now colour spreads, also grew. Tony Lewis, the former England player and well-known broadcaster and journalist, came in as Associate Editor and Vic Isaacs' the Hampshire scorer, is thanked for his help with the statistics. Another three years and Brian Croudy, Brian Heald and Barry McCaully receive thanks for their statistical help.

By 1982, the blurb on Lemmon states that he is now the author of five cricket books, not including the Annual. That number would multiply by ten over the next two decades. Such a mass of work meant minimal original research – most of the books were either biographies or histories of some kind. Lemmon therefore relied heavily on the commonly available source material, but within that limit his books achieved reasonable accuracy. David Hector Lemmon was born in North London in April 1931. He served in the R.A.F. then joined Shell-Mex before qualifying as a teacher. He was an ebullient character, who enjoyed speaking at dinners and other functions. He had just signed off the 1999 edition of the B&H Annual when he died at home in Southend in October 1998 aged 67.

Although county One Day cricket had begun in earnest with the Gillette Cup in 1963 and been reinforced by the John Player League six years later, even in the mid-1970s, when One Day Internationals were up and running and the first World Cup was staged, cricket statisticians as a body paid almost no attention to the records being created by this new form of Limited Overs cricket. The ACS perversely declined to put any One Day records in its Journal. *Wisden* for 1976 gave a page each to the records in the Gillette and Player competitions, then in the following edition reduced the John Player League section from full scorecards to potted scores. Unhappy with this state of affairs, Terry Alcock and Christopher Fuke proposed a society devoted to One Day records only. The group was formed in 1977 with Alcock as Chairman. Three of the leading lights in what was titled the 'Limited Overs Cricket Information Group' were Les Hatton, John Stockwell and Victor Isaacs. The group published a quarterly Newsletter, as well as an annual which gave seasonal statistics in each major limited overs competition for all players. In 1981 a *Gillette Cup Record Book* was published and the following year a similar book dealing with the B&H Competition. In retrospect their most useful publication contained the full scores of the John Player League matches for 1976. The group merged with the ACS in January 1986, by which time most statisticians had accepted that 'records' for the One Day games were useful and in demand by broadcasters and journalists.

Concerning the pioneers of this new set of cricket statistics, Alcock and Fuke soon faded from the scene, but three others deserve more than a passing mention. Victor Isaacs was born in Glasgow in August 1944. After leaving school he enlisted in the Army, retiring back to civilian life in 1974 and in April 1975 was appointed Hampshire scorer – he was a supreme 'figures-man'. He took over as the county's official record keeper after the death of Desmond Eagar in 1977. Later he became one of the first users of a computer for the purposes of cricket records and certainly the first to type into a computer all the matches ever played by a single county. In addition he was one of the first to compile comprehensive records for One Day Internationals and was the joint compiler of several record books related to these games. As has been noted he was also involved in the statistics for the *B&H Cricket Year*. A man of decisive principles, he could be doggedly determined when he had set his stall out. He retired as Hampshire scorer at the close of the 2005 season. His son, Richard Isaacs, is also a scorer and statistician, but in the world of broadcasters.

A second One Day statistician of note was Leslie Walter Hatton, who was connected with Worcestershire, but became the self-appointed keeper of the John Player Competition Records, in which capacity he reigned unchallenged. He compiled the record section for the Player League match programmes, which most counties used. A major work by Hatton was the *John Player League Record Book*, published by the ACS in 1987 and in a revised edition in 1993. Born in Wolverhampton in 1934, Hatton was an engineering draughtsman and a semi-professional musician. He was elected to the ACS Committee in 1978, was the driving force behind the ACS County Grounds booklets and compiled the Worcestershire edition of that series. In 1988 he took over the editorship of the ACS First-Class Counties Second Eleven Annual and his efforts to try and identify every current second eleven player as well as the compilation of a record section were legendary. In the ACS Famous Cricketers series he compiled the book on Don Kenyon. Very industrious, Hatton was a person on whose loyalty one could always depend. He died of cancer in February 2003.

John Stockwell edited the Limited Overs Group Quarterly as well as being the Group's Chairman from 1981 to 1985. He took over from Brooke as the editor of *The Cricket Statistician* from January 1986, but was forced to retire from the job in December 1987, and from the ACS Committee (which he had joined in 1982) due to business pressures. John Winston Stockwell was born in Weston-super-Mare in September 1947 and educated at RGS, Worcester. A chartered quantity surveyor, he is currently a construction consultant. He provided the statistics for the Gloucestershire Yearbook from 1985 to 1995 and contributed statistical appendices to a number of other publications, but his chief contribution to the ACS was probably the founding of the series of Statistical Surveys which commenced with the season 1864. These surveys continued for some twenty seasons before being superseded by the internet cricket sites.

Away from the ACS, an important book on a subject not previously researched in depth, was *Quilt Winders and Pod Shavers* published in 1979. It told the history of the major cricket bat and ball manufacturers. The author was Hugh Barty-King, a full-time industrial and social historian, who was educated at Winchester and Cambridge University, where he obtained a history degree. He has numerous non-cricket books to his name. The foreword was by Irving Rosenwater.

In the same year Derek Birley's book *The Willow Wand* was published, and caused some controversy. Birley wrote it in the aftermath of the Packer revolution of 1977. He rushed through three hundred years of cricket history, pointing out that those 'in charge', mainly the establishment at Lord's, had been always at loggerheads with the noble peasants, who acted as the cannon-fodder of the first-class game. Such figures as Lords Harris and Hawke, Pelham Warner and poor Neville Cardus were the major culprits. The fact that cricket simply mirrors the age in which it is played never seems to have dawned on Birley and he cheerfully plucks quotations from such authors as Arthur Carr, to suit his rather dodgy arguments. Born in Yorkshire in May 1926, he was educated at Hemsworth Grammar School and Cambridge University. After various posts in education, he was appointed Deputy Director of Education for Liverpool in 1964, then moved to Ulster in 1970, eventually retiring as Vice-Chancellor of Ulster University in 1991. An abrasive, rather large man, who was determined to get his own way, he spent his retirement in Cornwall where he wrote a three volume work on sport in Britain and *A Social History of English Cricket*, which demonstrated that he had learnt little from the errors made in his 1979 work. Birley died in May 2002. In 2010, *The Wisden Cricketer* magazine named the 50 best cricket books of all time, as selected by 42 of its contributors. The fact that Birley's 1979 book was voted no.1, can only demonstrate the paucity of historical knowledge within the magazine and its writers.

Two well-known cricketers and journalists tried their hands at telling cricket's history in a limited space in 1979. Robin Marlar was the author of *The Story of Cricket* for Marshall Cavendish; Trevor Bailey wrote *A*

History of Cricket for Allen & Unwin. Bailey squeezes everything prior to 1945 into 37 pages, before expanding through the years in which he played. The book is well-illustrated, but it really ought to have been his personal view of post-war cricket. Marlar does allow more space for the pre-1945 section, then moves into a sort of mini-encyclopedia, with brief scores of all Test Matches and a rather random selection of biographies. The short record section is compiled by C.J.Bartlett. The latter was born in Beckenham, Kent in July 1931 and educated at Christ's Hospital. He spent his working life as a personnel executive with London Transport. Bartlett was a founding member of the ACS, having already been a member of The Cricket Society for twenty years. He served as a committee member of the ACS from 1995 to 2006 and was for sometime the editor in charge of the Famous Cricketers series, and author of several of those books. Invaluable as a researcher on many ACS projects, he spent long hours at Colindale Newspaper Library, or checking Births & Deaths Registers.

The ACS Famous Cricketers series was launched in 1986 with Derek Lodge's book on J.B.Hobbs, which laid out his first-class career innings-by-innings in addition to a short biography, though a similar work on Geoff Boycott compiled by Steven Sheen had appeared in 1982 published by Hamlyns. Lodge preceded Bartlett as the editor of the ACS series. Sheen was elected to the ACS Committee in 1995 and served until 2008, being Marketing Manager for much of that period. He was to compile three titles in the Famous Cricketers series – Tom Hayward, Stan McCabe and F.R.Spofforth.

Both Marlar and Bailey's books suffer from a disease which inflicts so many publications – faulty picture captions. The proof reading of these is always the last task before the book goes to print and the captions are the first words read by possible purchasers – always a critical goldmine for reviewers.

Queen Anne Press commenced a new series in 1979 under the title 'Wisden Cricket Library'. The first two books to appear were an anthology of pieces from Wisden between the years 1864 and 1900, selected by the musician Benny Green and the *Wisden Book of Test Cricket 1876-77 to 1977-78* compiled by Bill Frindall. This book of Test cricket was the first to include all Tests since Arthur Wrigley's work in 1965. Frindall, like Wrigley, but unlike Webber, did not include match descriptions. The one new feature was second innings batting orders, but close of play scores were not included. The record sections of both books are similar. There are quite a number of corrections to scorecards, largely due to the researches of Geoffrey Saulez, the Sussex and England scorer. Born in Farnham, Surrey in 1916, Geoffrey Gordon Alfred Saulez was a qualified accountant, who took early retirement to devote himself to cricket statistics. He worked as a scorer for the B.B.C. and as a result went on several tours with the England team. He also scored for Sussex from 1977 to 1981 and for Surrey in 1989. Unlike the general run of statisticians, Saulez was an accomplished cricketer and during the war played in a number of good class matches in India; back in England he was a prominent member of Camberley C.C. Over the years he built up a season-by-season record for all first-class cricketers and he submitted occasional articles to various cricket magazines. He was a member of both The Cricket Society and the ACS. Saulez died in December 2004.

Queen Anne Press under its 'Wisden Cricket Library' published two major reference works in 1981. Frindall was the compiler of the *Wisden Book of Cricket Records*. His was an update of his own 1968 *Kaye Book of Cricket Records*, but with Robert Brooke as his principal adviser. As a result there were many additions and corrections to the previous volume (famously an extra 311 'centuries before lunch') Frindall largely followed the ACS Guides to First-Class cricket; the British Isles, Australia and New Zealand Guides had now been published, but the more difficult subject of Indian first-class matches had yet to be tackled. However Frindall made the silly mistake of stating that only eleven-a-side matches could be first-class and then failing to follow this edict through, especially in the case of players' career records. A.H.Wagg is credited with advising on the Indian problem, but there is no mention of the 1930-31 Vizianagram matches, which Wagg, as has been noted earlier, had researched.

The second 'Wisden Cricket Library' reference volume was much more ambitious – *Wisden Book of County Cricket*. The publishers gave the strong impression that Martin-Jenkins was the author. In fact he only wrote a brief overview of county cricket and the great bulk of the volume was statistical – 85 pages of essay, 355 pages of records edited by Frank Warwick. The latter, described as 'for nineteen years sports statistician for the *Daily Mail*, was completely out of his depth. The original idea was that a simple letter to the 17 first-class counties would result in 17 sets of comparable statistics, including career records of all county players. It was a pipe dream. The commissioning editor, Adrian Stephenson, had a meeting with Robert Brooke and myself at the eleventh hour and an effort was made to fill the gaps and unify the end product, but the result was not entirely satisfactory. At least the statistics in the main conformed to the ACS Guides.

1980 saw the publication of a new edition of *The World of Cricket*, now sponsored by Barclays Bank. E.W.Swanton remained the General Editor; Melford was replaced as Associate Editor by Woodcock. The cricket correspondent of *The Times*, John Charles Woodcock was born in Longparish, Hants, in August 1926. Educated at St Edward's, Oxford and Trinity College, Oxford, his strength was his knowledge of the contemporary cricket scene. His books have been mainly on English Test series. He was to be appointed editor of Wisden in 1981. He now lives in retirement in his native village.

The two Assistant Editors of the revised volume were Tony Winlaw, who had performed the same role for the first edition, and George Plumptre. The latter replaced Irving Rosenwater, who had moved to Australia as scorer and statistician for Packer's TV Channel. Copinger continued as the book's official statistician. Rosenwater of course had to be ditched because he had joined Packer's 'circus', but Plumptre seemed an odd replacement. Born in 1956, educated at Radley and Cambridge, he was an expert on garden design and a regular contributor to *Country Life* – at various times he had links with Bonhams and Sothebys. A lecturer, author, editor and freelance journalist, he was hardly the man to seek out the quirky errors made by the dozens of contributors.

The layout of the new book was altered from a strictly alphabetical arrangement of subjects to a series of sections, such as 'Biographies', 'International', 'Counties' and so on. The colour plates of the first edition had gone, but there were numerous black and white illustrations. Whilst David Frith, in his review notes "is there a greater single reference book? I doubt it", Robert Brooke is not so generous, his review pointing out that many of the errors in the first edition still remained, and perhaps Rosenwater might have weeded them out. The selection of names for the biographical section was biased to the modern, though many early heroes were noted in the historical text.

However in the same year as the book made its appearance, *The Complete Who's Who of Test Cricketers* was published. Rather surprisingly this was the first time a single work contained essays, some rather brief, on every Test player. The author, Christopher Martin-Jenkins, acknowledges the assistance of Michael Melford, Jim Coldham and Geoffrey Saulez, as well as Mervyn Shaw in Australia and Anandji Dossa in India. An odd note in the Preface states:

> 'Some career figures will, for simple lack of records, never
> be complete, but wherever possible the figures of any
> players who have reached a significant number of runs,
> wickets or catches have been given.'

The compiler has elected only to give a year of birth (and death if appropriate) for each player, thus side-stepping the problem of finding further data such as birthplace. Perhaps he should have omitted all first-class career figures?

On a more modest scale, 1981 saw the publication of the first cricket book by David Rayvern Allen. *A Song for Cricket*, issued by Pelham Books was, as the title implies, a history of cricketing songs. These had been particularly popular in the pre-First World War period. The author listed over 500 titles and the book runs to 219 pages with ample illustrations. Allen, who now has over 30 cricket titles to his name, was briefly a professional pianist after his National Service, but soon joined the B.B.C. where he spent the majority of his working life as a producer, often involved in programmes with musical connections. His second cricket book was even more obscure than the first and is mentioned at the very start of Chapter 1: *Samuel Britcher – The Hidden Scorer*, a 16 page booklet issued by J.R.Batten, a cricket book dealer. (it was in fact a reprint from an article published in *The Journal of The Cricket Society*). This work was expanded twenty years later into a sumptuous multi-volume production in the M.C.C. Library series, published by Christopher Saunders. The new tome reprinted all of Britcher's match score books, as well as Allen's revised work. Also in 1982 on a better-known subject, he wrote the biography of Sir C.Aubrey Smith, the actor and cricketer.

Two other writers, previously unknown in cricket book circles, had their first volumes published in 1981. Dr Michael Down was a lecturer at Nottingham University (and captain of the staff cricket team) when he researched his book *Archie* – the biography of A.C.MacLaren. By the time the book appeared the author was a scientist working in Pittsburgh, but in later years he returned to England and set up a business selling cricket books and publishing occasional high quality titles, including *Sketches at Lord's*, which reproduced the historically important Anderson lithographs of Victorian players. In *Archie*, apart from detailing MacLaren's cricketing career, which was well-known, Down dug into his not so illustrious business life which showed fecklessness and an unpleasant streak of arrogance. Down's only other historical work was the 1985 work *Is It Cricket?*, a review of English cricket since 1945, with particular emphasis on the financial and political aspects.

The second author is Eric Charles Midwinter, born in Manchester in February 1932 and educated at Cambridge University and at Liverpool. His book was *W.G.Grace. His Life and Times.* Both books were published by George Allen & Unwin, but there the similarity ends. Whilst Down concentrated on MacLaren the person, Midwinter concentrated more on the era in which Grace lived and added almost nothing to the actual life of W.G. which had not previously appeared in A.A.Thomson's biography of 1957. Midwinter had a degree in history – Down's degree was a scientific one – the difference shows. Midwinter went on to publish further cricket titles, but he was best known in cricketing circles as an active President of the ACS between 1997 and 2004, when his diplomatic skills were valuable in keeping the Association strong.

The Encyclopedia of Australian Cricket was published in 1980. The author was a journalist Malcolm Andrews, who had been the editor of *The World of Cricket* (the monthly magazine which ran from 1973 to 1979). The encyclopedia was not very profound and really required someone of Rosenwater's stature to fill the holes.

Chapter 17
The Booming Market for Cricket Books

The 1980s saw commercial cricket books by mainstream publishers grow in number through the entire decade. In 1981 33 cricket books were readily available in U.K. bookshops, by 1989 that number had risen into the 80s. These figures do not include reprints, of which there were a considerable number and do not include, of course, local annuals or the works issued by the ACS, nor are overseas books included except in cases where those books could be easily obtained in the U.K.

John Arlott continued to review all the titles submitted to *Wisden* and in the 1988 edition wrote:

> "The review, of 91 cricket titles, contains the largest number of outstanding contributions to the literature of the game issued in a single year. That is not reckoned since the beginning of this feature in *Wisden*, but through the history of cricket writing …. These publications embrace a number of quite unique contributions to writings on cricket, and the quality is uniformly high."

With hindsight it is difficult to agree with the final statement, for there were the usual clutch of ghosted autobiographies and 'compendium' works – 20 best batsmen, 50 great bowlers, 25 famous matches etc. – many of which were cobbled together to build up a publisher's cricket list.

The urge to publish also led to the duplication of two types of reference book. The first was a new style of 'record' book, breaking away from the Ashley-Cooper, Webber type with columns of statistics, providing lists such as every double-century, or every hat-trick. Instead there was a more detailed analysis of the actual current record, with illustrations where appropriate. Both books were published in 1983.

The Guinness Book of Cricket Facts & Feats by Bill Frindall and *The Hamlyn A-Z of Cricket Records* by the present writer, Peter Wynne-Thomas, both followed the format set out, on different subjects, by the two publishers. David Frith, in his review, suggests that the two books are on a collision course, but in reality, though both nominally covered the same ground, they were completely different animals. Both sold well enough (such was the demand for cricket titles) that the publishers later issued revised editions. The Hamlyn book stayed strictly with the A to Z format of the original *World of Cricket*, whereas Guinness split its book into sections, rather on the lines of the revised *World of Cricket*.

The second major 'clash' also involved the Hamlyn publishing group. Hamlyn commissioned Philip Bailey, Philip Thorn and Peter Wynne-Thomas to compile a book containing the basic biographical and statistical data on all cricketers, who had played in a first-class match in the British Isles from 1864 and to include the most notable players of the pre-1864 era. The book was to appear as a single volume.

Collins Willow commissioned Robert Brooke to compile a similar work but starting in 1744, though this would be issued in a number of volumes.

The Hamlyn Who's Who appeared in 1984. Reviewing the work, David Frith was generally happy with the end product, save for two points, firstly that each entry was given the forenames as they appeared on the relevant birth certificate – no nicknames were shown and no indication that players were sometimes better known by their second forename – secondly that the statistics adhered to the ACS Guides on first-class cricket and therefore both J.B.Hobbs and W.G.Grace were shown to have played in a different set of matches to those printed annually in *Wisden*. The book, over 1,000 pages in length, retailed at £30 and was published in conjunction with the ACS.

Collins Willow decided to issue a first volume covering players since 1945.

The one major difference from the Hamlyn version was that the statistics were in a separate section from the biographies – Hamlyn combined the two. The book appeared in 1985, priced at £25. The companion volumes never appeared, but the Hamlyn book was revised and updated in 1993.

The statistics in the Hamlyn book were almost entirely the work of Philip Bailey. Born in Epping in 1953, he was educated at Eltham College and Churchill College, Cambridge, where he read mathematics. At the time of the publication of the book he was employed as a computer programmer with the London Borough of Lewisham. He joined the committee of the ACS in November 1973 and apart from a six year break has served on the committee ever since, being (in 2010) easily the longest-standing member. Richard Streeton gave a profound description of Bailey in the 1993 history of the ACS:

> "Bailey, a quiet, retiring man, and a perfectionist by nature, would be nominated by most of his peers as possessing the most phenomenal brain for cricket statistics in the business. Bailey's mind invariably seems more agile than anyone else's where figures are concerned and his memory is extraordinary. He has had a hand in the majority of the statistics in ACS booklets and has also revelled in tracing birth and death certificates and other sources for previously unsuspected information."

He is certainly the outstanding cricket statistician of his generation and, in the opinion of the author, of all time. Statisticians since the 1930s had been checking the printed scores in *Wisden* against other sources in a piecemeal way, but Bailey set himself the task of checking all these scores against all the extant county scorebooks. From 1999 he was given the task of updating the first-class record section in *Wisden* and in more recent years has been the main provider of all records for the almanack. When the internet site Cricinfo began to build an historic base for all major cricket matches, Bailey left Lewisham Council to become fully involved in the Cricinfo programme. With the setting up of another cricket internet site CricketArchive, he moved to the new organisation and is constantly working not only to keep the site up-to-date, but also trying to reduce the number of errors in the scores which are held there. He was editor of *The Cricket Statistician* from 1988 to 2005. Apart from cricket, his other major interest is bridge. He has been chosen for England trials, having also represented Cambridge University and Kent.

As was noted in Chapter 15, Padwick's *A Bibliography of Cricket* was completed as a revised second edition in 1982, but was not actually published until 1984 and then in association with J.W.McKenzie, the leading secondhand cricket book dealer. The format was unaltered, Michael Pearce of the Cricket Society continued to be a major helper and Padwick also specially thanks Pat Mullins in Australia and S.S.Perera in Sri Lanka.

With the most obvious aspects of cricket's off-the-field interests now captured between book covers, those delving into the game's past began to explore new aspects of research.

Certain collectors had long been interested in cricket as illustrated in oil and water-colour. In 1941 a limited edition book had been published containing the paintings owned by Sir Jeremiah Colman. In 1955, the same publishers, Batsford, issued *The Game of Cricket* 'illustrated by a series of pictures in the museum of the Marylebone Cricket Club, principally from the collection of the late Sir Jeremiah Colman'. There was an introductory essay by Sir Norman Birkett and notes on the 34 paintings are by the M.C.C. Librarian, Diana Rait Kerr. The book is a splendid first dip into the world of cricket pictures.

The Noblest Game by John Arlott and Neville Cardus was published by Harrap in 1969, then reissued in 1989 by Bloomsbury with a new piece on cricket prints. There were 64 full-page colour illustrations, with descriptions of each on a facing page; the majority of the pictures are lithographs.

In 1982 a more specialist volume of pictures was published. For a number of years collectors had sought out the full-page cartoons in colour, which had been published in the weekly magazine *Vanity Fair*. Indeed they had a popularity among collectors almost from the first edition in 1869 with a cartoon of Disraeli. John Arlott was among the first to attempt a list of cricketers who had been featured. *The Cricketers of Vanity Fair* was a volume which it claimed contained full-size colour illustrations of all the cricketers. The author was Russell March. He had written occasional cricket articles for the press and in 1985 compiled a similar *Vanity Fair* book on jockeys.

In 1983 *John Player Art of Cricket* was issued by Secker & Warburg in conjunction with Imperial Tobacco. The authors were Robin Simon and Alastair Smart. It was the first book to attempt a comprehensive listing and illustration of cricket paintings as a genre. However the authors warn:

> "It (the book) makes no claim to completeness, but it does comprise nearly all the examples of cricket art of the eighteenth and nineteenth centuries that we have found most interesting".

Both authors had been lecturers at Nottingham University, Simon lecturing from 1972 to 1978 on the History of Art and Smart being Head of the Fine Art Department from 1956 to 1982. The book begins with a short essay on the early patrons and players and contains some minor errors. However a second essay on early pictures has great merit in that it unravels the myths with which previous writers had drowned Francis Hayman.

The book contains 32 colour plates and more than 100 monochrome. 163 pictures are given their provenance and there are notes on most artists, though details of the artist featured on the front cover eluded the authors. The book's major fault is the incomprehensible index. An exhibition of some of the paintings illustrated toured the country when the book was launched – Robin Simon expressed the view that a number of the paintings collected by Sir Jeremiah Colman were possibly 'fakes'. This caused something of a stir at the time.

With interest in cricket pictures and other artifacts related to the game, a new society was formed in October 1987, the 'Cricket Memorabilia Society'. Don Crossley was elected as Chairman, Tony Sheldon as Secretary, Keith Hayhurst as Treasurer, Anthony Collis as newsletter editor and Gordon Phillips as publicity officer. Its first quarterly magazine was published in June 1988. Within a year, Keith Hayhurst had taken over as editor and he remains the leading light of the organisation, which has proved a great success. In recent years, its quarterly magazine has devoted much of its space to reports of the many cricket memorabilia auctions which are now very much a feature of cricket collectors' lives. Keith Hayhurst effectively created the museum at Old Trafford in 1983 and was elected to the Lancashire County Cricket Club in 1988. He is also the county's honorary historian. He was author of *The Pictorial History of Lancashire County Cricket Club* published in 2000.

Gordon Phillips was the joint author of a book entitled *The Wisden Book of Cricket Memorabilia* which was published by Leonard Books three years after the Memorabilia Society was founded. The volume immediately became the textbook for anyone entering the world of cricket 'collecting' and was sub-divided into the various categories favoured by collectors. John Gordon Picton Phillips was born in Rhodesia in 1936 and emigrated to England in 1965. He joined *The Times* in 1970, retiring in 1982. He died in February 2003. His co-author was another *Times* employee, Marcus Williams. Educated at Oxford, he had begun his journalistic career with the *Oxford Mail*, before moving to *The Times* in 1980. He had a particular interest in postage stamps which had a cricketing connection and from 1980 to 1985 compiled a column in the *Wisden Cricket Monthly* on the subject. He also reported on cricket memorabilia auctions for *The Cricketer* during the 1980s.

Williams and Phillips were the joint authors of two volumes related to *The Times*. The first, *Double Century,* was a book of cricket extracts from the newspaper and the second a book containing cricket writings from the letters column.

Continuing the memorabilia theme, *Glorious Innings* appeared in 1987. This book compiled by Richard Bouwman featured the 'treasures' in the possession of Melbourne Cricket Club. At the time it was published Bouwman was Research Curator with the Australian Gallery of Sport at the Melbourne Cricket Ground. He was a graduate of Adelaide University and a former schoolmaster.

To follow the Melbourne book came *Treasures of Lord's* by Tim Rice, the well-known composer, published by Collins in 1989. There are quite a number of unfamiliar coloured illustrations.

If books on memorabilia were proving popular, then the same could be said of the statistical works issued by the ACS. Despite the existence of *Wisden*, the *Playfair Annual* and the *B&H Cricket Year*, no annual publication provided up-to-date career data for all the world's first-class cricketers. In 1985, the Limited Overs Statistical Group decided to merge with the ACS with the proviso that the ACS dropped its long standing attitude to 'One Day' statistics. The result was the inclusion in an annual containing all current first-class cricketers of their records in One Day matches as well as their first-class data. *The ACS International Cricket Yearbook* was first published in 1986 in conjunction with Hamlyns. The joint compilers were Philip Bailey, John Stockwell and Peter Wynne-Thomas. After two years Hamlyns decided the work was not a commercial proposition and from 1988, the ACS published the annual under its own imprint. In 1989 Philip Bailey became the sole compiler. The first issue contained 224 pages, but such has been the growth in top-class cricket that the 2010 edition had grown to 420 pages, though this does include nine pages detailing the careers of the leading women cricketers.

The year before this annual was launched the ACS first published a book containing the biographical details of cricketers who appeared in the First-Class Counties Second Eleven competition in the previous season – in effect it was a brother of the Minor Counties Annual issued by the ACS. The idea had been proposed by the Derbyshire statistician, Frank Peach; John Featherstone, who had been elected on to the ACS Committee in 1982, was appointed as compiler and editor. In 1985 he also took on the role of ACS Marketing Manager. Although born in Lincolnshire, Featherstone spent most of his life in Yorkshire and was employed by the Leeds City Council. A keen supporter of Yorkshire he was editor of Yorkshire's official magazine, *White Rose*. For five years he acted as Secretary to the Women's Cricket Association. He died in Dover, on the way to watch a soccer match, in February 1998, aged 59.

Another ACS series that was launched at this time (it was briefly alluded to under Les Hatton's biography) was the County Grounds series. Thus far there had been only one book that described in any detail the county grounds and this was Yardley and Kilburn's Homes of Sport : Cricket. The book confined itself to county grounds in current use (1952). This and Meynell's more limited volume have been noted in Chapter 10. Peebles had a book on Test Match Grounds published in 1967 and Alwyn Sampson was responsible for *Grounds of Appeal*, which contained the most charming sketches of county grounds, but again only those in use.

The ACS plan, on a county-by-county basis, was to give the detailed history of every ground ever used by the county team in a first-class or One Day equivalent, in a given county. It was an ambitious project. The series began with Nottinghamshire in 1984 by Peter Wynne-Thomas, followed by Worcestershire in 1985. As with other ACS series the books increased in detail as the years went by. The outstanding volume in the first ten years was Howard Milton's Kent. Milton commenced his book with the Dartford Brent ground of 1709 and the long history of county cricket in Kent meant much more detailed research than counties such as Nottinghamshire or Worcestershire. A professional librarian with the Ministry of Defence, Milton was appointed librarian to the Cricket Society in 1977 (a post he still holds) and from 1986 he took over responsibility for the Record Section in the Kent C.C.C. Yearbook (another position he still holds). He was responsible for Appendix I 1964-1984 of the History of Kent. In the ACS Famous Cricketers series, he compiled books on *F.E. Woolley* and *Lord Cowdrey*. He also wrote a separate history of the Bat & Ball Ground at Gravesend. It should be mentioned that the County Grounds series also contains photographs of each ground, or the site of each ground. Many of the photographs for the early books in the series were taken by John Featherstone. Unlike the original ACS County series, it was found impossible to maintain the publication of these County Grounds books on an annual basis and therefore 25 years on, two or three counties still remain to be researched and published – the original County series was completed in 1990 with the appearance of Sussex.

Whilst on the subject of the ACS it is worth noting that in 1987, the Association elected Richard Streeton as its first President. A keen cricket statistician, he was a cricket correspondent for *The Times* and was considered by his colleagues in the press boxes of county grounds and, indeed of many grounds overseas, as he toured with England, as the man to turn to for guidance on historical matters, especially those related to 'cricket records'. His only cricket book, a biography of P.G.H.Fender, won the Cricket Society Literary Award in 1981. Streeton was able to write it due to the prolonged strike which closed *The Times* for some months. Educated at King's School, Canterbury, Streeton (born 1931) commenced his journalistic career in the Midlands, notably on the *Nottingham Guardian*, then moved to Reuters before moving to a permanent spot with *The Times*. He was President of the ACS for ten years and worked conscientiously for the betterment of the Association, continuing to do so, even after his ten years in office ended. He died in Devon in 2006.

Moving from the ACS to the Cricket Society, the latter published no more major works following the issuing of the bibliography. The main publication therefore through the decade was the bi-annual Journal. Jim Coldham announced his retirement as Editor, after a fourteen year stint, in March 1984. The post was taken up by Clive Porter. Educated at Felixstowe Grammar School and Kent University, he was a schoolmaster based in Kent. He had occasionally performed the role of scorer for both radio and television. His only cricket book to date has been *The White Horse and the Kangeroo, Kent v Australians 1882-1977* which had been published in 1981. Between 1983 and 1985 he had a monthly series in *The Cricketer*, each month giving short essays on batsmen who had scored 100 hundreds. He was also an occasional letter writer to both *The Cricketer* and *Wisden Cricket Monthly*.

Another society which aspired to publications beyond the mundane society news was the Adelaide branch of the Australian Cricket Society. Its magazine *Cathedral End* was launched in January 1978 and was greatly expanded when Chris Harte became Editor in 1981. Harte then moved on to be editor of the *Australian Cricket Journal* which covered the Australian Cricket Society's branches throughout the continent. The Journal appeared between 1985 and 1990. In content this magazine was a cross between *The Cricket Society Journal* and *The Cricket Statistician*. Christopher John Harte was born in England, but moved to Australia in 1974. A journalist, he wrote several books on cricket tours as well as contributing to a variety of publications. In 1987 his book, *The History of The Sheffield Shield,* was published, the first comprehensive history of that competition. Harte gives potted scores of all the matches and nearly another hundred pages of statistics and tables. There is also a summary of the pre-Shield inter-colonial matches and a detailed essay on how the Shield competition was established through Lord Sheffield. The book is a good summary of the Shield and, as is indicated, is well supported with statistics. Harte next turned his attention to his adopted state and in 1991 published *The History of the South Australian Cricket Association*. Lavishly illustrated, its account of the Association is culled from the extant Minute Books and the local press reports. There are brief biographies of the players, with career records. Harte raised a number of controversial points, which upset the South Australian cricket authorities though he had been commissioned by the Cricket Association to write the book. He was taken to court for stealing 1,009 copies of the book, together with photographs and films, from the Cricket Association. Harte claimed that the photographs were going to be thrown away and that he took copies of the book because he had not been adequately paid. The court found in favour of the Cricket Association. Harte was given a 10-month suspended jail sentence and fined $A1,000, as well as paying $A20,000 in restitution.

Harte was also writing *A History of Australian Cricket* and this was published by Andre Deutsch in 1993 (it was part of a series of histories by the publishers). The book was written in a style more appropriate to the tabloid press, with suggestions of scandals that were not always supported by hard evidence. Harte returned in the early 1990s to live in England.

Harte's book in fact covered much the same ground as Jack Pollard's multi-volume Australian history. The first volume – *The Formative Years of Australian Cricket 1803-1893* – appeared in 1987 and ran to 344 pages. Pollard had covered much of the ground in his earlier writings, but the new work gave more detail and is well illustrated. Volume Two – *The Turbulent Years of Australian Cricket 1893-1917* came out later the same year, whilst *The Bradman Years. Australian Cricket 1918-1948* was published in 1988 and the final volume *From Bradman to Border. Australian Cricket 1948-1989* first appeared 1990. A fifth volume, *Highest, Most and Best. Australian Cricket Statistics* mainly by Ross Dundas, tied in the four history volumes.

Ross Lloyd Dundas, born in Mullumbimby, New South Wales in September 1953, might be considered Australia's first professional cricket statistician. He was trained as a computer operator and as such became interested in creating programmes to deal with cricket statistics. He was involved in the operation of the electronic scoreboard at Sydney in 1983 and since 1992 has been a consultant to the Australian Cricket Board as its official statistician. His *Complete Book of Australian Test Records 1877-1987* appeared in 1987. This work has been updated on several occasions since.

The study of cricket's history had developed into a subject on its own in Australia. In 1983 *Patrons, Players and The Crowd : The Phenomenon of Indian Cricket* was published by Longmans in 1980, the author being Richard Cashman, who was at the time an Associate Professor at the University of New South Wales. He was born in June 1940 at Hornsby, New South Wales, educated at North Sydney Boys' High School and the University of Sydney, Monash University and Duke University, USA. He then moved as Assistant Professor to the University of Rochester, New York, before transferring to New South Wales in 1972. He edited, with Michael McKernan *Sport : Money, Morality and the Media* in 1982. *Australian Cricket Crowds* and *'Ave a Go, yer Mug!* both appeared in 1984 and ten other titles have appeared under his name in more recent years. From 2004 he was Adjunct Professor, University of Technology, Sydney – an honorary position.

Another historian living in Australia who researched outside the confines of the actual performances on the field of play was Ric Sissons. *The Players, a Social History of the Professional Cricketer* published by Kingswood in 1988, deals with the contrasting fortunes of the amateurs and professionals in first-class and Test cricket throughout cricket's history and in particular with the post-Second World War 'shamateur'. The book was soundly researched, but rather let down by a lack of proof-reading. Sissons, who was employed in the publishing industry in Australia, had previously written *Cricket and the Empire*, yet another analysis of the 1932-33 Bodyline tour.

A more profound historian was Professor Derek West. A specialist in medieval French, he had spent much of his life in Canada, though a Yorkshireman by birth, and was a Professor at McMaster University in Ontario. Taking early retirement, he returned to England and began a detailed study of 19th century English professional cricketers. The result of his researches appeared in two volumes of biographies and the history of the professional travelling elevens of the 1840 to 1880 period. The first of these books to be printed, in 1988, was *The Elevens of England*, which dealt with the last-mentioned subject. Rather surprisingly this was an area of cricket history that had scarcely been surveyed, though John Arlott had begun some preliminary work in the 1950s. West had then published *Twelve Days of Grace*, a book containing the biographies of twelve Victorian professionals; later came *Six More Days of Grace* – another half dozen similar biographies. The books also contained some little known illustrations, culled from the press publications of the time. Professor West died in 2002.

1987 saw the appearance of David Frith's *Pageant of Cricket*. This splendid volume of pictures, arranged chronologically, tells the story of the game by both the pictures and the linked captions which accompany them. Its scope is worldwide and it is still the first port of call for anyone anxious to see the changes in appearance and dress of the players over its 250 year span.

Mention has been made of Christopher Harte's history of Australia; its publication had been preceded by two histories by the same publisher,

Andre Deutsch. The first was *A History of West Indies Cricket* by Michael Manley, who had been Prime Minister of Jamaica from 1972 to 1980 and was best known for his books on political themes. The book is hopelessly out of balance. Of its 576 pages, 510 are devoted to post-1945 cricket, and even then mainly Test Matches and One Day Internationals. The sparse notes on pre-1900 cricket started with the first inter-colonial game being played in 1846 (rather than the accepted 1865), so alarm bells rang very early on.

In 1990 came Mihir Bose's *A History of Indian Cricket*, again a substantial volume, 571 pages. Again the early history is reduced to a few pages – 47 pages cover the years 1792 to 1931 – but Bose has done a little more research than Manley. The book contains the full scores of all Indian Test Matches. Mihir Bose, at present the chief B.B.C. Sports analyst, was born in Calcutta, but came to England in 1969 and qualified as an accountant. He soon switched to journalism and has worked for both the *Sunday Times* and *Financial Weekly*, among other newspapers. His first cricket publication was a biography of Keith Miller, published in 1980. Bose's work was supplemented by *A Corner of a Foreign Field* by Ramachandra Guha, published by Picador in 2003. Guha was born in Dehradun in 1958 and educated in Delhi and Calcutta. Since 1995 he has been a full-time writer living in Bangalore. He combines social history with the history of cricket in Bombay. The tensions between the sides competing in the Bombay Tournament are related to the political push towards independence led by Gandhi and Jinnah – it is a thoroughly worthwhile book, reminding one of the work of C.L.R.James though again, the earliest days of Indian cricket are given but scant coverage. Guha had earlier published two other cricket books which are worthy of note, *Wickets in The East* and *Spin and Other Turns.*

It is appropriate here to note the vast volume on New Zealand cricket – nearly 500,000 words and a comprehensive selection of pictures – *Men in White* by Don Neely and Richard King. This prints the score of all matches, not just Tests, played by New Zealand Representative teams. The de luxe edition was retailed at £420. The principal author was Don

Owen Neely, born Wellington 1935. He played cricket for Wellington and became a Test Selector. The statistics were provided by Francis Payne, who had been appointed co-editor of the *Cricket Almanack of New Zealand* following the death of Arthur Carman in 1982. Payne was also the New Zealand official statistician and a scorer for Radio New Zealand.

Amid these heavyweight histories appeared a very lightweight item, *A History of Cricket* by Benny Green. He doesn't allow the facts to mar a good tale and the book cannot be taken seriously. Green was noted earlier for his quarrying of *Wisden* and editing a variety of extracts, mainly for Queen Anne Press and later Stanley Paul. He is better known as a jazz musician and broadcaster, frequently on television. Born in Leeds in December 1927, he died in 1998.

A slightly more serious book is *The Pictorial History of Cricket* by Ashley Brown, a Cambridge graduate. Half the work is devoted to post-1945 Test Matches and the first 45 pages take the story up to 1914. There is a very large picture content, but it is not in the league of David Frith's *Pageant*.

Amid all these books, most of which involved the authors in no original research, John Goulstone, mentioned in Chapter 12 as a major contributor to Rowland Bowen's *The Cricket Quarterly*, was publishing his own researches, both on cricket and other sports. *Sports Quarterly Magazine* was founded in 1977 and 20 editions were issued, the last in 1981. That publication was succeeded by *Sports History* which continued until 1987. Goulstone also compiled and published a number of other learned treatises. Only a rash author would go into print about 19th century sport without consulting Goulstone's work.

Wray Vamplew, who had worked on some sports projects with Richard Cashman – Vamplew spent 18 years in Australia and was Pro-Vice-Chancellor of Flinders University – returned to England taking up a post at De Montfort University. In 1988 Cambridge University published his *Pay Up and Play The Game*. This volume featured professional sport in Britain from 1875 to 1914, but only 20 out of 394 pages specifically feature cricket, which seems an imbalance since until 1900 cricket was the major team sport in the eyes of the public. In 2006 Vamplew was appointed editor of *The Journal of Sports History*.

In 1985 George Allen & Unwin published Michael Rundell's *The Dictionary of Cricket*, the first serious attempt at such a work since W.J. Lewis' book of 1934. Rundell was managing editor of English Language Teaching Dictionaries at Longman's. As such he would seem to have been the ideal person for the task. Unfortunately he was unaware of Professor John Ferguson's published additions to Lewis which had appeared in *The Cricket Quarterly* and *The Cricket Statistician*. Rundell, a Cambridge graduate, also failed to make a chronological systematic search through cricket publications issued since Lewis. The book was reissued in 1989, but no attempt was made to remedy the faults, which had been clearly pointed out in various book reviews – an opportunity lost. A later attempt at the same subject was John Eddowes' *The Language of Cricket*, published in 1997. In the introductory chapter, the author suggests that many early cricket words come from Northern France, thus reinforcing Rowland Bowen's theory for the origins of the game. Robin Marlar in his book review, praises the work, but hopes for a second edition when the many errors can be eliminated.

In the same year as Rundell's book, Derek Barnard's *An Index to Wisden Cricketers' Almanack 1864-1984* was published. The author was, at that time, the deputy headmaster of Tunbridge Wells Grammar School. The book updates Pogson's 1944 Index and improves upon it, but the author is not as thorough as J.H.St.J.McIlwaine, who indexed the eight volumes of *The Cricket Quarterly*. Its usefulness is that all the obituaries in the almanack are listed.

The 1980s saw a spate of biographies of retired, often deceased, cricketers, as opposed to today's increasing trend for biographies of current cricketers. David Lemmon was responsible for books on A.P.Freeman, J.W.H.T.Douglas and A.P.F.Chapman. They were workmanlike efforts, but revealed few glimpses of the real personality. Alan Ross wrote entertainingly about Ranjitsinhji, though a few years later Simon Wilde did a more thorough investigation into his non-cricketing activities. Gerald Howat tackled Walter Hammond and Christopher Douglas investigated

D.R.Jardine. Douglas, who was born in London in 1955, left school to join the theatre, appearing on the stage and on television. In 1980 he wrote a play based on the Bodyline series. This was broadcast on Radio 4; from this play stemmed his interest in Jardine's life.

The Family Fortune, published in 1978, told the story of a number of families who had produced several Sussex county cricketers. The author, Alan Hill, was residing in Sussex, having moved from his native Yorkshire, where he had worked as a sports journalist. Since 1980 he had written essays on specific cricketers for *The Cricketer*, but it was not until 1986 that Hill's first single biographical book appeared. It featured Hedley Verity and Hill interviewed a number of Verity's relatives. The book won The Cricket Society Literary Award. This proved the first of a number of biographies by the author – these were published regularly through the 1990s.

Chapter 18
A Spate of County Histories

An attempt had been made in the 1950s to publish histories of the first-class county clubs by Convoy Publications Ltd; in the 1970s Arthur Barker Ltd also began a county history series. Both these have been noted in Chapters 11 and 14. Neither series reached even the halfway point. In 1983 NatWest Bank sponsored a history of Gloucestershire, entitled *Gloucestershire Road*. The author, Grahame Parker, had played for the county and then been Secretary-Manager from 1968 to 1976. The main criticism of the work was that it tended to concentrate on the period, from 1932 onward when Parker was personally involved with the county. The early history was rather sketchy with no new research involved, however the book was well-illustrated and largely error-free.

Gloucestershire's western neighbours, Somerset, were the next county to be described. *Sunshine, Sixes and Cider* published by David & Charles, was written by the well-known journalist, David Foot. Born in East Coker, near Yeovil, he began his career with the *Western Gazette* before moving to various national papers, principally *The Guardian*. Foot was editor of *Ton-Up for Somerset 1875-1975* a 64-page publication celebrating the county's centenary, but his first landmark cricket book was *Harold Gimblett: Tormented Genius of Cricket*, issued by Heinemann in 1982. This showed a side of Gimblett of which the general public was oblivious.

Foot's Somerset history concentrates on the personalities of the players rather than the records and feats they achieved or performed – the book is certainly alive, but a different book might have centred on the actual

County Club and the terrible financial battle that the committee waged to prevent collapse.

The contrast between Foot's Somerset history and the next county saga – *Essex County Cricket Club: An Official History* is stark indeed. The co-authors are David Lemmon and Mike Marshall. It is twice the length of Foot's book. Marshall, who died in Southend in 1995 aged 81, was educated at King's, Canterbury and was a shipbroker in the City. He retired from business in 1975 and then served on various Essex C.C.C. sub-committees, later being appointed a Vice-President of the County Club. He owned a substantial cricket library and had an extensive collection of memorabilia, especially related to Essex. It was a solid work, but did not add much to the known history of the county and failed to give lively portraits of the players.

In 1986, Richard Wigmore, of Christopher Helm Publishers, decided, presumably on the strength of the three county histories just noted, to launch a uniform series of county histories and appointed Peter Arnold and Peter Wynne-Thomas as series editors. Peter Arnold was the author of numerous sports books, as well as being, until he retired, sports editor at Hamlyns. He was born in April 1931 in Croydon and educated at Wallington County School, after which he joined Temple Press, which merged with Newnes and finally with Hamlyns. In 1986 his book *The Illustrated Encyclopedia of Cricket* had been published by Marshall Cavendish.

The first books in the series – Kent by Dudley Moore, Glamorgan by Andrew Hignell, Middlesex by David Lemmon and Hampshire by Peter Wynne-Thomas with a personal view by John Arlott – all appeared in 1988. Taking the Glamorgan book as a typical example, the general history ran to 269 pages with about 70 photographs and a number of full scorecards. The more important players had single page biographies. The record section comprised a list of all players with brief details and career records, the results of all Championship matches and the usual selection of general records.

The most notable new name is that of Andrew Keith Hignell, who was born in September 1959 in Gloucester, but moved to Cardiff aged 18 months. Educated at Llanishen Grammar School and Exeter University, he was a master at Blundell's for six years before moving to Wells Cathedral School. In 2004 he left school-mastering to take up the post as archivist and First Eleven scorer at Glamorgan. Apart from his books, many of which will be mentioned later, he has contributed regular articles to the leading cricket journals. In 2005 he took over as Editor of both the Glamorgan C.C.C. Yearbook and *The Journal of The Cricket Society* (from Clive Porter). He is also the current Secretary of the ACS. His researches into early Glamorgan and South Wales cricket are to be commended as a model for other county historians.

In the 1970s and 80s the principal statistician for Glamorgan had been Wayne Thomas. Educated at Cardiff High School and University College, Cardiff, he was a lecturer and though he moved to Surrey through his work, he remained interested in both Glamorgan cricket and Welsh rugby; he had compiled *Glamorgan C.C.C. Book of Cricket Records 1921-1976* and *A Century of Welsh Rugby Players* in 1980.

The second batch of Helm histories was issued in 1989 – Yorkshire by Tony Woodhouse, Worcestershire by David Lemmon, Surrey also by David Lemmon, Lancashire by Peter Wynne-Thomas and Derbyshire by John Shawcroft. The last-named had previously written a Derbyshire history in 1970 (see Chapter 14). Anthony 'Tony' Woodhouse was born in Chapel Allerton in 1931. He worked in the family advertising business of Woodhouse & Sons Ltd of Leeds, but as a dedicated supporter of Yorkshire County Cricket spent much of his time following that county's fortunes. From 1957 to 1992 (when he suffered a serious road accident) he did not miss a single home Yorkshire match. In 1978 he was elected to the Yorkshire C.C.C. Committee and served until his accident. For more than thirty years he sent reports on the Yorkshire leagues to *The Cricketer*. He vied with Geoffrey Copinger as to which of them possessed the finest cricket library – his contained more than 12,000 titles. He was chairman of the ACS from 1981 to 1993. He died in Leeds in January 2003.

In 1990 and 1991, Helm published just one title a year – Gloucestershire by David Green and Warwickshire by Jack Bannister. Both authors were well-known county cricketers who had taken up journalism. Helm was then taken over by A. & C.Black. Three more county titles were issued by the new publishers – Nottinghamshire by Peter Wynne-Thomas, Leicestershire by Dennis Lambert and Northamptonshire by Matthew Engel and Andrew Radd. Engel, born June 1951, had been the cricket correspondent for *The Guardian* and in 1985 won the Sports Journalist of the Year Award. He took over as editor of the *Wisden Almanack* in 1993. Andrew Radd, Engel's junior by a decade, was and is a local broadcaster and journalist with the *Northampton Chronicle & Echo* and the *Northamptonshire Evening Telegraph*, where his love for local club cricket often comes to the fore. The Northamptonshire book was the final one to be printed – yet again a publisher had failed to complete a 'county' series.

The principal reason for the failure was not the poor financial return, but that other publishers saw an opportunity and jumped into county histories as the series progressed. Partridge commissioned *From The Sea End*, author Christopher Lee, *From the Stretford End*, author Brian Bearshaw and *From Sammy to Jimmy* author Peter Roebuck. Those books covered Sussex, Lancashire and Somerset. Astonishingly, Kingswood commissioned Eric Midwinter's *Red Roses Crest The Caps* (a third Lancashire history), while Crowood had Derek Hodgson, a local journalist, writing a rival to Woodhouse's Yorkshire history. Readers were spoilt for choice and the market was flooded.

The book by Christopher Lee is boldly sub-titled 'The Official History of Sussex County Cricket Club'. The author could be praised for explaining the background before the actual County Club was formed, but seven chapters (more than a third of the main text of the book) is surely over-egging the cake? These early chapters are a general waffle through early cricket history – nicely presented, but in a volume of this length not necessary. The record section begins with a list of Sussex villages and the dates when cricket was first recorded – John Goulstone published such a list in 1972, but the author clearly is blissfully unaware of this. Like the curate's egg the book is good in parts. Christopher Lee was the B.B.C.

Defence and Foreign Affairs Correspondent and at the time of writing this book he was a Research Fellow at Emmanuel College, Cambridge.

The Somerset history is by the county captain Peter Roebuck. Like the Sussex book it is an 'Official History', but unlike Lee, Roebuck doesn't dwell on the pre-county club period of Somerset cricket. In fact pre-1850 cricket in the county is a subject that is dire need of exploration. The book is published to celebrate 100 years of first-class cricket (a point that rather jars with many historians).

Hodgson's Yorkshire tome – *The Official History of Yorkshire CCC* - is certainly more readable than Woodhouse's Yorkshire, the latter being strictly solid fact, no opinions or flights of fancy permitted.

The establishment of *The Cricketer Quarterly* (in 1973) was noted in Chapter 14. Frindall assumed the editorship due to the death of Gordon Ross in 1985. The statistical team changed quite frequently over the years. A.H.Wagg died in 1980 and was replaced by Brian Heald. The latter was born in Hull in September 1938 and educated at Bridlington School. He was employed as a civil servant with HM Customs & Excise. Elected to the ACS Committee in 1988 he took over from John Stockwell as editor of the ACS Statistical Survey series. He was also heavily involved in the statistical side of the Essex Yearbook. He continued with *The Cricketer Quarterly* until 1988. Another statistician who assisted with the Statistical Surveys and indeed produced most of the actual statistical data was Don Ambrose, a bank manager from Lancashire. Ambrose built up a fine collection of cricket annuals and culled much information from them, especially checking league yearbooks, a source not generally tapped. He died in 2010.

Brian Croudy was added to *The Cricketer Quarterly* team in 1982 on the death of Michael Fordham. Born in Balham in December 1936 and educated at Salesian College, Battersea, Brian Albert Charles Croudy was elected to the ACS Committee in 1975 and specialised in overseas cricket, mainly New Zealand, India and North America. Starting in 1982 he took over from Geoffrey Copinger as the compiler of the first-class averages for the Press Association – the averages which appeared once or twice a week in the daily papers. This assignment he continued until 1991. From 1984 to 1998 he was also a major figure in checking the statistics for the *B&H Cricket Year* under David Lemmon. He worked tirelessly for the ACS. In the ACS Famous Cricketers series Croudy compiled books on W.Rhodes, B.Mitchell, H.W.Taylor and C.Blythe. In more recent years he has travelled to the United States to research the Halifax Cup and the players involved in that competition. Working for London Transport 'on the buses', the tales he told of that side of his life were more amusing than the TV series devoted to the subject!

Continuing the story of *The Cricketer Quarterly* to its conclusion, in 1986 Richard Lockwood and Andrew Longmore took over as editors from Frindall, but after two issues, Lockwood assumed sole command. The publication had lost its way and struggled to provide readers with all the overseas scores, which was its raison d'être. The magazine ceased in 2004 when *The Cricketer* and *Wisden Cricket Monthly* merged. Richard Lockwood had also been appointed Assistant Editor of *The Cricketer* in 1986, but moved to Bull Computers in 1990. That year he was also the compiler of *The Cricketer Digest of A Season*. This was a new concept, the first-class and limited overs scores for the 1990 season were combined with individual player's match-by-match data and the book appeared several months before *Wisden*. The demand for pure statistics proved much less than the publishers imagined – a second edition appeared covering 1991, but the project was then abandoned. The production of this annual was linked to a computer programme devised by Gordon Vince and thus the start of the revolution that would transform cricket statistics.

As the ACS series on county grounds made steady progress, a book on current grounds, substantially updating Yardley's book of 1952 was published. *The Wisden Guide to Cricket Grounds* was issued by Stanley Paul in 1989. The principal author was William Ahmed Powell, born in Lahore in 1964. A graduate member of the Chartered Institute of Building, he was a member of the ACS Committee for four years during the 1990s and was also on the Cricket Memorabilia Society Committee. A major feature of the new book was the detailed plans of each current first-class ground in England and Wales. Information on how to travel to each ground was given, as well as the basic ground records and a short history. These histories were written by Alex Bannister, a well known cricket journalist with the *Daily Mail* and a regular contributor to *The Cricketer*. He retired from journalism in 1979 and died in December 2006.

The book was expanded in a second edition in 1992; this included grounds in Scotland and Ireland and some Minor County venues. Powell also wrote the ACS Grounds books on Middlesex and Surrey. In 1994 *Cricket Grounds Now and Then* used some of the information in Powell's Guide, but its principal feature was photographic, giving mainly aerial photographs of grounds at the present time and in the inter-war period.

The finest book on first-class cricket grounds came, not from the ACS series, or indeed another English writer, but from Richard Christen. *Some Grounds To Appeal* was published by the author in 1995. A4 in size and 240 pages, plus 64 pages of colour plates, the book gives detailed histories of the 39 Australian grounds used for first-class cricket to 1995, as well as details of several other 'important' venues. There are many historic photographs and maps, but the author also took the numerous aerial photographs. An eight page supplement adds the two most recent grounds and some addenda. The work gives historians for all the other cricket playing countries something to which they might aspire. Richard Christen was born in Sydney in November 1941 and educated at Parramatta High School. He was a member of the Australian Regular Army until retirement. He also proposed a similar work on South African grounds, but this unfortunately did not materialize.

The promotion of Durham to first-class status prompted three books – *Durham – The Birth of a First-Class County* by Ralph Dellor, *From Minor to Major* by Simon Hughes and *Past, Present & Future* by Jack Bannister and David Graveney. Dellor, a journalist by profession, had been involved in editing the programmes that were issued to accompany Sunday League matches. He was born in Essex and educated at Brentwood and Portsmouth University. For several years he assisted with the annual *The Cricketers' Who's Who* and since 2003 has been connected with Sportsline Media

Ltd. Graveney and Hughes were both Durham cricketers at the time. Hughes later went into journalism and more recently TV commentary. .

The earliest source book on Durham was *Fifty Years History of the Durham County Cricket Club 1882-1931* written by the then County Hon Secretary, William Bell. Of its period it was an excellent publication. In 1983, the County scorer, Brian Hunt, compiled a centenary book, building on Bell's work.

If no publisher managed a complete series of county histories, there was an appetite for histories of the County Championship, no less than three appearing in quick succession, all by authors previously noted. *A History of The County Cricket Championship* by Robert Brooke was issued by Guinness in 1991, to celebrate 100 Years of Championship cricket, thus avoiding the pitfalls into which Webber had tripped (see Chapter 11). This was principally a statistical work with a page devoted to each season, plus 61 pages of general records. *The Illustrated History of County Cricket* by Eric Midwinter, published by Kingswood, appeared the following year. The main section contains essays of about eight pages each on the individual counties and the other section is a general history. *Cricket's Champion Counties* by David Lemmon, issued in 1991 by Breedon, included both the County Champions and the Counties who won One Day Competitions.

Readers could also enjoy no less than three general histories of cricket – Martin-Jenkins' *Cricket – A Way of Life: The Cricketer Illustrated History of Cricket*; *Cricket: An Illustrated History* by David Rayvern Allen and *The Wisden Illustrated History of Cricket* by Vic Marks, the Somerset player. Ashley Brown's book has previously been noted.

Another angle tried by publishers was a series of Who's Who books on a county-by-county basis. The ACS had produced its set of booklets on the subject and the Who's Who giving every first-class cricketer had resulted. The plan with these new books was to add marginally more statistics and provide photographs of the players. The first to be published was on Warwickshire by Robert Brooke and David Goodyear. It was issued in 1989 and its main fault was the very poor quality of the photographs.

David William Goodyear was born in Birmingham in 1938 and employed by Cadburys. He was at one time the official historian to Aston Villa F.C. and wrote a history of that club.

Brooke and Goodyear tackled Worcestershire next. Both volumes were published by Robert Hale, who took subscriptions prior to publication in order to protect themselves against loss. Lancashire, again by Brooke and Goodyear, appeared in 1991, this time under the Breedon imprint. Glamorgan, by Andrew Hignell and Yorkshire by Tony Woodhouse came out in 1992. Sales were disappointing and here the series ceased.

A fresh view of the county scene was a series of record books launched by Limlow Books in 1993 – the first volume covering Hampshire had in fact been awaiting a publisher for some time before Limlow took the plunge. The author was Victor Isaacs, the Hampshire scorer and the format was similar to that devised by Roy Webber for his Playfair Record Book, but with additions such as the career records of all the county players. Like most other 'county' series, this one failed to complete the course, but only just! The final book, covering Northants was published in 2000 and compiled by Philip Bailey, but Sussex's author failed to provide a long-promised manuscript.

Most of the compilers were connected with their county's yearbook and have been noted previously in that capacity, but a few other names, some of whom later became yearbook editors, deserve notice. Michael Ayers (Surrey) was the county scorer from 1990 to 1994 and edited the county yearbook record section from 1991 to 1995. He was also for a time editor of *The Scorer*, a magazine designed for county scorers. David Baggett (Derbyshire) assisted Frank Peach with the county yearbook and was editor from 2001 to 2006. A qualified banker and computer consultant, he was born in Derby in March 1933 and educated at Derby School. A well-known local cricketer and latterly an umpire who stood in some County Second Eleven matches, he served on the Committee of the County Club for seven years and was President of the ACS from 2004 to 2007. Roy Wilkinson (Yorkshire) was a founding member of the ACS and an editor of the Yorkshire Yearbook from 1975. The Rev Malcolm Lorimer

(Lancashire), a Methodist minister, had taken over from Charles Oliver as compiler of the Record Section of the county yearbook in 1987 and since 1996 has been the yearbook editor. A member of the ACS Committee from 1988 to 2003 he was the Association's chairman for ten years. Over the last decade Lorimer has been responsible for the compilation and/ or publication of a number of books relating to Lancashire. He is the Lancashire C.C.C. librarian and is also heavily involved with the Cricket Memorabilia Society. Keith Gerrish (Gloucestershire) is both the current county scorer and editor of the yearbook. He was appointed as scorer in 1996, after retiring. He was the editor and compiler of the First Class Counties Second Eleven Annual, taking over in 2004 following the death of Les Hatton. Gerrish retired as the annual's editor after the appearance of the 2010 edition.. Michael Hill retired as editor of the Somerset Yearbook after the 2003 edition and Richard Walsh took over for 2004. Eddie Lawrence compiled a photographic history of Somerset C.C.C. in 1991 and has been the author of several other books relating to the county, but the record book was compiled by Nigel Johns. Lawrence died in 2010.

Another publisher decided on a different approach. Spellmount, a small firm in Tunbridge Wells, commissioned Dean Hayes to write books containing the biographies of a selection of players from a given county. The series commenced with *Lancashire Cricketing Greats* in 1989. Hayes, who was born in Bolton in 1949, was a primary school headmaster and like Goodyear, began his sports history interest with soccer – especially Bolton Wanderers. Kent and Gloucestershire followed Lancashire in 1990 and Yorkshire appeared in 1991. The title then altered to *Famous Cricketers of ....* Essex appeared in 1991 under the new heading, with Middlesex in 1992. Glamorgan was published by Christopher Davies in 1996. The essays on the individual players in all these books were pleasant enough, but with little original research undertaken, the errors from previous works were often repeated. Like the four general histories noted the books added nothing to the information that many readers had already acquired – perhaps some of the illustrations were the main attraction.

There were, however, books for the more erudite students of cricket history. David Rayvern Allen's volume *Early Books on Cricket* appeared in 1988 and gave more detailed descriptions of the early volumes listed in 'Padwick'. Ronald Willis researched the origins of the Ashes urn and his book *Cricket's Biggest Mystery: The Ashes* had been published in Australia in 1982 and in England the following year. Willis, born in North Yorkshire, worked as a journalist on the *Yorkshire Evening Post*, before emigrating to Australia in 1976. He researched the background of Florence Morphy and the family for whom she worked, as well as the Earls of Darnley.

Breedon, the Derby-based publishers, decided to issue a series of books providing the detailed scores of first-class matches played in the inter-war period. The compiler was Jim Ledbetter and the series began with the 1939 season. After the initial book, the series was taken over by Limlow Books, but then the ACS assumed publication with the 1930 edition. Jim Ledbetter, born in Nottingham in September 1933, was educated at High Pavement School and Hatfield College, Durham University. He was latterly a history lecturer at Nottingham Trent University. He joined the Committee of the ACS in 1990 as Honorary Treasurer and was Chairman from 2002 to 2004. Ledbetter also compiled two books in the Famous Cricketers series – F.H.Tyson and C.V.Grimmett.

In Australia, statisticians and historians, no doubt due to the influence of Roger Page, were increasingly active. Yet another attempt was made to float a national Australian cricket annual. This time it was a purely solo effort, with no commercial backing. *Allan's Australian Cricket Annual* first appeared in 1987-88. Allan William Miller, the proprietor, compiler and editor, was born in April 1967 in Whyalla, South Australia and educated at Newton Moore School, Bunbury. The page size of the new annual was A4 and the early editions were typed out on a Canon typewriter. The end product looked home-spun, as indeed it was, however the data Miller gathered for all the major matches played in Australia was more comprehensive than anything before attempted. Information such as the times of play and the times of any weather interruptions, the attendances and receipts, names of the 12th men and of the scorers was included. The score of the not out batsman at the fall of each wicket was another first. By the third edition Miller had added biographies of all current first-class players in Australia and the notes were not the mundane routine stuff – one typical opening description gives a flavour – 'Like Dad's old Fordson tractor, Scott Hookey doesn't usually fire first up, but once he's started he can go all day.' A quite remarkable point regarding the third edition is that Miller's office at home was destroyed by fire which burnt much of the correspondence and data received, but he did not despair – he began again.

It was most unfortunate that the Wisden organization decided to launch *Wisden Cricketers' Almanack Australia* in 1998, based on the format of the English version. Miller was approached to help, but decided to continue on his own. Miller's last annual appeared in 2001 – an inspired publication sadly missed. Allan Miller is now in waste management. The *Wisden Australia*, despite commissioning the big names of the day, edited successively by Gideon Haigh, Warwick Franks, Christian Ryan and Greg Baun, ceased after eight editions, the last being 2005-06. There was also a *Pocket Wisden Australia* that survived four editions.

In 1991 came the first of two volumes which would contain every first-class match score for Australia. *First-Class Cricket in Australia Volume 1 1850-51 to 1941-42* was compiled by Ray Webster and edited by Allan Miller. The former is a retired bank official, who was born in April 1941 at East Brunswick and educated at Camberwell High School. Volume 2 appeared in 1997 and completed the scores to 1976-77. The match scores, though not quite as detailed as in *Allan's Annual*, are well researched and correct many earlier errors. Most significantly the scores contain a note stating from where the details have been gleaned.

Australia also saw the appearance in 1991 of a 'Waghorn'. *Early Cricket in Sydney 1803-1856* was originally compiled by James Scott, who died in 1962. The manuscript ran to 1,000 pages. Richard Cashman and Stephen Gibbs edited this down to 261 pages and the result was the publication of many hitherto 'forgotten' references to cricket in the first half of the 19th century.

It was more difficult for statisticians to locate the detailed scores of Pakistan matches, even though these games did not commence until 1947-48. Abid Ali Kazi was responsible for having these matches published in a series of five books, which cover matches up to 1974-75 and were printed between 1997 and 2003. Abid Ali Kazi with Nauman Bader were largely involved in the foundation of the Pakistan Association of Cricket Statisticians & Scorers. A similar organization had been set up in 1987 in India, publishing a Journal and other statistical material with Mohandas Menon and Vasant Naik as the leading members.

Chapter 19
Biographies Multiply

From the late 19th century, with books such as Coxhead's *Cricket Records*, through Lester's *Bat v Ball*, Home Gordon's *Cricket Form At A Glance*, E.L.Roberts's numerous publications to Webber's *Playfair Book of Cricket Records* and its successors by Bill Frindall, the cricket reading public had been kept abreast of cricket statistics relating to first-class cricket. The growth of Test cricket saw Test record books appear, initially just England v Australia, but then Test cricket in general with Webber's *Playfair Book of Test Cricket* and its successors by Wrigley and Frindall. Frindall's final volumes containing full scores of all Tests appeared in 2000, since when commercial publishers have moved toward so-called encyclopedias which give very limited statistical information. The ACS *Who's Who of Cricketers* published in 1982 and reissued in 1993 gave biographies of all first-class cricketers in the British Isles. In Australia Webster's books containing all first-class match scores in that country was noted in the last chapter; *The Oxford Companion to Australian Cricket* was published in 1996 with Richard Cashman heading a list of contributors. This was Australia's equivalent of *The Barclays World of Cricket*. Through the 1980s there had been a steady interest in the history of Australian cricket. This growth had been, if anything, increased since then. A splendid illustration of this is the *Oxford Companion*, since it lists no less than 102 contributors. It is impractical to provide data on all these writers and researchers, those who wish to can refer to the three pages of contributors printed in that work.

The introduction of the internet was to make these great volumes almost superfluous. County and club yearbooks and their overseas companions gave statistics purely for the clubs they served.

The story of how Simon King founded CricInfo in Minnesota in 1993 and how that particular internet bubble expanded and at the turn of the century exploded, with its founder being sidelined by his fellow directors and resigning, is for another place, but King's initiative had a profound effect on the humble amateur cricket statistician. Through CricInfo and its off-shoot CricketArchive, the detailed score of every match of note was available at the touch of a button and out of that resource came all the basic records and cricketing biographies of the vast majority of players. The innocent hobby of cricket's 'anoraks' was altered beyond recognition.

Pure statisticians in the generally accepted cricket definition were sidelined and publishers now moved toward cricket books which were the fruits of historical research. People such as John Goulstone had pioneered in-depth study of contemporary documents and in the process demolished many half-truths. Irving Rosenwater, in a letter to the present writer, commented:

> 'The writing of cricket history is not the cavalier process that some people see it as, to be undertaken at a whim, and just copying what is common knowledge. Some writers go through a whole career on that basis. Cricket history is an extremely demanding branch of scholarship, indulged in alas far too frequently – with predictable results – by persons unfitted for this demanding task.'

In England a largely unexplored area of cricket research had been Minor Counties cricket. The ACS had begun to publish books on Minor Counties, county-by-county, containing basic player details and career records. The first to appear, in 1993, was Lincolnshire, largely researched by Ken Trushell, see Chapter 15. There was a three year gap before Tony Percival completed the second county – Cheshire in 1996. Progress was very slow for two reasons. First, unlike the first-class counties, the match scores themselves were not always complete and second, again unlike the first-class counties, almost no biographical research had been done.

Percival was, like Ken Trushell before him, very much involved in the county cricket of his chosen shire – at the time of writing he is the Hon Secretary of the County Club – and this made research easier than it might have been. Anthony Barry Percival was born in Stretford, Manchester in August 1937 and educated at Sale Grammar School; he is a retired bank manager. In carrying out his biographical research he worked very much in conjunction with Philip Thorn, but Percival widened his horizons beyond Cheshire and in 2003 compiled a similar book on neighbouring Staffordshire. With the death of Philip Thorn, he has continued to research biographies of Minor County players from other counties.

The person who set himself the task of researching and trying to compile complete scorecards for every Minor County Championship match is Tony Webb. The job is a long, tedious affair involving the checking of literally hundreds of provincial newspapers, since in many cases no county scorebooks, other than for recent years, are extant. The ACS began the publication of these match scores, on a season-by-season basis in 2004, with 1895. The detail far exceeds the information for the first-class scores as published by the ACS and indeed now reproduced on internet web sites. A flavour of the work undertaken by Webb can been gleaned from a note quoting his sources for a particular game, in this case Oxfordshire v Bucks in 1895:

> 'Abingdon Herald 20 July; Jackson's Oxford Journal 20 July; Oxford Chronicle 20 July; Oxford Times 20 July; Bucks Advertiser 20 July; Bucks Herald 20 July; South Bucks Free Press 19 July; The Cricket Field 27 July; Sporting Life 18-19 July; The Sportsman 17,18,19 July.'

Tony Webb was born in South Croydon in January 1943 and educated at Seaford College and Dublin University. Prior to retirement he was Director of Education and Training for the Confederation of British Industry.

Activity among the Minor Counties was not confined to Tony Webb, Tony Percival and their immediate band. Cambridgeshire, that county once briefly first-class, had been on the ACS stocks for thirty years.

Stephen Harper-Scott made some progress, but it is only in recent years that Willie Sugg has been gradually working his way, line-by-line through the county's 19th century newspapers and has so far published three of a series of booklets which will cover the period from 1700 to 1870. In 2006 Tony Percival compiled the standard ACS booklet on the county.

Two Minor County histories have emerged in recent years. *Cricket in Hertfordshire* by R.G.Simons was issued in 1996 and this deals with both club and county cricket. The author was born in Watford in March 1922, educated at Berkhamsted and played county cricket for Hertfordshire from 1939 to 1969.

A History of Bucks County Cricket Club, as its title implies, is principally devoted to the County Club. The author, Douglas Miller, was born in Knutsford in October 1937 and educated at Wellington and Trinity Hall, Cambridge. By profession he is a market researcher – and a keen local cricketer. His first cricket book was *Cricket Grounds of Gloucestershire* in the ACS series, which is an excellent work. He has also written biographies of Don Shepherd, Charles Palmer, Allan Watkins and Jack Bond. Miller retired as Chairman of the ACS in March 2008, after a vigorous term of four years.

Another series, instigated by the ACS on cricket below first-class level concerned the ICC Trophy. The first book, which was published in 1989, covered the Trophy matches of the first three competitions and was mainly compiled by Darren Senior; the second volume covering 1990 and 1994 was compiled by Richard Streeton and the third covering 1997 by Peter Griffiths and Darren Senior. The latter was at one time employed at Headingley by Yorkshire C.C.C., but has now moved to the teaching profession

The current Surrey scorer, Keith Booth, who worked in retailing and university administration, before retiring to take up county scoring, has been actively researching various aspects of cricket's history. Following a book on Michael Atherton, Booth wrote *Knowing The Score*, a history of scoring, in 1999, which focused too much on Surrey and the South East, but *His Own Enemy* telling the tragic story of Ted Pooley and then *The*

Father of Modern Sport, about C.W.Alcock were more profound. His most recent book is a biography of George Lohmann.

David Frith had three books published, all of which have an Anglo-Australian flavour. The first, in 1994, *Stoddy's Mission*, was devoted to the 1894-95 England tour to Australia and effectively expanded a section of Frith's earlier biography of A.E.Stoddart. In 1999 came *The Trail Blazers*, which related H.H.Stephenson's tour to Australia and the third was *Bodyline Autopsy*, which should be, but won't be, the final word on the England tour of 1932-33. In between all this work came the sacking of Frith as editor of the magazine he had founded, *Wisden Cricket Monthly,* in 1996. The following year he had published *Caught England, Bowled Australia*, his autobiography. In 1990 his book *By His Own Hand* contained essays on noted cricketers who had committed suicide (expanded and updated as *The Silence of The Heart* in 2001).

It is appropriate here to bring the saga of the mainstream English cricket magazines up to date. Frith left *Wisden Cricket Monthly* in March 1996. John-Paul Getty had bought the *Wisden Almanack* in 1993 and, it is rumoured, unknowingly acquired Frith's magazine at the same time. Frith's autobiography gives a blow-by-blow account of the next three years, ending in his departure. Steven Lynch, who had been Frith's assistant editor since January 1986, was a cricket 'nut'. Born in Surrey in 1957, he had joined the staff of M.C.C. at Lord's on leaving school and by 1979 had been appointed M.C.C. Office Manager. He first came to notice by winning the difficult annual quiz of the magazine in three successive years. His first letter to *The Cricketer* had been published in January 1974, regarding bowlers no-balled for throwing. Lynch has remained with the Wisden organization ever since. From the magazine he moved on to the internet site, Wisden.com and then to CricInfo when that merged with Wisden.com. He was the editor of those sites, a feature of which for some ten years has been the 'Ask Steven' section. Lynch is currently Deputy Editor of the *Wisden Almanack*..

Two subjects which have never ceased to interest cricket writers are Hambledon and W.G.Grace. Three books on the former have appeared in recent years. Ashley Mote wrote *The Glory Days of Cricket*, published in 1997, which he followed up the following year with a new version of Nyren's book, having uncovered an early manuscript whilst researching the history of Hambledon. There are some doubts about the origins of this manuscript. Ashley Mote, born in London, in January 1936, was a journalist who later worked for Unilever. He was elected as an MEP for UKIP, but was imprisoned in 2007 for benefit fraud.

In 2000 *Start of Play*, written by David Underdown, was issued. This is mainly centred on Hambledon, although sub-titled 'Cricket and Culture in Eighteenth Century England'. References to 18th century cricket north of the Home Counties are conspicuous by their absence. The author goes to great lengths to describe the class of people who played cricket in the south-eastern corner of England, it is as if cricket was not played outside that area. Underdown, a professional social historian, runs through the 17th century background of Kent and Sussex with a practiced hand.

A year later John Goulstone's book *Hambledon: The Men and The Myths* appeared. The author built on the works of Ashley-Cooper, filling in the gaps in the latter's published researches and correcting errors where necessary. Goulstone's book is very much a work of reference, unlike the other titles mentioned where the writers' opinions have floated to the top.

A final postscript to Hambledon comes in the form of Neil Jenkinson's *Here's The Hambledon Club*. The book traces the story of cricket in Hambledon from the time of its decline at the close of the 18th century up to 2000. Jenkinson was also the author of *Richard Daft* in the ACS biographical series.

The second historical monument, W.G.Grace, saw three volumes issued to celebrate the 150th anniversary of his birth. Robert Low's *W.G.* ran to 312 pages; Simon Rae's *W.G.Grace. A Life* used up 548 pages. With no major contemporary documents emerging in recent years, the authors had to rely on facts which had been long in the public domain. They also had to decide which of the numerous W.G. stories had any basis in fact. For both Low and Rae, this was the only venture into cricket writing.

Low, a Scot, was a 'proper' journalist and war correspondent in, inter alia, Vietnam and Kosovo, before writing a number of historical novels, set in the Viking era. Rae has been a poet and broadcaster, for example presenting 'Poetry Please' on B.B.C. Radio 4, and at the time of writing has a share in a provincial theatre company.

In contrast to these two biographies, the third book, by Joe R. Webber, is 1,102 pages in length and A4 in page size. The book stays strictly to the facts – the statistical facts. The author attempted, and probably succeeded, to trace every match in which Grace was involved. Contemporary newspapers were scoured, and after a detailed list of every game, comes a multitude of statistical tabling. For Webber the book was a one-off – he had not been particularly interested in cricket statistics before the project and after publication by the ACS, he resigned from the Association to pursue other fields of study.

In Chapter 18 it was noted that the publisher, Spellmount, started a series of county books giving biographies of the most notable players. In 2000 another publisher, Tempus, launched a similar series, 'One Hundred Greats'. Each book contained hundred players from a given county, with usually a single page biography and photograph. By and large these biographies did little more than (in the case of deceased players) repeat their obituaries. Obviously the 'top' hundred players of a county are the players whose details are already known and in a few hundred words, the authors could have little room for any more obscure facts they might unearth. Therefore any criticism of the books centred purely on the selection of the players included. The quality clearly depended on the individual author, but unlike Spellmount, Tempus endeavoured to find a new author for each title: The list, in chronological order reads: Glamorgan (A.K.Hignell), Yorkshire (M.Pope & P.E.Dyson), Worcestershire (L.W.Hatton), Leicestershire (D.A.Lambert), Sussex (John Wallace), Gloucestershire (A.K.Hignell), Hampshire (N.Jenkinson), Surrey (J.R.Lodge), Warwickshire (R.Brooke), Middlesex (R.Brooke), Nottinghamshire (J.Ledbetter), Durham (M.Appleby), Kent (D.Robertson & H.Milton), Lancashire (K.Hayhurst), Northants (A.Radd), Somerset

(E.Lawrence)

In addition Hignell compiled 100 First-Class Umpires, based on the same criteria. Using mainly the same authors, Tempus began a second series 'Fifty Finest Matches'. At the time of writing, about one-third of the first-class counties have been covered.

Several historians and statisticians mentioned in the above series merit more than a passing note. Mick Pope, born in Swinton in April 1964 and educated at Swinton C.S., was a member of the ACS Committee from 1994 to 2007 and the Association's Marketing Manager for five years. From 1985 he has contributed articles to various cricket publications. He is Secretary of the Wombwell Cricket Lovers and has been editor of their magazine *The 12th Man*. He is currently researching 18th century cricket in Yorkshire and has been author, or co-author of several books relating to Yorkshire cricket, notably biographies of Roy Kilner, Alonzo Drake and Major Booth. Pope has recently discovered the detailed score of the famous Sheffield & Leicester v Nottingham match of 1826, the most important feature of this discovery being that the full bowling analysis is shown.

Paul Dyson, who co-authored the Tempus book with Pope, was educated at Wath-on-Dearne Grammar School and Leeds University, where he studied music. He was head of music at Easingwold School. He has published several books on cricket statistics including *The Counties and Test Cricket, Benson & Hedges Cup Record Book* and *A Century of Headingley Tests*. He has also provided statistical records for several biographies; like Pope he has written articles for the cricket press.

Jerry Lodge is a leading member of the Surrey Statistical Group, based at The Oval. The brother of Derek Lodge, he was born in Sutton in May 1934 and educated at Rutlish School. Retiring as a director of an international insurance brokers, he was Honorary Treasurer of the ACS from 1999 to 2007 and wrote several books in the Association's 'Famous Cricketers' series, included a revised edition of his brother's book on Jack Hobbs. Among his other works are *Surrey C.C.C., A History since 1945, Fifty Finest Matches: Surrey* and a book on the Surridge family.

The ACS 'Famous Cricketers' series ended with the 100th title – *R.Benaud*. the author was Daniel Herborn, Assistant Curator at Sydney Cricket Ground Museum, the book coming out in 2007. Several authors who compiled more than one book in the series merit inclusion in this work, notably Dr Keith A.P. Sandiford, who was born in Barbados in 1936 and was, in 2006, Professor Emeritus of History at the University of Manitoba. He was the author of no less than nine titles – E.D.Weekes, C.L.Walcott, F.M.M.Worrell, G.S.Sobers, W.W.Hall, M.D.Marshall, J.D.C.Goddard, S.Ramadhin and A.L.Valentine. Apart from this impressive series, Sandiford has had several books published on the development of cricket in Barbados, including *Combermere School and Barbadian Society*, *The Elite Schools 1865-1966* and *Cricket Nurseries of Colonial Barbados*, all of which give fresh insight into the game on the author's native island.

Geoff Wilde, born in Southport in 1940 and educated at Merchant Taylor's, Crosby, had a career in accountancy. His books featuring J.B.Statham and G.E.Tyldesley set new standards for the statistical aspects of the Association. A keen supporter of the ACS, he is a fierce critic of those whose aspirations in the statistical field fall short of the levels he tries to maintain. Gerald Hudd, born in Portskewett, Monmouth, in January 1942, spent his working life in the prison service. He was the compiler of ten of the 'Famous Cricketers', namely T.W.Graveney, R.T.Simpson, C.A.Milton, T.E.Bailey, K.R.Miller, I.T.Botham, C.W.L.Parker, J.H.Wardle, J.C.Laker and T.W.J.Goddard. The books are workmanlike, competent statistical biographies. Hudd was also the compiler of *Test Cricket History at Old Trafford 1884-1998.*

Hugh Garrod, born Bristol in 1943, is the head of a primary school in Bedfordshire. He is the author of the books on A.O.Jones and G.L.Jessop. The former had connections with Dunstable, where Garrod is involved in the local History Society and Jones is given an excellent biography with his statistics. Since Brodribb had previously written Jessop's biography, the Jessop 'Famous Cricketer' book is more strictly confined to that player's statistical record. Derek Carlaw is also the author of two titles, F.W.Tate and W.L.Murdoch. A journalist by profession, Carlaw has lived in Canterbury since 1978, is a regular contributor to the Kent C.C.C. Yearbook and is co-author of the most recent Appendix to the Harris Kent History.

Roger Heavens, born in East Ham in 1948, is a land surveyor by profession. He compiled the Arthur Haygarth booklet in the ACS series, but he is better known as a publisher of cricket books. His firm undertook the re-publication of the 15 volumes of Haygarth's S&B and then published, for the first time, both Volume 16 and Volume 17 in the style of the originals. He has also published indices to each of the earlier volumes. He also published the first volume of Ian Maun's *From Commons to Lord's*.

Peter Griffiths, born in Mansfield in 1948, was the co-author of three 'Famous Cricketers', James Lillywhite, John Wisden and Ivo Bligh. Griffiths was educated at Queen Elizabeth's Grammar School, Mansfield and Manchester University. He co-authored Volume 2 of Padwick's *Bibliography of Cricket* with Stephen Eley, published in 1991. Between 1997 and 1999 he was joint compiler of five volumes of the *ACS First-Class Match List*, which effectively merged the individual First-Class Guides into a uniform series. Like Heavens he has also published books, most notably the series of county record books. His main expertise is in computer programming and he currently runs CricketArchive, which has on its site the detailed scores of all major matches as well as numerous lesser games. In addition the site contains biographical and statistical details for all players who appeared in major matches, plus sundry other cricketers. Griffiths was a member of the ACS Committee from 1993 to 2008.

Wesley Harte, born in Crawfordsburn, Co.Down, and educated at the Methodist College, Belfast, is a retired Civil Servant. He has compiled four books in the Famous Cricketers series – M.P.Donnelly, B.Sutcliffe, C.S.Dempster and R.J.Hadlee.

Brian Stanley Bassano, born in East London, South Africa in 1936, compiled the book on G.A.Faulkner. A journalist by profession, he was at times Manager and Secretary of Border C.U. and played a major role in trying to integrate cricketers of all races when the racist laws were rescinded in South Africa. His most important book was *The History of South African Cricket Volume IV 1947-1960*. In addition he wrote *MCC in South Africa 1938-1939*, *South Africa in International Cricket 1888-1970* and tour books covering the 1931-32 South Africans to Australia and the 1935-36 Australians in South Africa. His son has played first-class cricket for Derbyshire. Bassano died in Launceston, Tasmania in July 2001 and his books on G.A.Faulkner and on the 1922-23 tour to South Africa were published posthumously.

Norman Rogers, born in Coventry in 1944, is a Sales Manager for a local company. He compiled the book on H.E.Dollery, and had previously published a biography of W.E.Hollies.

A major flaw with many of the Famous Cricketers books, especially the earlier ones, was that authors frequently based their statistics on match scores printed in *Wisden*, even though the actual scorebooks for many of the matches were extant. Geoff Wilde, who did work from the Lancashire scorebooks for his volumes, unearthed no less than fifty differences between the scorebook and the scores printed in *Wisden* . If other authors had carried meticulous checking on a similar scale, perhaps the series would have continued after the 100th book. As it was the ACS Committee decided that all the data was now on line and the books were superfluous.

The ACS series on 'counties', having completed the first-class 'counties' for both the British Isles (Ireland had been compiled by Edward Liddle and Scotland by Richard Miller) and Australia, moved on to South Africa. 'Transvaal Cricketers' was issued in 1995, since when books on Natal, Western Province, Border and Northerns have been published. The principal compiler and researcher for all these volumes has been Robin Isherwood.

With the establishment of domestic first-class cricket in Sri Lanka, Zimbabwe and later Bangladesh and the absence of cricket annuals which published detailed first-class scores in those countries, the ACS decided to fill the gap by issuing its own Sri Lankan, Zimbabwean and Bangladeshi publications. These were very largely the work of Philip Bailey, but with the assistance of Sa'adi Thawfeeq in Sri Lanka and Sohel Awrangzeb in Bangladesh. In Zimbabwe however, John Ward, a long standing ACS member, provided the information at the time when he was the official statistician for that country.

Whilst touching on Sri Lankan cricket mention has to be made of S.S. 'Chandra' Perera, who for some thirty years was the island's principal cricket historian and statistician, as well as acting as scorer for the Sri Lankan team. In 1969 he had published *Four Score & Ten*, the history of the Royal v St Thomas match series. The book ran to 260 pages and gave the full scores of all the matches between the two schools as well as articles and statistics. In 1986 he published *The History of the Royal College*, a 602-page volume, celebrating 150 years of the school, which had a large cricket content. Perera was also responsible for numerous booklets that celebrated cricket tours to Sri Lanka, or matches on the island. It was disappointing that Sri Lanka in recent years was unable to publish an annual along the lines of S.P.Foenander's *Ceylon Cricketers' Companion* of the 1920s, since the ACS books did not venture beyond the first-class scene.

A final paragraph on the ACS's latest series. These are a sequence of biographies between 100 and 150 pages in length and feature players for whom no 'commercial' biography has been printed. Unlike in the 'Famous Cricketers' series, the actual statistical content is relegated to half a dozen, or fewer pages at the back. Those published to June 2010 include Allan Watkins and Jack Bond (Douglas Miller), Johnny Briggs (Stuart Brodkin), George Duckworth (Eric Midwinter), Ernie Jones (Bernard Whimpress), Rockley Wilson (Martin Howe), Bill Copson (Kit Bartlett), Richard Daft (Neil Jenkinson), Ernest Hayes (Keith Booth) and J.H.King (A.R.Littlewood). The editor of the series is David Jeater, who joined the ACS Committee in 2007. He had written the Famous Cricketers book on Percy Perrin, as well as a number of articles for *The Cricket Statistician,* in particular on first-class umpires and also first-class cricketers who were noted for their skills in 'racket games'. He was born in

Brighton in 1944 and educated at Vardean School and Hertford College, Oxford; by profession he was a Town Planner.

Chapter 20
Historians Dig Deeper

The previous chapter may give the impression that the ACS monopolized the publication of historical and statistical books during the last decade or so, but in fact there were plenty of other worthwhile books on aspects of cricket history, if not so many on statistics now that the internet covered that branch so thoroughly.

In 2004 however the Sussex Record Society published Tim McCann's book *Sussex Cricket in the Eighteenth Century*. This work expanded on the volume published by the Squires some fifty years before. The principal content of the book contains Sussex cricket references from 1702 to 1800, but pre-1700 references are dealt with in the lengthy Introduction. Sussex being such an early county in cricketing terms the book contains many new references and does give the source of those references. Timothy J. McCann is the Assistant County Archivist at West Sussex Record Office and had previously researched into the archives of the Dukes of Richmond, who were very heavily involved in promoting 18th century cricket.

However, many of the historical items published in the British Isles in recent years centred on aspects which are too narrow to command a place in a book such as this – a typical example is *Foreign And Fantastic Field Sport: Cricket in County Tipperary* by Patrick Bracken, published in 2004. Regrettably readers will have to search the latest Bibliography *Post Padwick: The Gibbs Extension of Padwick's Bibliography: 1990-2006* to find items such as the Tipperary example, rather than check the present book. Stephen Gibbs, based in Australia, had published a bibliography of Don

Bradman and a bibliography listing about 1,000 items missed from the two volumes in *Padwick*, before he issued his 628 page volume of cricket publications since 1990. It is a most ambitious undertaking and a most useful work, but he seems to have used printed listings of books, rather than the more difficult task of searching out works that, due to their limited circulation, do not find their way into dealers' catalogues.

In contrast to Gibbs' book two authors have published bibliographies confined to a single county. Martin Wilson's book covers Northamptonshire and Duncan Anderson's, Nottinghamshire. These are both works that the two authors have spent almost a lifetime in compiling. It is hoped that other counties may follow their lead.

Martin Wilson has produced several other specialist volumes, including *An Index to Waghorn, Dawn's Early Light* (listing cricket notices in America before 1820), and *An Eighteenth Century German View of Cricket*, which is the republication and translation of a 1796 German book describing cricket, together with some early references to the game being played in Germany. He is heavily involved in the search for 18th century cricket references and has in the recent past developed into perhaps the leading authority on early cricket history. His book *First Cricket In…*, published by Christopher Saunders in 2009, was initially based on the work of Rowland Bowen. It lists the first cricket references in each English County and then in countries throughout the world. There are many instances where Wilson has been able to update Bowen's list and, just as important, Wilson has noted the contemporary source for the great majority of his notes, a sad omission by Bowen. He has been a frequent contributor of articles to the ACS Journal, and has unearthed the earliest-known references to cricket in, for example, Ceylon and at Oxford University. In 2010 he discovered the first 'new' Hambledon score since the days of Ashley-Cooper. Born in Rushden in 1964 and educated locally and at Durham University, he is a chartered accountant and author of many books on taxation.

Echoes From A Golden Age was published by Boundary Books in 2010. The book was the history of the famous photographic firms in Brighton prior to the First World War, namely those run by Foster and Hawkins, specializing in cricketing portraits. The author was Duncan Anderson, mentioned above. He was born in Cleethorpes in 1952, educated at Oundle and is a chartered accountant by profession. The firms issued postcards of players at the end of the Victorian era through to 1914 and the book gives numerous examples of their work.

A Favourit' Game by Andrew Hignell, also ends in 1914, but has a longer time span, beginning with the earliest reference to cricket in South Wales in 1783. The author explains how the building of the railways helped to spread the game through that part of the country. Hignell also wrote *Rain Stops Play,* a work that analysed the effect of the climate on the first-class counties in the Championship. Hignell has written several other books on Glamorgan cricket, including the biographies of Maurice Turnbull and John Clay.

Across the world, Greg Ryan compiled *The Making of New Zealand Cricket 1832-1914* which followed a similar theme to Hignell's book. Both authors dug deep into the archives and built on a great deal of original research. Greg Ryan has a history degree from Canterbury University and teaches New Zealand history.

New Zealand also has its own cricket bibliography, compiled by Rob Franks and published by Christopher Saunders in 2006. Saunders has been responsible for the publication of many books of cricket scholarship in recent years and historians owe a great debt to him. Franks lists over 1,500 items, many for the first time, but a fair proportion are match programmes which usually were not included in *Padwick.*

The United States saw the publication of *The Tented Field: A History of Cricket in America* by Tom Melville, educated at Ripon College and the University of Wales, and a teacher by profession. The author confines American cricket before 1838 to a brief six page chapter and the story effectively stops in 1914. So the work ought to be American cricket 1838 to 1914. Given that limitation, it expands on Lester's book of 1951, but as Martin Wilson demonstrated in *Dawn's Early Light* there is still much to explore in the early history of the States.

George B. Kirsch's *Baseball and Cricket: the Creation of American Team*

Sports 1838-72 gives us exactly what the title states. A scholarly work befitting its author's background as a history professor and a plethora of endnotes refer the reader to sources (particularly contemporary newspapers) which will be invaluable to later researchers. Before leaving America, one must mention *Cricket in America, 1710–2000* by P.David Sentance. The '1710' of the title promises more thorough treatment of the earliest period of American cricket. However, the years to 1838 are covered in no more than two or three pages, though later periods are dealt with more thoroughly.

In South Africa Andre Odendaal researched and wrote *The Story of an African Game: Black Cricketers and the Unmasking of one of Cricket's Greatest Myths. South Africa 1850-2003*. This work reveals the extent of non-white cricket in South Africa from early mission school cricket through to the present time. It is well illustrated and deals thoroughly with its subject. Odendaal was a professor in history and heritage studies at the University of the Western Cape and is the author of many books on South African politics and sport.

In Australia, Bill Reynolds researched below 'first-class' level to compile *A History of Country Week Cricket in Western Australia 1907-2007*. The book contains notes on the 243 clubs that have been involved in Country Week Carnivals during the hundred years, as well as a season-by-season report on the matches. Biographies of the principal personalities are also included. The book is complementary to Anthony Barker's *The WACA*, which was published in 1998. William Perival Reynolds was born in Yarloop, Western Australia in December 1938 and worked on the family farm, before becoming an agricultural consultant.

Other notable present-day Australian cricket historians include Ross Smith and Kenneth Williams. Smith, born in December 1956 in Launceston, is employed in the Community History Centre in Launceston. Apart from his research into Tasmanian cricket he has specialized in recording all the sixes hit in Test Match cricket. Kenneth Williams, born in East Malvern in December 1944 and educated at Melbourne University, was a school teacher by profession. He was largely responsible for the revised ACS Guide to First-Class Cricket in Australia. His book *For Club and Country* details the biographies of Test cricketers with Melbourne connections and he has also written on club cricket in Victoria.

Alf Batchelder is one of a group of researchers and authors who are involved in the projects connected to the Melbourne Cricket Club library and museum. No less than ten of his publications are listed in *Post Padwick*, all of them directly or indirectly featuring the MCG. *The Yorker*, which was published from 1993 to 2003, was a magazine which contained very useful cricket book reviews, as well as historical articles relating to the MCG. For example an abridged version of James Ricci's 'MCG Curators' was published in the magazine. The General Editor was John Owen.

Philip Derriman, originally a journalist in England, joined the *Sydney Morning Herald*. His first major cricket book was *The Grand Old Ground*, being the history of Sydney Cricket Ground. This was followed by *True to the Blue* the history of the NSW Cricket Association and, among other works, a biography of Don Tallon.

Bernard Whimpress is the curator of the museum at the Adelaide Oval. He is the founding editor of *Baggy Green*, the Journal of Australian Cricket, which began publication in 1998. He was written a number of books including *Clem Hill's Reminiscences* and a biography of Ernie Jones in the Lives in Cricket Series.

A. 'Alf' B.M. James has written and published numerous works, most of which are of a statistical nature. One of his early projects, entitled *Averages & Results of Australian First-class Cricket* was issued in several volumes, the first covering 1850-51 to 1914-15 came out in 1985. Generally his publications are in limited editions, some limited to as few as four or five copies. *Post Padwick* lists 15 titles.

Charlie Wat, like Alf James, tends to plough his own furrow. His publications, under the imprint Cricket Stats Publications, were statistical, many of them being updated on an annual basis. Examples are *Test Records of Australian Players*; *The LOI Record of the Australian Players*; *Australian First-class Season; Register of Australian Cricketers*. His first publications came out in the 1980s. Many of course are superseded by information on the internet.

Ric Finlay, based in Tasmania, wrote the Famous Cricketers series book on A.F.Kippax, published in 1993, having compiled *Island Summers*, a history of Tasmanian representative cricket, the previous year. Currently a Committee member of the ACS, he is now more involved in computer programmes related to cricket statistics.

Ronald Cardwell published *The A.I.F. Cricket Team* in 1980 and since then has issued a number of interesting booklets on Australian cricketing topics, including, in recent years brief biographies on W.A.Brown, R.N.Harvey and A.R.Morris.

A lesser item with cricketing as a side issue is *Football's Forgotten Tour* by John Williamson, which tells for the first time of Arthur Shrewsbury's effort to claw back the money lost on the 1887-88 England tour to Australia. It is a fascinating saga.

The increased interest in cricket history has resulted in the reprinting of many rare cricket books. Sporting Handbooks published facsimile editions of the early *Wisdens*, covering the years 1864 to 1878. Willows Publishing has continued this process and facsimiles are available for most seasons up to 1945.

Two projects which were, perhaps, more ambitious, were the facsimiles of Britcher and Denison. Both these were undertaken by Christopher Saunders. The Britcher reprint of 15 Britcher annuals and an accompanying volume by D.R.Allen is the more valuable project, since the extant copies of Britcher annuals are exceedingly rare. The set of Denisons follows a similar pattern, with facsimiles of his annuals and a biography (plus numerous appendices) by Allen.

Roger Heavens, who has previously been mentioned in connection with the reprinting of *Scores & Biographies,* published a reprint of Bentley's scores, again with an introduction by Allen. In 1989, Heavens was also responsible for re-issuing the two volumes of Buckley's cricket notices. Perhaps someone might publish all the manuscript notes that Buckley collected and remain largely forgotten in the archives at Lord's. J.W.McKenzie reprinted Epps' Scores, again with an introduction by

Allen, and has been responsible for the reprinting of several of the early books relating to England tours.

During 2007 and 2008 there has been a spate of anguished biographies or autobiographies by present-day cricketers; with psychiatrists now a feature of Test and County squads, this is hardly a surprise. These do not however come within the remit of this present work. Other books have concentrated on events and personalities of the past fifty years or so. Stephen Chalke published his perceptive biography of Tom Cartwright in 2007 and in 2008 a collection of his own essays from the *Wisden Cricketer*.

Gideon Haigh, a Melbourne journalist, in 1993 wrote *The Cricket War* which detailed the Packer Affair. Since then he has built up a reputation as a cricket historian and his biographies of W.W.Armstrong and Jack Iverson have been well received. As has previously been noted he was for a time Editor of *Wisden Australia*. He has also published books on Test Series involving Australia. Gideon Clifford Davidson Haigh was born in London, but raised in Geelong. He has been described as the natural successor to Neville Cardus.

A more difficult research project however was Tony Laughton's *Captain of the Crowd.*. This biography of Albert Craig, the Surrey Poet, was one of the outstanding 'historical' cricket books of the last ten years, published by Boundary Books and running to over 300 pages with many fresh illustrations. He has also published a book on the early collector A.D.Taylor.

On a much larger canvas, Sir John Major, the former Prime Minister, wrote *More Than A Game*, which in the main describes the development of cricket from its earliest beginnings until the 1870s, but then gives a briefer description of cricket to the First World War. It is a work for the general reader, which adds no fresh facts, nor does it pose any new theories with regard to the game's origins.

The *Wisden Almanack* for 2009 was edited by the *Sunday Telegraph* cricket correspondent, Scyld Berry, who took over from Matthew Engel in 2008. The editor lists well over a hundred people who have contributed to the latest edition, but the Deputy Editors are Harriet Monkhouse, Hugh Chevallier, who joined *Wisden* in 1999, and Steven Lynch. Harriet Monkhouse, born in 1962 and coming from Manchester, is an Oxford graduate, who joined the *Almanack* in 1990 and as the editor of the day noted 'she has altered the work pattern of more than a decade. For that I am especially grateful'. Whether the word decade should be changed to century is an open question. Harriet was elected to the Committee of the ACS in 1996 and has also been a unobtrusively sound adviser to the Association. Steven Lynch has been previously noted. Philip Bailey is now described as the 'Chief Statistician'. To accommodate other material the section devoted to U.K. cricket has been reduced. All the domestic One Day matches now only appear as potted scores and Minor County and Second Eleven competition results, averages and reports have been severely curtailed. The splendid Births & Deaths section of Ashley-Cooper has become four pages and 172 names. However all Test players are contained in a separate section as are most current first-class players, which means that a large number appear in both lists. A & C Black are presently the publishers.

Overseas the annual for New Zealand maintains its high standard, South Africa's now fails to give the detailed scores of all first-class matches and in 2008 there were no national annuals for West Indies, Australia or India (save for the Board's publication which is almost impossible to find). This latter work was entitled *Cricontrol Statistical Annual* edited by Sudhir Vaidya until 1996-97. The title was then changed to *BCCI Statistical Annual* edited by Mohandas Memon until 2001-02. Vaidya then resumed the editorship. The work is very comprehensive and includes junior cricket. A number of Indian Ranji Trophy sides have had publications issued, the most impressive being *The Spirit of Chepauk* by Subbiah Muthiah – this was the 150 year history of Madras C.C.

The increasing reliance by statisticians on the internet sites for both first-class and even more so for 'List A' One Day and Twenty-Twenty matches. It should be noted that the ACS, mainly through Philip Bailey, introduced the system of classifying Limited Overs Matches and those which are considered of the equivalent to 'First-Class' are given 'List A' status and used by CricketArchive and other bodies for compiling players' career records. For the best part of a century, cricket statisticians compiled either first-class records, usually for their particular team, or, from the 1890s, Test Match data. The advent of top class Limited Overs cricket, first at domestic, then at International, level added a whole new raft of 'records'. The recent emergence of Twenty-Twenty cricket adds two more facets, so that the ordinary cricket follower can be easily confused as 'records' fall almost match-by-match.

The 2009 Wisden contains the following note in its book review section 'All first-class counties produce handbooks of varying quality.' No mention is made of Minor County handbooks, some of which are excellent. A splendid summary of all the first-class counties' annuals was written by Clive Porter and published in *The Journal of The Cricket Society* Volume 23, no.2, Spring 2007. The book review section of the *Wisden Almanack* has still not recovered from the retirement of John Arlott.

The major change on the U.K. cricket magazine front was the merger in 2003 of the *Wisden Cricket Monthly* and *The Cricketer*. The first hybrid appeared in October 2003 under the editorship of John Stern, but with Matthew Engel as the 'Editor-in-Chief', linking the magazine, in theory, more closely to the *Almanack*. In 2008 John Stern continued as editor. A number of other U.K.-based cricket magazines have come and generally gone over the past two decades. They have been almost entirely focused on current affairs, usually with a greater picture content. The magazines that regularly feature historical and statistical work are *The Journal of The Cricket Society* whose current editor is Andrew Hignell and *The Cricket Statistician* (the journal of the ACS) with Simon Sweetman in charge. Prior to Sweetman taking on the editorship in 2006, both Philip Thorn and Mark Asquith had short spells as editor.

Richard Hill launched *Cricket Lore* at the end of 1991. This was announced as being issued ten times a year and was devoted in the main to historical subjects, but rather like Bowen's *The Cricket Quarterly* did discuss current matters. The magazine continued until 2005, but never seemed too sure of its readership and its articles were aimed more at the general cricket enthusiast than the dedicated historian or statistician.

At the time of writing the major historical project, which has been briefly noted earlier is *From Commons to Lord's*, Ian Maun's compilation of all known 18th century references to cricket. Volume One was published by Roger Heavens in 2009 and covered the years 1700 to 1750, including many references not published in a cricket work before, a number of which come from works of fiction. The volume was edited by Roger Packham and Martin Wilson. Roger Packham has long been an expert on early cricket and worked with John Goulstone on projects in the 1980s. Importantly the book brought together the researches of Waghorn, Buckley and many others including the Sussex volume by McCann, noted at the beginning of this chapter. Volume Two, covering 1751 to 1770, was published in 2011.

Ian Maun was born in 1949 and educated at RGS High Wycombe and Pembroke College, Cambridge. Formerly a schoolmaster by profession, he has in recent years been a language lecturer at Exeter University

Books on cricket's history as a whole continue to be published. In 2009, the broadcaster and former county cricketer, Simon Hughes, had his work *And God Created Cricket* published. It has been described as history strung together in an entertaining and conversational manner. Clearly no in-depth research was undertaken, but it serves as a gentle introduction to the game, with not too many blunders.

A more serious tome issued in 2010 is *The Cricketer's Progress: From Meadowland to Mumbai* by Eric Midwinter, which traces cricket's history in tandem with the social and political happenings of each era. It is similar to Derek Birley's social history, but without the factual errors of the latter.

The ACS has continued to issue books of match scores in the last two years. Philip Bailey has acted as editor and compiler of the first-class match series which at the time of writing has reached 1924. John Bryant has acted as editor and compiler of a new series *ACS Overseas First Class Annual*, which publishes the scores of all first-class matches played outside the British Isles. The reason behind the publication has been the gradual ceasing of national annuals, in particular India, West Indies and Australia.

John Bryant, who is a member of the Committee of the ACS, was born in Waltham Abbey in 1956, educated at Goff's School, Cheshunt and is a Policy Leader for the National Housing Federation. Bryant was editor of a book of 'Great' matches played in England between 1772 and 1800, published by the ACS in 2011. A panel of researchers, led by Martin Wilson and Keith Warsop checked the scores published in Haygarth's *Scores & Biographies* and other earlier sources, against contemporary press details. This checking revealed a remarkable number of changes to the 'accepted' versions of the scores and was a work of major importance.

Philip Paine has been a frequent contributor to cricket magazines, though his name is chiefly associated with a set of volumes detailing the final resting places of cricketers. He has combed numerous graveyards working on this self imposed task. He also did valuable work on establishing the history and location of the Montpelier Ground in what is now South London.

With cricketing publications of an ever more diverse nature being researched and published, it has been impossible within the limited scope of this book to include every work on cricket's history and statistics. As was noted in the initial Introduction, the three Bibliographies are the ideal source for readers who wish to delve further into the subject.

Appendix One
Peter Wynne-Thomas
By Keith Warsop

In a book telling the story of the historians of cricket it would be surprising if a reader was unable to find the name of Peter Wynne-Thomas who has been at the forefront of the game's researchers for some four decades. However, with his customary modesty the author of this volume has omitted all but passing reference to himself so that the duty of covering his achievement has been deputed to a long-time colleague.

Peter Wynne-Thomas was born in 1934 and educated at Lancing College in Sussex. At the age of eight he moved with his family to Nottingham and when county cricket resumed at the end of the Second World War he gravitated to Trent Bridge where he followed Nottinghamshire in the heyday of Walter Keeton, Charlie Harris, Joe Hardstaff, Harold Butler, Arthur Jepson and the young Reg Simpson.

This led him to compile the players' seasonal averages and eventually to attempt to record the doings of all Nottinghamshire cricketers, both statistical and biographical. In this task he used the best of models — Arthur Haygarth, the compiler of *Scores and Biographies*. Like Haygarth, Wynne-Thomas visited or sent questionnaires to old players or their descendants as well as touring cemeteries to transcribe the inscriptions on cricketers' graves.

In the 1960s both he and I were early contributors to Rowland Bowen's *Cricket Quarterly* and it was through Bowen that we made contact. From the mid-1960s I joined Wynne-Thomas in his quest for old Nottinghamshire cricketers, including the visits to graveyards, and slowly his research turned into a book — *Nottinghamshire Cricketers 1821-1914*. When published in 1971 it won the Cricket Society's "Book of the Year" award and set him on a cricket writing career which eventually pushed his professional job of architectural consultant into the background.

When Bowen decided to end the *Cricket Quarterly*, moves were made to keep it going and Wynne-Thomas was the man set to take over as its editor. At the last minute Bowen had a change of heart as he felt the CQ was too personally bound up with himself to allow it to be run by anyone else.

Soon afterwards, in 1973, the Association of Cricket Statisticians was formed and, apart from a few months in 1974, Wynne-Thomas was at its heart, first as treasurer and then from July 1974 as secretary until he retired in 2006. He was deeply involved in the many ACS publishing enterprises, contributing a number of volumes himself as well as undertaking the typesetting for many of the early booklets and for years he checked, sub-edited and did the art work for these productions.

From April 1977 to May 1979 Wynne-Thomas and Robert Brooke issued their own monthly magazine, *Cricket News*, and it was in 1979 that Wynne-Thomas became archivist at Trent Bridge, the year in which the follow-up to his first Nottinghamshire volume appeared — *Nottinghamshire Cricketers 1919-1939*. He had already edited the county's annuals from 1975 and once ensconced at Trent Bridge he became a focal point for an avalanche of queries on all things cricket; historical, statistical and trivial.

In the 1980s Wynne-Thomas began a fruitful partnership with the publisher Hamlyn which saw in rapid succession *England on Tour* (1982), *The Hamlyn A-Z of Cricket Records* (1983) and *The Complete History of Cricket Tours at Home and Abroad* (1989) which incorporated the *England on Tour* material. The A-Z of records was modelled on a similar Hamlyn publication for football edited by Phil Soar who included all the Football and Scottish League tables from the start. Using this example, Wynne-Thomas gave every County Championship and Sunday League table as well as the leading averages each season from 1864, thus getting away from the standard book of cricket records which usually consisted of endless list after endless list. Instead, Wynne-Thomas also gave some background context and comment on the various records involved. Different areas were tackled with *Cricket in Conflict* (Newnes, 1984), written jointly with Peter Arnold, which covered various cricket rows over the years, and *Give Me Arthur* (Barker, 1985), a biography of the great Nottinghamshire batsman Arthur Shrewsbury which made use of the cricketer's own diaries.

However, Wynne-Thomas' most important achievement in these years was his collaboration with Philip Bailey and Philip Thorn on the *Who's Who of Cricketers* (Newnes, 1984), a 1,144-page epic which gave biographical details of all participants in British first-class cricket from 1864 as well as the most prominent of earlier players. The main division of labour was that Bailey provided the career figures, Thorn a mountain of biographical data and Wynne-Thomas the important contribution of writing brief but readable entries for the huge number of players covered as well as typing the manuscript. An updated edition came out in 1993.

In 1988 the Trent Bridge ground had been in existence for 150 years so to mark this occasion came *Trent Bridge. A history of the ground to commemorate the 150th anniversary 1838-1988* in which Wynne-Thomas indulged in a full-scale history of the county rather than restricting himself solely to the story of the ground. A 32-page supplement appeared in 1994.

That was not Wynne-Thomas' only tilt at a Nottinghamshire history at this time. In the early 1990s the publisher Helm brought out a series of county histories to which he contributed volumes on Hampshire and Lancashire as well as Nottinghamshire.

At this period Wynne-Thomas was also editing the Nottinghamshire Yearbook (formerly the annual) as well as writing articles for a variety of cricket publications but his major attention was focused on a wider field than just Nottinghamshire. *The History of Cricket. From the Weald to the World* (HM Stationery Office, 1997) not only covered all available research into the game's past as well as including some impressive theories of the author's, but convincingly demolished some of the myths and wackier ideas about cricket's origins.

Perhaps the most pioneering work of all was *Nottinghamshire Cricket Grounds* (Nottinghamshire County Council, 2001) whose title implies coverage of the grounds used by the county club but whose scope is explained in the sub-title "being a tour and survey of 463 past or present grounds in the County with a Ploughman's Lunch or two", this last phrase referring to the many village pubs called at for refreshment over the course of three years of research. Wynne-Thomas' industry is apparent not just in the pursuit of many lost grounds but also in the diagrams he provides for a large number of those still existing. At its publication this was a unique achievement which has since inspired a few other researchers to start on a similar quest in their own counties.

One major achievement, however, still lacks a publisher. This is Wynne-Thomas' monumental *Index to The Cricketer 1921-2004* which he compiled over some twenty years in time off from his other cricket labours. It exists in the Trent Bridge library on hundreds of index cards but needs to be transferred into typescript. Many researchers have made valuable use of it so its preservation in more permanent form is an urgent necessity. Meanwhile, for Peter Wynne-Thomas, work continues on the latest Nottinghamshire annual.

Appendix Two
Statistics in the Computer Age
By David Kendix

From the mid-1980s onwards, the work and scope of the cricket statistician, that had remained essentially unchanged throughout cricket history, was fundamentally altered through the advent of the home computer and then the internet.

This allowed two significant changes in the way statisticians worked. The computer allowed information on players and scores to be captured on databases or spreadsheets. This data could then be manipulated, allowing searches for records or compilation of averages to be carried out instantly. Then the internet allowed information to be globally accessible, shared and exchanged, updated and corrected. The provision of cricket statistics became a real-time commercial service, with an ever broadening range of outputs and uses. This Appendix covers some of the pioneers in the harnessing of computer power and cricket statistics, generating materials that could not feasibly have been delivered in earlier generations.

The building blocks of most cricket statistics are a set of complete and accurate scorecards of international or first-class matches. While it was a founding goal of the ACS to classify all such matches and make their records as accurate as possible, it needed the computer to make this information usable and accessible. However, the original rationale for placing scorecards on computer in a form that allowed statistical analysis, as opposed to merely for typesetting purposes, came from an unlikely source.

Although arguments over the relative merits of batsmen and bowlers had raged throughout cricket history, the statistical tools for making such comparisons remained resolutely blunt for well over a century. There were simply batting averages and bowling averages. Of course it was well recognised that traditional averages could never properly distinguish between performances made against strong or weak opponents, on friendly or treacherous pitches, or in a winning or losing cause. It was only with computers that it became possible to create an objective method to factor in such differences; the result being player ratings.

Rob Eastaway (b 1963) is an author, speaker and occasional broadcaster, particularly in the field of the public understanding of maths. In 1984 he was introduced by a mutual friend to Gordon Vince, who had successfully built a computerised cricket simulation game; the modern version of the 'Howzat' dice game or 'Oval' card game played by earlier generations of schoolboys. An article on this new computer simulation appeared in *The Cricketer* in 1986 and prompted former England captain Ted Dexter to contact Vince and Eastaway. Dexter saw how golf had player rankings and wondered why cricket could not do the same. The three of them worked on the concept over that winter and, with sponsorship from Deloittes, launched the first set of Test cricket rankings in June 1987. This generated significant media coverage, the idea of announcing who was the number one batsman and bowler in the world at that time being an innovative way to promote the game. In 1988, the BBC started showing players' world rankings as part of its coverage, further raising its profile. Then in 1991, Graham Gooch became the world's top ranked batsman, an achievement that resonated with UK press and public opinion.

Soon after the international ratings first appeared, there was a call for a similar approach to be applied to the English county game. Dexter, in his new capacity as Chairman of Selectors, would be a welcome recipient of any data purporting to show who really were the best performing county cricketers. By suitably adapting their Test methodology, Vince and Eastaway duly delivered a set of county batting and bowling rankings, which with sponsorship became the Whyte & Mackay rankings. In order to maintain the Test and county rankings, Vince needed to enter on to his computer the scorecard of each match as it was played. He created a program that allowed the information within a match scorecard to be extracted automatically and input into the rankings model. The program also checked the scorecard for internal consistency, ensuring not only that all the totals tallied, but that items such as falls of wicket were consistent with the development of an innings.

The fortuitous by-product of this exercise was that other scorecard statistics, beyond those captured for the rankings model, could be readily extracted from the typed-up scorecards. In particular, at any point during the county season, a comprehensive set of county or national batting or bowling averages could be generated.

The next step was to apply the international ranking model retrospectively, thereby recreating the ratings that players would have achieved at all stages in their careers. This generated statistics that objectively compared players from different eras, at least to the extent to which they each dominated their contemporaries. But since this involved Vince entering all past Test scorecards into his template, it suddenly became possible to generate automatically virtually any set of Test records capable of being derived from a scorecard.

So, motivated by Ted Dexter's dream of a set of world Test rankings, and with the consequent need for a database that captured scorecard data, the first major step in the computerisation of cricket statistics had been achieved.

As well as being used by various television companies and news agencies, Vince also provided his program to local cricket clubs who could then input their past and future scorecards and thereby generate their own set of player and historical records.

During the 1990s, a variety of 'rival' player ratings were devised, competing for coverage and credibility. Then in 1998, Dexter, Eastaway and Vince, now sponsored by PwC, launched the ODI ratings. As other methods fell into disuse, these were increasingly being referred to by the media as the official world ratings. Finally in 2003, the ICC formally adopted the ratings, securing sponsorship first from LG and then Reliance Mobile.

With the emergence of the internet, the Cricinfo website became the natural home for typed-up international scorecards. At this point, anyone with computer access could, either by subscribing to a database or by going online, look up scores of matches that were previously glimpsed only by those fortunate enough to have the relevant reference books. Making source data available to anyone interested in cricket statistics was the next key step in allowing new and original research to be undertaken.

The twin channels for further progress were to expand the breadth of scores available and to increase the ability to search the data, allowing ever more tailored information to be extracted. Andrew Samson in South Africa and Ric Finlay in Australia both developed their own offline databases incorporating a significant range of first-class scorecards and more search functionality. The latter was made available on a subscription service with emailed updates. These proved highly popular with television and radio commentators, allowing queries to be answered instantly while the prompt for the query was still topical. To know whether a new record has been set, one no longer needed to know what the previous record was, nor even whether it had ever been researched previously, but only to be able to create the relevant search from the required database.

The culmination of the computerisation of cricket statistics has been the phenomenon that is CricketArchive, founded by Peter Griffiths and Philip Bailey in 2003 with the original aim of capturing the scorecard of every first-class match and List A match. With this task completed by 2004, it then broadened its scope to almost all levels of the game for which authoritative scorecards exist, including minor counties, club matches, age group and women's cricket. As at June 2011, it contained around 270,000 match scorecards and 400,000 player profiles and its rate of growth appears limited only by the appetite of statisticians around the world to submit new scores or enhanced details of past matches. An unusual occurrence can be spotted in a first-class match somewhere in the world and within minutes a query can be run on CricketArchive and an email distributed chronicling any precedents for the occurrence in any of the 53,000 first-class matches to have been played over the previous two centuries.

Beyond the electronic compilation of historic information, there have been two other uses of cricket statistics made possible by computing power, which have each in their own way transformed how the game is played or reported. Yet in both cases, the pioneers would not necessarily have seen themselves as cricket statisticians, but as people who happened to apply their commercial, computing or mathematical skills to the game of cricket.

In the late 1980s, premium rate telephone services began providing live commentary on all county matches. This alerted the ECB to the fact that scores of county matches was an asset valued by millions of cricket followers, yet one that provided no commercial return to English cricket. Journalists had for years phoned through updates from the ground, typically at 30 minute intervals. But if scores could be generated electronically in real time, directly from the official scorers, with access to these feeds being made commercially available to the media, then this would be a service that would have some value. In a joint venture with the Press Association (PA), the ECB introduced in 1993 the mandatory scoring of county cricket by computer, then two years later, once the technology was deemed reliable enough, it was expanded to cover international matches.

The official scorer would enter each ball bowled into the 'Cricket Record' program, the information would travel through a modem to PA, where it would create instant scorecards that would always reconcile. These could then be placed on the PA website and formatted according to its clients' needs, providing page-ready copy for newspapers. Without the scope for transcription errors, the reliability of scorecards compiled by Wisden increased dramatically. Just as significantly, for the first time, averages could be generated in real time and published at any point in the season. So the traditionally laborious process of producing end of season averages was no longer a task at all, being an automatic by-product of computer scoring. Even the intermediate step of typing up scorecards had been removed; statistics in real time allowed commentators to feast on an ever broader range of statistical offerings.

So as we move into the second decade of the 21st century, we find that the capturing and use of scores and records on computer is no longer limited to the first-class game or to 'serious' statisticians. Software packages tailored to even the most modest club or village team can allow full searchable records of scores and player biographies to be compiled online, with multiple users updating and enhancing the information. Meanwhile cricket scoring packages such as Total Cricket Scorer allows the subscriber to score the match and provide live online feeds.

The publication of cricket statistics research has flourished on the internet. Any number of websites and blogs have appeared with regular and original output appearing from, amongst others, Steven Lynch, S Rajesh, George Binoy and Travis Basevi. Broadcasters such as Sky TV appoint their own statisticians such as Benedict Bermange and Richard Isaacs to keep the commentators nourished with statistics generated from their laptops. The transformation of the cricket statistician from the intricate and laborious hobby to the mass media driven supplier of real time data is complete.

Perhaps the most important and pragmatic application of computing to cricket statistics was undertaken by two English academics in the mid-1990s, with their research changing limited overs cricket worldwide. In 1992, the result of an evenly poised World Cup semi-final was decided when rain led to a two over interruption. Throughout the 30 year history of one-day cricket, anomalous or unfair results had arisen once the weather played a part, but such a flaw had become unsustainable in the form of the game that had become commercially dominant.

Frank Duckworth (b. 1939) a retired mathematical scientist and editor of the news magazine of the Royal Statistical Society and Tony Lewis (b. 1942) a university lecturer and authority in Operational Research, had met in 1995 and realised that rain stoppages was a problem that needed solving using the tools of their trade. Their key conceptual breakthrough was the realisation that when a team is batting they are trying to maximise their score subject to two constraints, their limited overs and their limited wickets (i.e. being all out). Therefore they needed to understand how in practice these two constraints operated. This required substantial quantities of source data, which fortunately for them had just started to become accessible online through ball-by-ball records of recent limited overs matches. With this data they created a series of tables that described how on average teams tended to marshal their twin resources (remaining overs and wickets). Thus when an interruption occurred, they could adjust the target score by an amount that reflected the resources lost, thereby maintaining the size of the advantage held by the 'winning' team.

The Duckworth Lewis method, subsequently known simply as D/L was scrutinised by ECB and ICC, before being used for the first time in an ODI at the start of 1997. As more data was collected, the formula was refined, with a more sophisticated version being launched for professional cricket in 2003 which would run only on a computer, rather than using look-up tables. As with player ratings, others put forward their versions, but none has yet eclipsed the D/L method. In 2001, ICC adopted it as the required standard for international cricket and it has since been used at domestic level across the world. Their eponymous creators received MBEs in 2010 for "services to Mathematics and to Cricket".

Appendix Three
ACS Statistician of the Year

2010	Martin Wilson
2009	Ian Maun
2008	Peter Griffiths
2007	Tony Percival
2006	Krish Reddy
2005	Tony Webb
2004	Tim McCann
2003	Abid Ali Kazi
2002	Geoff Wilde
2001	No award
2000	Don Ambrose
1999	Brian Croudy
1998	Joe Webber
1997	Ray Webster
1996	Vic Isaacs
1995	Bill Frindall
1994	Howard Milton
1993	Philip Bailey, Philip Thorn and Peter Wynne-Thomas
1992	Kit Bartlett
1991	Les Hatton
1990	Richard Lockwood
1989	Robert Brooke
1988	Andrew Hignell
1987	Philip Bailey
1986	George Russ

Appendix Four
List of ACS Officers and Committee Members
1973-2011

The following have been ACS officers:

President
R.M.Streeton 1987-1997
E.C.Midwinter 1997-2004
D.J.Baggett 2004-2007
M.J.K.Smith 2007-

Chairman
R.W.Brooke 1973-1979
D.A.Lambert 1979-1981
A.Woodhouse 1981-1993
M.G.Lorimer 1993-2002
A.J.Ledbetter 2002-2004
D.Miller 2004-2008
D.Kendix 2008-2011
R.H.L.Moulton 2011

Vice-Chairman
J.Featherstone 1982-1987

Secretary
D.A.Lambert 1973-1974
R.W.Brooke 1974
P.Wynne-Thomas 1974-2006
A.K.Hignell 2006-

Treasurer
P.Wynne-Thomas 1973-1974
P.R.Thorn 1974
K.S.C.Trushell 1974-1985
D.Q.Harvey 1985-1990
A.J.Ledbetter 1990-1999
J.C.Lodge 1999-2007
R.Gibbons 2007-

Marketing Manager
 J.Featherstone 1987-1993
L.W.Hatton 1993-1994
S.Sheen 1995-2002
M.Pope 2002-2006

Editor of The Cricket Statistician
R.W.Brooke 1973-1985
J.W.Stockwell 1986-1988
P.J.Bailey 1988-2005
P.R.Thorn 2005
P.Wynne-Thomas and K.Warsop (joint) 2005
M.Asquith 2006
A.K.Hignell 2006
S.Sweetman 2006-

The complete list of those who have served on the committee as members or
ex-officio members is:

M.Asquith 2006
P.J.Bailey 1973-1976; 1982-
D.J.Baggett 2004-2007
C.J.Bartlett 1995-2006
R.W.Brooke 1973-1986
J.Bryant 2008-
B.A.C.Croudy 1975-1985; 1986
J.Featherstone 1982-1993
R.Finlay 2006-

D.R.Gallagher 1973

P.D.Griffiths 1993-2008

D.Q.Harvey 1985-1990

L.W.Hatton 1978-2003

B.Heald 1988-2006

A.K.Hignell 1993-1994, 2006-

R.H.Isaacs 2006-2008

V.H.Isaacs 1981-1988

D.Jeater 2007-

D.Kendix 2005-

D.A.Lambert 1973-1974; 1976-1981

A.J.Ledbetter 1990-1999; 2000-2005

D.H.A.Lodge 1989-1996

J.Lodge 1999-2007

M.G.Lorimer 1988-2003

J.D.Mace 1986-1989

E.C.Midwinter 1997-2004

D.Miller 2003-

R.W.S.Miller 1978-1981

R.H.L.Moulton 2009-

H.F.Monkhouse 1996-

H.Nathan 2006-

M.Pope 1994-2006

W.A.Powell 1993-1995, 1997-1999

A.Samson 2003-2007

S.Sheen 1995-2008

J.W.Stockwell 1982-1986

R.M.Streeton 1985-1997

S.Sweetman 2008-

P.R.Thorn 1973-1974

K.S.C.Trushell 1974-1985; 1987-1993

M.Wilson 2011-

A.Woodhouse 1981-1993

P.Wynne-Thomas 1973-1974; 1974-2006

Appendix Five
ACS Publications and Amendments
Compiled by Peter Griffiths

First-class Match Guides

1. A guide to first class cricket matches played in Australia (31p., 1977)
2. A guide to first class cricket matches played in Australia second edition (96p., 1983)
3. A guide to first class cricket matches played in The British Isles (40p., 1976)
4. A guide to first class cricket matches played in The British Isles second edition (40p., 1982)
5. A guide to important cricket matches played in The British Isles 1709-1863 (40p., 1981)
6. A guide to important cricket matches played in The British Isles 1707-1863 (40p., 1985)
7. A guide to first class cricket matches played in India (208p. 1986)
8. A guide to first class cricket matches played in New Zealand 1863-1980 (120p., 1981)
9. A guide to first class and other important cricket matches in North and South America compiled by C.J.Clynes (32p., 1987)
10. A guide to first class cricket matches played in Pakistan (52p., 1989)
11. A guide to important cricket matches played in South Africa (38p., 1981)
12. A guide to first class cricket matches played in Sri Lanka (32p., 1987)
13. A guide to first class cricket matches played in The West Indies (64p., 1984)
14. Complete first-class match list volume 1 1801-1914 (85p., 1996)
15. Complete first-class match list volume 2 1914/15-1944/45 (71p., 1997)
16. Complete first-class match list volume 3 1945-1962/63 (69p., 1997)
17. Complete first-class match list volume 4 1963-1980/81 (81p., 1998)
18. Complete first-class match list volume 5 1981-1998 (150p., 1999)

Match Scorebooks

19. Great cricket matches 1772-1800 (300p., 2010)

20. Important cricket matches 1801-1819 (125p., 1996)

21. Important cricket matches 1820-1829 (104p., 1996)

22. Important cricket matches 1830-1838 (136p., 1995)

23. Important cricket matches 1839-1844 (158p., 1994)

24. Important cricket matches 1845-1849 (156p., 1994)

25. Cricket matches 1850-1854 (167p., 1992)

26. Cricket matches 1855-1859 (170p., 1989)

27. Cricket matches 1860-1863 (163p., 1984)

28. First class cricket matches 1864-1866 (159p., 1979)

29. First class cricket matches 1867-1869 (158p., 1980)

30. First class cricket matches 1870-1872 (168p., 1980)

31. First class cricket matches 1873-1874 (133p., 1980)

32. First class cricket matches 1875-1876 (152p., 1980)

33. First class cricket matches 1877-1878 (184p., 1981)

34. First class cricket matches 1879-1880 (174p., 1981)

35. First class cricket matches 1881 (96p., 1981)

36. First class cricket matches 1882 (132p., 1981)

37. First class cricket matches 1883 (123p., 1981)

38. First class cricket matches 1884 (145p., 1982)

39. First class cricket matches 1885 (137p., 1982)

40. First class cricket matches 1886 (140p., 1983)

41. First class cricket matches 1887 (116p., 1983)

42. First class cricket matches 1888 (144p., 1983)

43. First class cricket matches 1889 (107p., 1983)

44. First class cricket matches 1890 (144p., 1983)

45. First class cricket matches 1891 (122p., 1984)

46. First class cricket matches 1892 (141p., 1985)

47. First class cricket matches 1893 (167p., 1985)

48. First class cricket matches 1894 (191p., 1985)

49. First class cricket matches 1895 (224p., 1986)

50. First class cricket matches 1896 (224p., 1988)

51. First class cricket matches 1897 (232p., 1988)

52. First class cricket matches 1898 (215p., 1990)

53. First class cricket matches 1899 (248p., 1992)

54. First-class cricket matches 1900 (236p., 1994)

55. First-class cricket matches 1901 (247p., 1996)
56. First-class cricket matches 1902 (280p., 1997)
57. First-class cricket matches 1903 (256p., 1999)
58. First-class cricket matches 1904 (266p., 2000)
59. First-class cricket matches 1905 (282p., 2002)
60. First-class cricket matches 1906 (262p., 2003)
61. First-class cricket matches 1907 (286p., 2004)
62. First-class cricket matches 1908 (276p., 2005)
63. First-class cricket matches 1909 (281p., 2005)
64. First-class cricket matches 1910 (268p., 2006)
65. First-class cricket matches 1911 (300p., 2006)
66. First-class cricket matches 1912 (314p., 2007)
67. First-class cricket matches 1913 (274p., 2008)
68. First-class cricket matches 1914 (282p., 2008)
69. First-class cricket matches 1914/15-1919 (263p., 2008)
70. First-class cricket matches 1920 (263p., 2009)
71. First-class cricket matches 1921 (332p., 2009)
72. First-class cricket matches 1922 (309p., 2010)
73. First-class cricket matches 1923 (347p., 2010)
74. First-class cricket matches 1924 (342p., 2011)
75. First-class cricket a complete record 1926
    compiled and edited by Jim Ledbetter (239p., 2009)
76. First-class cricket a complete record 1927
    compiled and edited by Jim Ledbetter (248p., 2008)
77. First-class cricket a complete record 1928
    compiled and edited by Jim Ledbetter (244p., 2007)
78. First-class cricket a complete record 1929
    compiled and edited by Jim Ledbetter (246p., 2005)
79. First-class cricket a complete record 1930
    compiled and edited by Jim Ledbetter (267p., 2002)
80. Sri Lanka first-class scores 1988-89 (48p., 1994)
81. Sri Lanka first class matches season 1989-90 compiled by Philip J. Bailey
    (44p., 1994)
82. Sri Lanka first class matches season 1990-91 compiled by Philip J. Bailey
    (52p., 1995)
83. Sri Lanka first-class matches season 1991-92 compiled by Philip J. Bailey
    (60p., 1996)

84. Sri Lanka first-class matches 1992/93 compiled by Philip J. Bailey (67p., 1997)

85. Sri Lanka first-class matches 1993/94 compiled by Philip J. Bailey (43p., 1997)

86. Sri Lanka first-class matches 1994/95 compiled by Philip J. Bailey (79p., 1998)

87. Sri Lanka first-class matches 1995/96 compiled by Philip J. Bailey (111p., 1998)

88. Sri Lanka first-class matches 1996/97 compiled by Philip J. Bailey (104p., 1999)

89. Sri Lanka first-class matches 1997/98 compiled by Philip J. Bailey (70p., 1999)

90. Sri Lanka first-class matches 1998/99 compiled by Philip J. Bailey (125p., 2001)

91. Sri Lanka first-class matches 1999/2000 compiled by Philip J. Bailey (102p., 2002)

92. Sri Lanka first-class matches 2000/01 compiled by Philip J. Bailey (138p., 2002)

93. Sri Lanka first-class matches 2001/02 and 2002 compiled by Philip Bailey (131p., 2004)

94. Sri Lanka first-class matches 2002/03 and 2003 compiled by Philip Bailey (117p., 2004)

95. Sri Lanka first-class matches 2003/04 and 2004 compiled by Philip Bailey (105p., 2005)

96. Sri Lanka first-class matches 2004/05 and 2005 compiled by Philip Bailey (80p., 2006)

97. Sri Lanka first-class matches 2005/06 and 2006 compiled by Philip Bailey (113p., 2008)

98. Zimbabwe first-class matches 1993/94 (22p., 1995)

99. Zimbabwe first-class matches 1994/95 compiled by John Ward (28p., 1995)

100. Zimbabwe first-class matches 1995/96 compiled by John Ward (20p., 1996)

101. Zimbabwe first-class matches 1996/97 compiled by John Ward (12p., 1997)

102. Zimbabwe first-class matches 1997/98-2005/06 compiled by Philip Bailey (151p., 2006)

103. Bangladesh first-class and one-day matches 2000/01 compiled by Philip Bailey (67p., 2002)

104. Bangladesh first-class matches 2001/02 compiled by Philip Bailey (37p., 2004)

105. Bangladesh first-class matches 2002/03 and 2003 compiled by Philip Bailey (23p., 2004)

106. Bangladesh first-class matches 2003/04 and 2004 compiled by Philip Bailey (37p., 2004)

107. Bangladesh first-class matches 2004/05 and 2005 compiled by Philip Bailey (39p., 2006)

108. Bangladesh first-class matches 2005/06 compiled by Philip Bailey (38p., 2008)

109. Overseas matches 2007/08 edited by John Bryant (576p., 2010)

110. The minor counties championship 1895 edited by Tony Webb (79p., 2004)

111. The minor counties championship 1896 edited by Tony Webb (77p., 2005)

112. The minor counties championship 1897 edited by Tony Webb (105p., 2005)

113. The minor counties championship 1898 edited by Tony Webb (112p., 2006)

114. The minor counties championship 1899 edited by Tony Webb (114p., 2006)

115. The minor counties championship 1900 edited by Tony Webb (128p., 2007)

116. The minor counties championship 1901 edited by Tony Webb (150p., 2008)

117. The minor counties championship 1902 edited by Tony Webb (139p., 2008)

118. The minor counties championship 1903 edited by Tony Webb (148p., 2009)

119. The minor counties championship 1904 edited by Tony Webb (190p., 2010)

120. The minor counties championship 1905 edited by Tony Webb (164p. 2011)

Cricket Yearbook

121. ACS cricket yearbook 1986 compiled by Peter Wynne-Thomas, Philip Bailey and John Stockwell (224p.)

122. ACS international cricket yearbook 1987 compiled by Peter Wynne-Thomas, Philip Bailey and John Stockwell (224p.)

123. ACS international cricket yearbook 1988 compiled by Philip Bailey, John Stockwell and Peter Wynne-Thomas (96p.)

124. ACS international cricket yearbook 1989 compiled by Philip Bailey (207p.)

125. ACS international cricket yearbook 1990 compiled by Philip Bailey (224p.)

126. ACS international cricket yearbook 1991 compiled by Philip Bailey (232p.)

127. ACS international cricket yearbook 1992 compiled by Philip Bailey (232p.)

128. ACS international cricket yearbook 1993 compiled by Philip Bailey (248p.)

129. ACS international cricket yearbook 1994 compiled by Philip Bailey (256p.)

130. ACS international cricket yearbook 1995 compiled by Philip Bailey (256p.)

131. ACS international cricket yearbook 1996 compiled by Philip Bailey (270p.)

132. ACS international cricket yearbook 1997 compiled by Philip Bailey (280p.)

133. ACS international cricket yearbook 1998 compiled by Philip Bailey (280p.)

134. ACS international cricket yearbook 1999 compiled by Philip Bailey (283p.)

135. ACS international cricket yearbook 2000 compiled by Philip Bailey (288p.)

136. ACS international cricket yearbook 2001 compiled by Philip Bailey (312p.)

137. ACS international cricket yearbook 2002 compiled by Philip Bailey (319p.)

138. ACS international cricket yearbook 2003 compiled by Philip Bailey (337p.)

139. ACS international cricket yearbook 2004 compiled by Philip Bailey (332p.)

140. ACS international cricket yearbook 2005 compiled by Philip Bailey (340p.)

141. ACS international cricket yearbook 2006 compiled by Philip Bailey (341p.)

142. ACS international cricket yearbook 2007 compiled by Philip Bailey (375p.)

143. ACS international cricket yearbook 2008 compiled by Philip Bailey (384p.)

144. ACS international cricket yearbook 2009 compiled by Philip Bailey (424p.)

145. ACS international cricket yearbook 2010 compiled by Philip Bailey (420p.)

146. ACS international cricket yearbook 2011 compiled by Philip Bailey (480p.)

Overseas First-class Annual

147. ACS overseas first-class annual 2009 edited by John Bryant (654p.)

148. ACS overseas first-class annual 2010 edited by John Bryant (685p.)

Minor Counties Annual

149. Minor counties who's who 1976 edited by Robert Brooke (31p.)

150. Minor counties who's who and annual 1977 compiled by Brian Hunt,
      Jack Burrell and Robert Brooke (32p.)

151. Minor counties annual 1978 edited by J.R.Burrell, B.Hunt, R.W.Brooke and
      P.Wynne-Thomas (32p.)

152. Minor counties annual 1979 edited by R.W.Brooke and P.Wynne-Thomas (32p.)

153. Minor counties annual 1980 compiled by Brian Hunt (32p.)

154. Minor counties annual 1981 edited and compiled by Brian Hunt and
      Robert Brooke (i, 33p.)

155. Minor counties annual 1982 edited and compiled by Brian Hunt and
      Robert Brooke (i, 34p.)

156. Minor counties annual 1983 edited and compiled by Brian Hunt and
      Robert Brooke (i, 33p.)

157. Minor counties cricket annual and official handbook 1984 (48p.)

158. Minor counties cricket annual and official handbook 1985
      edited by David Armstrong (56p.)

159. Minor counties cricket annual and official handbook 1986
      edited by David Armstrong (56p.)

160. Minor counties cricket annual and official handbook 1987
     edited by David Armstrong (56p.)
161. Minor counties cricket annual and official handbook 1988
     edited by David Armstrong (56p.)
162. Minor counties cricket annual and official handbook 1989
     edited by David Armstrong (56p.)
153. Minor counties cricket annual and official handbook 1990
     edited by David Armstrong (56p.)
164. Minor counties cricket annual and official handbook 1991
     edited by David Armstrong (56p.)
165. Minor counties cricket annual and official handbook 1992
     edited by David Armstrong (60p.)
166. Minor counties cricket annual and official handbook 1993
     edited by Dacid Armstrong (60p.)
167. Minor counties cricket annual and official handbook 1994
     edited by David Armstrong 4(60p.)
168. Minor counties cricket annual and official handbook 1995
     edited by David Armstrong (64p.)

First-class Counties Second XI Annual

169. First-class counties second XI annual 1985 (40p.)
170. First-class counties second XI annual 1986 (39p.)
171. First-class counties second XI annual 1987 (40p.)
172. First-class counties second XI annual 1988 (39p.)
173. First-class counties second XI annual 1989 (43p.)
174. First-class counties second XI annual 1990 (52p.)
175. First-class counties second XI annual 1991 (52p.)
176. First-class counties second XI annual 1992 (56p.)
177. First-class counties second XI annual 1993 (60p.)
178. First-class counties second XI annual 1994 (64p.)
179. First-class counties second XI annual 1995 (64p.)
180. First-class counties second XI annual 1996 (68p.)
181. First-class counties second XI annual 1997 (64p.)
182. First-class counties second XI annual 1998 (68p.)
183. First-class counties second XI annual 1999 (72p.)
184. First-class counties second XI annual 2000 (72p.)
185. First-class counties second XI annual 2001 (72p.)

186. First-class counties second XI annual 2002 (72p.)
187. First-class counties second XI annual 2003 (72p.)
188. First-class counties second XI annual 2004 (64p.)
189. First-class counties second eleven annual 2005 (64p.)
190. First-class counties second eleven annual 2006 (68p.)
191. First-class counties second eleven annual 2007 (72p.)
192. First-class counties second eleven annual 2008 (72p.)
193. First-class counties second eleven annual 2009 (76p.)
194. First-class counties second eleven annual 2010 (78p.)
195. First-class counties second eleven annual 2011 edited by Howard Clayton (98p.)

British Isles Teams series

196. Berkshire Cricketers 1844-2008 by Tony Percival (56p., 2008)
197. Sir Julien Cahn's team 1923 to 1941 by Peter Wynne-Thomas (16p., 1994)
198. Cambridge University cricketers 1820-1992 (102p., 1992)
199. Cambridgeshire cricketers 1819-2006 (68p., 2007)
200. Cheshire cricketers 1822-1996 (70p., 1997)
201. Derbyshire cricketers 1871-1981 (38p., 1982)
202. Essex cricketers 1876-1986 (36p., 1987)
203. Glamorgan cricketers 1888-1987 (30p., 1988)
204. Gloucestershire cricketers 1870-1979 (36p., 1979)
205. Hampshire cricketers 1800-1982 (46p., 1982)
206. Irish cricketers 1855-1980 (40p., 1980)
207. Kent cricketers 1834-1983 (56p., 1983)
208. Lancashire cricketers 1865-1988 compiled by Malcolm G. Lorimer and Don Ambrose (50p., 1989)
209. Leicestershire cricketers 1879-1977 (27p., 1977, limited ed. of 750 copies)
210. Lincolnshire cricketers 1828-1993 (52p., 1993)
211. Liverpool & District Cricketers 1882-1947 by Don Ambrose (32p., 2002)
212. Middlesex cricketers 1850-1976 (52p., 1976, limited ed. of 700 copies)
213. Minor Counties ListA Cricketers by Richard V.Isaacs (162p., 2009)
214. Northamptonshire cricketers 1905-1984 (24p., 1984)
215. Northumberland cricketers 1867-2010 (68p., 2011)
216. Nottinghamshire cricketers 1835-1978 (36p., 1978)
217. Scottish cricketers 1905-1980 (31p., 1981)
218. Shropshire cricketers 1844-1998 by Tony Percival (61p., 1999)
219. Somersetshire cricketers 1875-1974 (36p., 1974, limited ed. of 500 copies)

220. Staffordshire cricketers 1872-2002 by Tony Percival (75p., 2003)
221. Surrey cricketers 1839-1980 (50p., 1980)
222. Sussex cricketers 1815-1990 by Philip Bailey and Philip Thorn (48p., 1990)
223. Warwickshire cricketers 1843-1973 compiled by Robert Brooke (36p., 1973, limited ed. of 350 copies)
224. Worcestershire cricketers 1899-1974 compiled by Philip Thorn (31p., 1974, limited ed. of 500 copies)
225. Yorkshire cricketers 1863-1985 (47p., 1986)

Overseas Teams series
226. New South Wales cricketers 1855-1981 (64p., 1981)
227. Queensland cricketers 1892-1979 (38p., 1979)
228. South Australian cricketers 1877-1984 (63p., 1984)
229. Tasmanian cricketers 1850-1982 (40p., 1982)
230. Victorian cricketers 1850-1978 (64p., 1978)
231. Western Australian cricketers 1892-1983 (39p., 1983)
232. Border cricketers 1897/98 - 1997/98 by Robin Isherwood and Philip Bailey (35p., 1999)
233. Natal cricketers 1889/90-1996/97 by Robin Isherwood and Philip Bailey (40p., 1997)
234. Transvaal cricketers 1889/90-1993/94 by Robin Isherwood and Philip Bailey (48p., 1995)
235. Western Province cricketers 1889/90-1995/96 by Robin Isherwood and Philip Bailey (43p., 1996)
236. Northerns Cricketers 1937/38 - 1999/2000 by Robin Isherwood and Philip Bailey (32p., 2000)
237. New Zealand Cricketers 1863/64 - 2010 by Tony McCarron (240p., 2010)
238. Barbados cricketers 1865-1990 by Philip Thorn (31p., 1991)
239. Jamaica cricketers 1894/95-1994/95 by Philip Bailey, Bill Lane and Philip Thorn (22p., 1996)
240. European cricketers in India, Ceylon and Burma by Philip Thorn and Philip Bailey (56p., 1998)
241. Rest of the World, Commonwealth and International XI cricketers by Keith Warsop (48p., 2006)

Famous Cricketers Series
242. No 1: J.B.Hobbs by Derek Lodge (44p., 1986)

243. No 1: J.B.Hobbs (second edition) by Jerry Lodge (88p., 2001)

244. No 2: W.H.Ponsford by Anthony George (23p., 1987)

245. No 3: V.M.Merchant by Philip Bailey (28p., 1988)

246. No 4: F.E.Woolley by Howard Milton (84p., 1988)

247. No 4: F.E.Woolley (second edition) by Howard Milton (111p., 1998)

248. No 5: George A. Headley by R. K. Whitham (30p., 1989)

249. No 6: Harold Larwood by Peter Wynne-Thomas (56p., 1990)

250. No 7: Cyril Washbrook by Malcolm Lorimer and Roy Cavanagh (51p., 1990)

251. No 8: Martin Donnelly by Wesley Harte (28p., 1990)

252. No 9: J.C.Clay by Andrew Hignell (71p., 1991)

253. No 10: W.W.Armstrong by Ken Williams (64p., 1991)

254. No 11: Frank Tarrant by Lee Semmens (71p., 1991)

255. No 12: Ranjitsinhji by Simon Wilde (32p., 1992)

256. No 13: Walter Hammond by Neil Barnard (88p., 1992)

257. No 14: Graeme Pollock by Anthony D. Collis (40p., 1992)

258. No 15: W.G.Grace by Derek Lodge (99p., 1993)

259. No 16: Duleepsinhji by Rex Roberts and Simon Wilde (32p., 1993)

260. No 17: Alan Kippax by Ric Finlay (34p., 1993)

261. No 18: Brian Statham by Geoffrey Wilde (104p., 1993)

262. No 19: Ray Lindwall by Warwick Torrens 60p., 1993)

263. No 20: George Parr by Peter Wynne-Thomas (39p., 1994)

264. No 21: Brian Close by C.J.Bartlett (64p., 1994)

265. No 22: A.R.Morris by Peter Hartshorn (22p. 1994)

266. No 23: Bert Sutcliffe by Wesley Harte (94p., 1994)

267. No 24: F.R.Spofforth by Steven Sheen (54p., 1994)

268. No 25: P.B.H.May C.B.E. by Derek Lodge (47p., 1995)

269. No 26: Frank Tyson by Jim Ledbetter (56p., 1995)

270. No 27: Colin Blythe by Brian Croudy (94p., 1995)

271. No 28: P.A.Gibb by Kit Bartlett (43p., 1995)

272. No 29: Everton DeCourcy Weekes by Keith A.P.Sandiford (48p., 1995)

273. No 30: Clem Hill by Keith Walmsley (83p., 1996)

274. No 31: Hanif Mohammed by Salim Parvez (50p., 1996)

275. No 32: D.G.Bradman by Derek Lodge (36p., 1996)

276. No 33: Clyde Leopold Walcott by Keith A.P.Sandiford (46p., 1996)

277. No 34: Tom Hayward by Steven Sheen and Kit Bartlett (72p., 1997)

278. No 35: C.S.Dempster by Wesley Harte (53p., 1997)

279. No 36: Tony Lock by Chris Overson (109p., 1997)

280. No 37: Frank Mortimer Maglinne Worrell by Keith A.P. Sandiford (57p., 1997)
281. No 38: D.V.P.Wright by Ian Phipps (91p., 1997)
282. No 39: D.C.S.Compton by Brian Croudy and Kit Bartlett (76p., 1998)
283. No 40: Neil Harvey by Michael Richardson (50p., 1998)
284. No 41: T.G.Evans by Jerry Lodge (62p., 1998)
285. No 42: Gary Sobers by Keith A.P.Sandiford (86p., 1998)
286. No 43: Tom Graveney by Gerald Hudd (96p., 1998)
287. No 44: Sir Alec V. Bedser C.B.E. by Jerry Lodge (77p., 1999)
288. No 45: Hedley Verity by Barry Rickson (70p., 1999)
289. No 46: Bert Ironmonger by Warwick Franks (67p., 1999)
290. No 47: John Wisden by Peter Griffiths and Kit Bartlett (50p., 1999)
291. No 48: George Giffen by Graham Groom (57p., 1999)
292. No 49: Don Shepherd by Bob Harragan (85p., 1999)
293. No 50: Reg Simpson by Gerald Hudd (60p., 2000)
294. No 51: Don Kenyon by Les Hatton (62p., 2000)
295. No 52. Malcolm Marshall by Vic Isaacs and Dave Allen (111p., 2000)
296. No 53. George Geary by Dennis Lambert (89p., 2000)
297. No 54. Stan McCabe by Steven Sheen (40p., 2000)
298. No 55. Arthur Milton by Gerald Hudd (78p., 2000)
299. No 56. Laurence Barnard Fishlock by Kit Bartlett (47p., 2000)
300. No 57. W.M.Woodfull by Dr.Greg McKie (40p., 2000)
301. No 58. Trevor Bailey by Gerald Hudd (114p., 2001)
302. No 59. Aubrey Faulkner by Brian Bassano (36p., 2001)
303. No 60. Ernest Tyldesley by Geoff Wilde (88p., 2001)
304. No 61. Wes Hall by Keith A.P.Sandiford (49p., 2001)
305. No 62. Ken Barrington by Jerry Lodge (68p., 2001)
306. No 63. A.O.Jones by Hugh Garrod (98p., 2001)
307. No 64. Jas.Lillywhite, jun. by Peter Griffiths and Kit Bartlett (50p., 2002)
308. No 65. Len Hutton by Barry Rickson (73p., 2002)
309. No 66. Wilfred Rhodes by Brian Croudy (155p., 2002)
310. No 67. Ivo Bligh by Peter Wynne-Thomas and Peter Griffiths (17p., 2002)
311. No 68. Fred Tate by Derek Carlaw (58p., 2002)
312. No 69. G.Boycott by Paul Booth (114p., 2002)
313. No 70. Keith Miller by Gerald Hudd (52p., 2002)
314. No 71. J.D.C.Goddard by Keith A.P.Sandiford (39p., 2003)
315. No 72. Lord Cowdrey of Tonbridge, C.B.E. by Howard Milton (106p. 2003)
316. No 73. Sonny Ramadhin by Keith A.P.Sandiford (54p., 2003)

317. No 74. Bill Edrich by Jerry Lodge (72p., 2003)
318. No 75. Arthur Haygarth by Roger Heavens (30p., 2003)
319. No 76. J.N.Crawford by Nigel Hart
     edited and assisted by Bernard Whimpress (47p., 2003)
320. No 77. W.L.Murdoch by Derek Carlaw (56p., 2003)
321. No 78. Bruce Mitchell by Brian Croudy (40p., 2004)
322. No 79. Richard Hadlee by Wesley Harte (138p., 2004)
323. No 80. E.G.Wynyard by Keith Warsop (52p., 2004)
324. No 81. C.W.L.Parker by Gerald Hudd (112p., 2004)
325. No 82. H.E.'Tom' Dollery by Norman Rogers (68p., 2004)
326. No 83. Ian Botham by Gerald Hudd (120p., 2004)
327. No 84. G.L.Jessop by Hugh Garrod (72p., 2004)
328. No 85. Derek Underwood by Philip Crofton and Kit Bartlett (138p., 2004)
329. No 86. John Edrich by Jerry Lodge (78p., 2005)
330. No 87. J.H.Wardle by Gerald Hudd (80p. 2005)
331. No 88: Herbert Wilfred Taylor by Brian Croudy (39p., 2005)
332. No 89. F.S.Jackson by James P.Coldham (54p., 2005)
333. No 90. Roy Edwin Marshall by Keith A.P.Sandiford (76p., 2005)
334. No 91. J.C.Laker by Gerald Hudd (89p., 2005)
335. No 92. Ian Chappell by Bob Harragan and Lawrie Colliver (58p., 2006)
336. No 93. Keith Fletcher O.B.E. by Derek J. Noble (112p., 2006)
337. No 94. Alfred Lewis Valentine by Keith A.P.Sandiford (40p., 2006)
338. No 95. P.A.Perrin by David Jeater (83p., 2006)
339. No 96. Clarrie Grimmtt by Jim Ledbetter (68p., 2006)
340. No 97. Eddie Paynter by Kit Bartlett (40p., 2006)
341. No 98. Tom Goddard by Gerald Hudd (101p., 2006)
342. No 99. Bob Taylor by Jerry Lodge (102p., 2007)
343. No 100. Richie Benaud by Daniel Herborn (82p., 2007)

Lives in Cricket
344. No 1: Allan Watkins by Douglas Miller (113p., 2007)
345. No 2: Johnny Briggs by Stuart Brodkin (109p., 2007)
346. No 3. George Duckworth by Eric Midwinter (75p., 2007)
347. No 4. Ernie Jones by Bernard Whimpress (92p., 2007)
348. No 5. Rockley Wilson by Martin Howe (115p., 2008)
349. No 6. Bill Copson by Kit Bartlett (92p., 2008)
350. No 7. Richard Daft by Neil Jenkinson (147p., 2008)

351. No 8. Ernest Hayes by Keith Booth (124p., 2008)

352. No 9. J.H.King by A.R.Littlewood (151p., 2009)

353. No 10. John Shepherd by Paddy Briggs (137p., 2009)

354. No 11. C.P.Lewis by Bob Harragan and Andrew Hignell (121p., 2009)

355. No 12. Ric Charlesworth by Tony Barker (112p., 2009)

356. No 13. A.P. 'Bunny' Lucas by David Pracy (139p., 2010)

257. No 14. Jack Bond by Douglas Miller (145p., 2010)

258. No 15. Michael Falcon by Stephen Musk (152p., 2010)

259. No 16. Joe Hardstaff by Roger Moulton (142p., 2010)

260. No 17 Fuller Pilch by Brian Rendell (148p., 2010)

261. No 18 F.R.Foster by Robert Brooke (132p., 2011)

262. No 19 Frank Sugg by Martin Howe (136p., 2011)

Grounds Series

363. Cricket grounds of Derbyshire by John Shawcroft (75p., 2008)

364. Cricket grounds of Durham by Steven Draper (52p., 2006)

365. Cricket grounds of Essex by Bob Harragan (65p., 2007)

366. Cricket grounds of Glamorgan by Andrew Hignell (50p., 1985)

367. Cricket grounds of Gloucestershire by Douglas Miller (80p., 2000)

368. Cricket grounds of Hampshire (28p., 1988)

369. Cricket grounds of Kent by Howard Milton (104p., 1992)

370. Cricket grounds of Lancashire by Malcolm Lorimer and Don Ambrose (72p., 1992)

371. Cricket grounds of Leicestershire by E. E. Snow (40p., 1987)

372. Cricket grounds of Middlesex by William Powell and Philip Bailey (48p., 1990)

373. Cricket grounds of Nottinghamshire by Peter Wynne-Thomas (32p., 1984)

374. International cricket grounds of Scotland by Duncan McLeish (72p., 2005)

375. Cricket grounds of Somerset by Bob Harragan (60p., 2005)

376. Cricket grounds of Surrey by William A. Powell (64p., 2001)

377. Cricket grounds of Warwickshire by Robert Brooke (36p., 1989)

378. Cricket grounds of Worcestershire by Les Hatton (32p., 1985)

379. Cricket grounds of Yorkshire by Steven Draper (77p., 1995)

Test Match Grounds Series

380. No 1: Trent Bridge Test Records 1899-1996 by Jim Ledbetter (84p., 1997)

Survey Series

381. 1863: a statistical survey (42p., 1998)
382. 1864: a statistical survey (32p., 1985)
383. 1865: a statistical survey (36p., 1985)
384. 1866: a statistical survey (36p., 1987)
385. 1867: a statistical survey (36p., 1991)
386. 1868: a statistical survey compiled by David Robertson (37p., 1992)
387. 1869: a statistical survey compiled by Don Ambrose (39p., 1994)
388. 1870: a statistical survey compiled by Don Ambrose (44p., 1995)
389. 1871: a statistical survey compiled by Don Ambrose (47p., 1995)
390. 1872: a statistical survey compiled by Don Ambrose (48p., 1996)
391. 1873: a statistical survey compiled by Don Ambrose (50p., 1997)
392. 1874: a statistical survey compiled by Don Ambrose (56p., 1997)
393. 1875: a statistical survey compiled by Don Ambrose (63p., 1999)
394. 1876: a statistical survey compiled by Don Ambrose (63p., 2000)
395. 1877: statistical survey - a review of the season compiled by Don Ambrose
      (62p., 2001)
396. 1878: statistical survey - a review of the season compiled by Don Ambrose
      (76p., 2003)
397   1879: statistical survey - a review of the season compiled by Don Ambrose
      (62p., 2004)
398. 1880: statistical survey - a review of the season compiled by Don Ambrose
      (71p., 2005)
399   1881: statistical survey - a review of the season compiled by Don Ambrose
      (71p. 2006)

Miscellaneous

400. Unpublished scores 1 (53 leaves, 197-)
401. 16 unpublished Australian scores (ii, 16p., 1976)
402. Warwickshire cricket record book compiled by Robert W. Brooke (96p., 1982)
403. John Edward Shilton's book: the triumphs and disasters of a Warwickshire
      cricketer by Robert Brooke (64p., 1984)
404. John Player Special League cricket record book 1969 to 1986
      compiled by Les Hatton (128p., 1987)
405. Kent versus Surrey compiled by George Russ (16p. including covers, 1987)
406. I.C.C. Trophy competitions 1979, 1982, 1986 (ii, 113p., 1989)
407. I.C.C. Trophy competitions 1990 & 1994 (119p., 1995)

408. I.C.C. Trophy Kuala Lumpur 1997 edited by Peter Griffiths (108p., 1997)
409. One day International cricket records by V. H. Isaacs and R. K. Whitham (92p., 1990)
410. Sunday League record book 1969 to 1992 compiled by Les Hatton (158p., 1993)
411. Benson and Hedges Cup record book 1972-1994 compiled by Paul Dyson (163p., 1996) (note that it actually covers the years 1972-1995)
412. Gillette Cup and NatWest Trophy Record Book 1963-1996 compiled by Victor and Richard Isaacs (237p., 1997)
413. England Under-19: Test matches and one-day internationals by Howard Clayton, Peter Griffiths and Derek Sederman (129p., 1996)
414. 99 not out: scorecards and statistics of women's Test Matches 1934-1996 compiled by Arthur Stanford and Marion R.Collin (156p., 1996)
415. Twenty-one years of the ACS by Richard Streeton (57p., 1993)
416. Country House Cricket Grounds of Leicestershire and Rutland (48p., 1998)
417. The Chronicle of W.G. by J.R.Webber (1,102p., 1998)
418. Horan's Diary: The Australian Touring Team 1877-1879 edited by Frank Tyson (358p., 2001)
419. F.S.Ashley-Cooper: A Biographical Sketch & Bibliography by Peter Wynne-Thomas (40p., 2003)
420. Philadelphia and North American Cricketers 1878-1972 by Mark Leopard (24p., 2004)
421. First-Class on Tour by Keith Warsop and Philip Thorn (20p., 2005)
422. A History of Bucks County Cricket Club by Douglas Miller (166p., 2006)
423. Clem Hill's Reminiscences edited by Bernard Whimpress (102p., 2007)
424. Gubby Under Pressure by Brian Rendell (106p., 2007)
425. Two Stalwart Scottish Cricketers: John Kerr and Jimmy Aitchison by Duncan McLeish (38p., 2008)
426. Cricket's Wartime Sanctuary: The First-Class Flight to Bradford by Tony Barker (196p, 2009)
427. Golden Mondays: The Story of Cricket's Bank Holiday Matches by John Shawcroft (213p., 2011)

Cricket Statistician
428. No. 1, June 1973 (6p.)
429. No. 2 (8p.)
430. No. 3 (28p.)

431. No. 4, February 1974 (i, 31p.)
432. No. 5, May 1974 (32p.)
433. No. 6, August 1974 (36p.)
434. No. 7, October 1974 (38p.)
435. No. 8, Winter 1974 (43p.)
436. Index to contents - no. 1 to no. 8 compiled by Brian Croudy (3p., 1975)
437. No. 9, Spring 1975 (44p.)
438. No. 10, Summer 1975 (36p.)
439. No. 11, Autumn 1975 (41p.)
440. No. 12, Winter 1975 (38p.) - called Winter 1976 on the cover
441. No. 13, Spring 1976 (36p.)
442. No. 14, Summer 1976 (38p.)
443. No. 15, Autumn 1976 (40p.)
444. No. 16, December 1976 (44p.)
445. No. 17, March 1977 (36p.)
446. No. 18, July 1977 (40p.)
447. No. 19, October 1977 (36p.)
448. No. 20, December 1977 (46p.)
449. No, 21, March 1978 (i, 25p.)
450. No. 22, June 1978 (i, 25p.)
451. No. 23, October 1978 (i, 24p.)
452. No. 24, December 1978 (i, 24p.)
453. No. 25, March 1979 (i, 33p.) - called April 1979 on the cover
454. No. 26, June 1979 (i, 31p.)
455. No. 27, October 1979 (24p.)
456. No. 28, December 1979 (i, 33p.)
457. No. 29, March 1980 (i, 28p.)
458. No. 30, June 1980 (i, 28p.)
459. No. 31, October 1980 (i, 29p.)
460. No. 32, December 1980 (ii, 38p. including covers)
461. No. 33, March 1981 (i, 29p.)
462. No. 34, June 1981 (i, 32p.)
463. No. 35, October 1981 (36p.)
464. No. 36, December 1981 (44p.)
465. Index to The Cricket Statistician 1973 to 1981 issues no. 1 to no. 36 inc. compiled by L. T. Newell and L. Hatton (24p., 1981)
466. No. 37, March 1982 (36p.)

467. No. 38, June 1982 (32p.)
468. No. 39, October 1982 (40p.)
469. No. 40, December 1982 (32p.)
470. No. 41, March 1983 (48p.)
471. No. 42, June 1983 (32p.)
472. No. 43, October 1983 (32p.)
473. No. 44, December 1983 (64p.)
474. No. 45, March 1984 (40p.)
475. No. 46, June 1984 (36p.)
476. No. 47, October 1984 (32p.)
477. No. 48, December 1984 (48p.)
478. No. 49, March 1985 (40p.)
479. No. 50, June 1985 (40p.)
480. No. 51, Autumn 1985 (48p.)
481. No. 52, Winter 1985 (44p.)
482. No. 53, Spring 1986 (48p.)
483. No. 54, Summer 1986 (48p.)
484. No. 55, Autumn 1986 (48p.)
485. No. 56, Winter 1986 (48p.)
485. No. 57, Spring 1987 (40p.)
486. No. 58, Summer 1987 (48p.)
487. No. 59, Autumn 1987 (48p.)
488. No. 60, Winter 1987 (48p.)
489. No. 61, Spring 1988 (40p.)
490. No. 62, Summer 1988 (48p.)
491. No. 63, Autumn 1988 (48p.) - incorrectly called no. 62 on title page
492. No. 64, Winter 1988 (48p.)
493. No. 65, Spring 1989 (40p.)
494. No. 66, Summer 1989 (48p.)
495. No. 67, Autumn 1989 (48p.)
496. No. 68, Winter 1989 (48p.)
497. No. 69, Spring 1990 (40p.)
498. No. 70, Summer 1990 (48p.)
499. No. 71, Autumn 1990 (48p.)
500. No. 72, Winter 1990 (48p.)
501. No. 73, Spring 1991 (40p.)
502. No. 74, Summer 1991 (48p.)

503. No. 75, Autumn 1991 (48p.)

504. No. 76, Winter 1991 (48p.)

505. No. 77, Spring 1992 (40p.)

506. Index to The Cricket Statistician issues 1-77 compiled by Peter Griffiths (87p., 1992)

507. No 78, Summer 1992 (48p.)

508. No 79, Autumn 1992 (48p.)

509. No 80, Winter 1992 (48p.)

510. No 81, Spring 1993 (40p.)

511. No 82, Summer 1993 (48p.)

512. No 83, Autumn 1993 (48p.)

513. No 84, Winter 1993 (48p.)

514. No 85, Spring 1994 (40p.)

515. No 86, Summer 1994 (48p.)

516. No 87, Autumn 1994 (48p.)

517. No 88, Winter 1994 (48p.)

518. No 89, Spring 1995 (40p.)

519. No 90, Summer 1995 (48p.)

520. No 91. Autumn 1995 (48p.)

521. No 92, Winter 1995 (48p.)

522. No 93, Spring 1996 (40p.)

523. No 94, Summer 1996 (48p.)

524. No 95, Autumn 1996 (48p.)

525. No 96. Winter 1996 (48p.)

526. No 87 Spring 1997 (??p.)

527. No 98. Summer 1997 (48p.)

528. No 99. Autumn 1997 (48p.)

529. No 100. Winter 1997 (100p.)

530. Subject index to The Cricket Statistician issues 1-100 compiled by Peter Griffiths (88p., 1998)

531. No 101. Spring 1998 (48p.)

532. No 102. Summer 1998 (48p.)

533. No 103. Autumn 1998 (48p.)

534. No 104. Winter 1998 (48p.)

535. No 105. Spring 1999 (40p.) - incorrectly called summer on the cover

536. No 106. Summer 1999 (48p.)

537. No 107. Autumn 1999 (48p.)

538. No 108. Winter 1999 (48p.)
539. No 109. Spring 2000 (40p.)
540. No 110. Summer 2000 (48p.)
541. No 111. Autumn 2000 (48p.)
542. No 112. Winter 2000 (48p.)
543. No 113. Spring 2001 (40p.)
544. No 114. Summer 2001 (48p.)
545. No 115. Autumn 2001 (48p.)
546. No 116. Winter 2001 (48p.)
547. No 117. Spring 2002 (40p.)
548. No 118. Summer 2002 (48p.)
549. No 119. Autumn 2002 (48p.)
550. No 120. Winter 2002 (48p.)
551 No 121. Spring 2003 (40p.)
552 No 122. Summer 2003 (48p.)
553. No 123. Autumn 2003 (48p.)
554. No 124. Winter 2003 (48p.)
555. No 125. Spring 2004 (40p.)
556. No 126: Summer 2004 (48p.)
557. No 127: Autumn 2004 (48p.)
558. No 128: Winter 2004 (48p.)
559. No 129. Spring 2005 (40p.)
560. No 130. Summer 2005 (48p.)
561. No 131. Autumn 2005 (48p.)
562. No 132. Winter 2005 (48p.)
563. No 133. Spring 2006 (40p.)
564. No 134. Summer 2006 (48p.)
565. No 135. Autumn 2006 (56p.)
566. No 136. Winter 2006 (56p.)
567. No 137. Spring 2007 (48p.)
568. No 138. Summer 2007 (56p.)
569. No 139. Autumn 2007 (56p.)
570. No 140. Winter 2007 (56p.)
571. No 141. Spring 2008 (56p.)
572. No 142. Summer 2008 (56p.)
573. No 143. Autumn 2008 (56p.)
574. No 144. Winter 2008 (56p.)

575. No 145. Spring 2009 (56p.)
576. No 146. Summer 2009 (56p.)
577. No 147. Autumn 2009 (56p.)
578. No 148. Winter 2009 (56p.)
579. No 149. Spring 2010 (56p.)
580. No 150. Summer 2010 (56p.)
581. No 151. Autumn 2010 (56p.)
582. No 152. Winter 2010 (55p.)
583. No 153. Spring 2011 (56p.)
584. No 154. Summer 2011 (56p.)

ACS Membership Bulletin
585. No 1. September 2008 (4p.)
586. No 2. December 2008 (4p.)
587. No 3. June 2009 (7p.)
588. No 4. September 2009 (4p.)
589. No 5. December 2009 (4p.)
590. No 6. March 2010 (4p.)
591. No 7. June 2010 (4p.)
592. No 8 September 2010 (4p.)
593. No 9. December 2010 (4p.)
594. No 10. June 2011 (4p.)

Members' List
15 November 1975 (6p.)
4 December 1978 (12p.)
1 November 1986 (20p. including covers)
March 1990 (30p.)
May 1995 (20p.)

Rules
Rules 1973 (1p.)
Rules July 1986 (2p.)
Draft rules September 1986 (4p.)
Draft rules May 1993 (8p.)
Draft rules February 1996 (8p.)

Index

INDEX

INDEX

INDEX